Introducing race and gender i

Introducing race and gender into economics is the first book to provide a detailed model of how issues of race and gender can be integrated into the teaching of an introductory economics course. The book's innovative structure mirrors a typical introductory course and suggests alternative examples and approaches which have a race and/or gender perspective.

Part I provides a framework for reconstructing the teaching and study of economics from a race and gender perspective.

Parts II and III give ten practical examples of race and gender topics which can be incorporated into introductory courses in both microeconomics and macroeconomics.

Part IV provides a wider perspective by contextualising issues of race and gender. The five essays include a feminist critique of economics study and an analysis of the problems of race, gender, and economic data.

Introducing race and gender into economics is a much needed addition to the literature on the teaching and study of economics. Its combination of theoretical discussion and practical examples make it an extremely useful text for students and teachers at all levels.

Robin L. Bartlett is a Professor in Economics at Denison University, Ohio, and Chair of the Committee on the Status of Women in the Economics Profession.

Introducing race and gender into economics

Edited by
Robin L. Bartlett

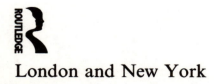

London and New York

First published 1997
by Routledge
11 New Fetter Lane, London EC4P 4EE

Simultaneously published in the USA and Canada
by Routledge
29 West 35th Street, New York, NY 10001

© 1997 Robin L. Bartlett

Typeset in Times by Pure Tech India Ltd., Pondicherry
Printed and bound in Great Britain by Mackays of Chatham, Kent

British Library Cataloguing in Publication Data

A catalogue record for this book is available from the British Library

Library of Congress Cataloguing in Publication Data

A catalogue record for this book has been requested

ISBN 0–415–16282–3 (hbk)
ISBN 0–415–16283–1 (pbk)

Contents

List of figures

List of tables

List of contributors

Robin L. Bartlett
Professor of Economics, Denison University, Granville, OH

Carolyn Shaw Bell
Professor Emerita, Wellesley College, Lexington, MA

Robert Cherry
Professor of Economics, Brooklyn College of the City University of New York

Rosemary T. Cunningham
Associate Professor of Economics, Agnes Scott College, Decatur, GA

Vernon J. Dixon
Associate Professor of Economics, Haverford College, Haverford, PA

Marianne A. Ferber
Professor of Economics and Women's Studies, University of Illinois, Urbana

Sherryl Davis Kasper
Assistant Professor of Economics, Maryville College, Maryville, TN

William M. Kempey
Professor of Economics, Kean College of New Jersey, Union, NJ

Louise Laurence
Associate Professor, Towson State University, Baltimore, MD

Margaret Lewis
Assistant Professor of Economics, College of Saint Benedict, St Joseph, MN

Robert L. Moore
Professor of Economics, Occidental College, Los Angeles, CA

Akira Motomura
Associate Professor of Economics, Stonehill College, North Easton, MA

Pamela J. Nickless
Associate Professor of Economics, University of North Carolina, Asheville, NC

Rachel A. Nugent
Assistant Professor of Economics, Pacific Lutheran University, Tacoma, WA

Kathy Parkison
Assistant Professor, Indiana University, Kokomo, IN

Janice Peterson
Associate Professor of Economics, State University of New York, Fredonia, NY

Irene Powell
Associate Professor of Economics, Grinnell College, Grinnell, IA

Margaret A. Ray
Assistant Professor of Economics, Mary Washington College, Fredericksburg, VA

Jane Rossetti
Assistant Professor of Economics, Franklin and Marshall College, Lancaster, PA

James D. Whitney
Associate Professor of Economics, Occidental College, Los Angeles, CA

Preface

This is a book intended to generate and develop ideas on how to integrate race and gender issues into introductory economics courses. Integrating race and gender issues into the introductory course is important because over 900 colleges and universities offer introductory economics. The content of these courses is heavily dependent upon the content of the introductory texts. Studies have shown that most texts contain very little material dealing with race and gender issues. Those books that do tend to put such issues into special chapters, and often treat them in stereotypic ways. Thus introductory courses generally have very little material that deals with economic concepts and policies from the perspective of race and gender.

While the content of courses and textbooks is largely standardized throughout the country, students have become more diverse. Slightly more than half of all college students are now female, and racial and ethnic backgrounds are increasingly eclectic. Textbooks that deal with economic concepts as if race and gender considerations do not exist, or are not important, have little relevance to a growing proportion of students. Reacting to these concerns, the National Science Foundation funded a proposal for three five-day summer workshops on integrating the latest scholarship on women and minorities into the introductory economics course. Participants chosen for the workshops came from across the country and were seasoned instructors representing a cross-section of faculty from small liberal arts colleges, large research universities, historically black colleges, and women's colleges.

During the workshops there were large group presentations and small group discussions designed to model a variety of effective teaching techniques in a simulated classroom environment, not unlike the ones many participants find themselves in. Using what they had learned from attending these workshops, several participants developed examples in their own voice for use in this book. Many of these examples begin with an introduction discussing course goals, targeted students, teaching techniques, and institutional constraints. Next, a free-standing race- and/or gender-focused-lecture, discussion, or simulation is developed. Lastly, some authors reflect on the exercise, with a discussion of troubling points that may arise and how to handle them.

HOW TO USE THIS BOOK

The target audience of this volume is teachers of introductory economics courses. There is a growing realization that the time has come for more inclusive teaching in introductory economics courses. At present, however, few instructors know how to do this, and existing textbooks are of little help. Concerned instructors often think the way to remedy this situation is for them to become acquainted with the vast amounts of available research on race and gender issues in economics.

We demonstrate an alternative, more efficient and productive, approach: instructors are shown how to analyze traditional economic concepts from a race and gender perspective. The microeconomic and macroeconomic exercises can be used in a traditional introductory economics course along with a standard introductory economics textbook. The final section of the book provides a context within which to reconstruct an introductory economics course. The complete volume will help instructors become more comfortable with the race and gender material and gain greater competence in handling it. Most important, non-traditional students, male and female, are far more likely to find economics relevant to them and to want to go on in the field.

STRUCTURE

Part I of the book develops a framework within which to begin integrating race and gender into introductory economics. Part II provides six microeconomic examples, and Part III provides five macroeconomic examples. Part IV provides examples of how to handle stereotyping, learning differences, and problematic data.

ACKNOWLEDGMENTS

The editor has benefited greatly from her work with Susan Feiner as Co-Principal Investigator on two National Science Foundation grants (NSF-DUE 9154159 and NSF-DUE 9354006) which sponsored three workshops on "Improving Introductory Economics by Integrating the Latest Scholarship on Women and Minorities." The first workshop was at the College of William and Mary, 1993; the second was at Denison University, 1994; and the last workshop was at Wellesley College, 1995. The author would like to thank each of these institutions, HarperCollins, and McGraw-Hill for their substantial contributions to the workshops. Finally, the author would like to thank Judy Thompson for typing and formatting the entire text. Her comments, suggestions, and support were greatly appreciated. She worked tirelessly with various versions of the manuscript. Jennifer Bailey ('98) worked diligently at formatting references and giving a student's point of view. Angie Tooill worked as my student assistant for the first two years and kept the correspondence flowing. Finally, the editor would like to thank Marci McCaulay and Carol Singer. Their support is greatly appreciated.

Robin L. Bartlett

Part I

Integrating race and gender: a framework

This part of the book is an introduction to integrating race and gender issues into an introductory economics course. Robin Bartlett, in "Reconstructing Economics 190 R&G: Introductory Economics from a Race and Gender Perspective," discusses a way to begin reconstructing an introductory economics course within the framework of course development. This chapter reviews the four elements of course design and discusses where race- and gender-related issues may play a part in encouraging or discouraging students in the subject.

It includes an examination of how economics is communicated to students on the first day of class through the demographic characteristics of the professor, the course syllabus, and textbook. It looks at the interactions between the professor and the student and how those first impressions are important, particularly for the non-traditional student of economics.

Next, the Macintosh model of integrating race and gender into any course is presented. The five interactive stages of the Macintosh model are developed and a new, more inclusive course syllabus for introductory economics is presented. The new course syllabus not only explicitly mentions race and gender issues, but also outlines how the material will be presented and how students will be evaluated. A unique feature of the course is its pedagogy. Students are given the option of taking the course by themselves or as part of a cooperative group as a team.

While the syllabus presented is still work in progress, it provides some suggestions of the changes it is necessary to make with respect to content, methodology, and pedagogy.

1 Reconstructing Economics 190 R&G: Introductory Economics course from a race and gender perspective

Robin L. Bartlett

On the first day of introductory economics, students form impressions of their instructor and of economics. Their first reactions to instructors and their more visible characteristics such as gender, race/ethnicity, age, dress, and able-bodiness are important. From these reactions, students form opinions and expectations about their instructors. On the first day of class, students also form first impressions about economics and whether or not they will like it. They form these opinions and expectations from reactions to the course syllabus and from the required textbook(s). Students examine these documents and try to figure out what they will learn, how they will learn it, and what will be expected of them. Finally, students watch how the instructor interacts with different students, and in particular, with themselves. They do a quick cost/benefit analysis and either keep the textbook(s) or fill out a drop-add slip.

AN INTRODUCTORY ECONOMICS COURSE SYLLABUS

While little can be done to change students' first impressions of their instructor, this book will focus on students' impressions of introductory economics and how it is taught from a race and gender perspective. The course syllabus displayed in Figure 1.1 is typical of ones for one-semester introductory economics courses. Syllabi for two-semester or two-quarter courses focus on either introductory microeconomics or macroeconomics each term and tend to cover more topics. Independent of course length, however, most syllabi look remarkably similar. Key bits of information about the time, meeting place, and instructor are located at the top of the first page. Course objectives, if explicit, are outlined under the course title and number. A list of required texts follows, along with a schedule of dates and chapters to be covered on these dates. Sometimes the chapter headings are included to indicate topics. At the end of the syllabus are course requirements: the number of exams to be taken, the weight given each exam in calculating the student's final grade, and other course assignments such as readings, quizzes, short papers, bonus points, etc. Course syllabi often read as if they were legal documents. Rarely do introductory economics

Figure 1.1 A syllabus: Economics 190 R&G: Introductory Economics

Economics 190 R&G: Introductory Economics
Department of Economics
Denison University

Instructor: Robin L. Bartlett
Office: Knapp 210
Office Hours: 1:30–2:30 MTWR
Phone: X6574

Required Texts:
  Bailey, Jennifer L. and Thompson, Judy A. *Understanding Economics Tomorrow*, tenth edition (Granville, OH: Doers, 1996).

Course Goals:
  1. To learn the basic concepts and definitions used by economists.
  2. To learn the basic models of supply and demand used by economists.
  3. To learn how to apply the basic models of supply and demand to economic issues and problems.

Course Outline:
  August 29 to September 2
    Day 1 Introductions and Expectations
    Day 2 The Science of Choice   Chapter 1
    Day 3 Scarcity   Chapter 2
    Day 4 Global Scarcity   Chapter 2

  September 5 to September 9
    Day 1 The Law of Demand   Chapter 3
    Day 2 Changes in Demand   Chapter 3
    Day 3 The Elasticity of Demand   Chapter 3
    Day 4 The Law of Supply   Chapter 4

  September 12 to September 16
    Day 1 Changes in Supply   Chapter 4
    Day 2 The Elasticity of Supply   Chapter 4
    Day 3 Supply and Demand   Chapter 4
    Day 4 Market Analysis   Chapter 5

  September 19 to September 23
    Day 1 Price Controls   Chapter 5
    Day 2 Quantity Controls   Chapter 5
    Day 3 Review for Hourly Exam   Chapter 5
    Day 4 First Hourly Exam

  September 26 to September 30
    Day 1 Return and Discussion of First Hourly Exam
    Day 2 Production   Chapter 6
    Day 3 Profits   Chapter 6
    Day 4 Marginal Analysis   Chapter 6

  October 3 to October 7
    Day 1 Marginal Costs   Chapter 6

Day 2 Marginal Costs and Price   Chapter 6
Day 3 Monopoly   Chapter 7
Day 4 Monopoly vs. Competition   Chapter 7

October 10 to October 14
Day 1 Factor Markets   Chapter 8
Day 2 Changes in the Demand for Labor   Chapter 8
Day 3 Unions and Wages   Chapter 8
Day 4 Market Failures   Chapter 9

October 17 to October 21
Day 1 Government Intervention   Chapter 9
Day 2 Poverty   Chapter 9
Day 3 International Trade   Chapter 10
Day 4 Free Trade   Chapter 10

October 24 to October 28
Day 1 Review
Day 2 Second Hourly Exam
Day 3 Return and Discussion of Second Hourly Exam
Day 4 Aggregate Economic Activity   Chapter 11

October 31 to November 2
Day 1 Past Periods of Growth   Chapter 11
Day 2 Business Cycles   Chapter 12
Day 3 The Circular Flow   Chapter 12
Day 4 No Class

November 7 to November 11
Day 1 Government Policies   Chapter 13
Day 2 Taxes and Outlays   Chapter 13
Day 3 Money and Interest Rates   Chapter 14
Day 4 The Demand for and Supply of Money   Chapter 14

November 14 to November 18
Day 1 The Fed   Chapter 15
Day 2 Monetary Policy   Chapter 15
Day 3 Review for Third Hourly Exam
Day 4 Third Hourly Exam

November 21 to November 25–Thanksgiving Break!

November 28 to December 2
Day 1 Return Third Hourly Exam
Day 2 Economic Disagreements   Chapter 16
Day 3 Who is Right?   Chapter 16
Day 4 No Class

December 5 to December 9
Day 1 Inflation and Unemployment   Chapter 17
Day 2 Growth   Chapter 18
Day 3 Stabilization   Chapter 19
Day 4 Wrap-up and Evaluations

December 12 to December 16
   Day 1 Final Exam 9:00–11:00 am (Section 04)
   Day 2 Final Exam 9:00–11:00 am (Section 06)

Course Requirements:
A.	Three Hourly Exams (100 Points Each)	300
B.	A Final Exam (200 Points)	200
C.	Class Participation (100 Points)	100
	TOTAL POSSIBLE POINTS	600

Calculation of Course Grade:

Percent of Total	Minimum Points	Grade
97–100	582+	A+
92–96	552+	A
90–92	540+	A−
87–89	522+	B+
83–86	498+	B
80–82	480+	B−
77–79	462+	C+
73–76	438+	C
70–72	420+	C−
67–69	402+	D+
63–66	378+	D
60–62	360+	D−

course syllabi paint a very exciting and inclusive picture of what students will learn in coming weeks and how they will go about learning.

When planning a course, introductory instructors usually find an old syllabus from a previous semester or borrow one from a colleague who has just taught the course. Before putting pen to paper, or fingers to keyboard, however, take a close look at an introductory economics course syllabus or the one found in Figure 1.1. Use a highlighter pen to mark those places in the syllabus where race and gender issues are explicitly mentioned. If the syllabus is like the one presented above, this task will not take long.

Next, open any introductory economics textbook and count the number of times race and gender issues are mentioned in the first chapter, or even in the next ten chapters. Go to the textbook's index and find where race and gender issues are mentioned. How often do the words "women," "race," or "ethnicity" appear? Feiner and Morgan (1987) did such an analysis and found that race and gender issues were rarely mentioned in introductory economics textbooks, and when they were, they were often found in separate chapters on "women's issues" or "minority concerns." Feiner and Morgan also found that, while sexist language was avoided, women and people of color were often included in stereotypic ways when economic concepts were illustrated. An update of the Feiner and Morgan study showed that little progress had been made (Feiner 1993). An unbalanced representation of women and people of color is not unique to economics.

Rosser (1990) found the same problems in a select set of science textbooks in which gender-neutral presentations were accompanied by examples and illustrations which were frequently stereotypical.

The introductory economics course syllabi and textbook are two important vehicles for communicating to students what economics is all about. The syllabus serves as a road map—informing students of what road the instructor is going to take them down (what topics will be covered) and how they are going to travel it (the pedagogy). The text serves as a reference manual—a reservoir of economic concepts—a detailed write-up of the terrain to be covered. A quick look at the introductory economics syllabus and a flip through the pages of an introductory economics textbook may give students the wrong impression of economics as a subject with little to say about race and gender-related issues. If the subject with its limited textbook applications is still of interest to them, the graphical or mathematical presentation of economics may be less attractive to some students than the methods of theorizing in other subjects. As a result, good students may shy away from economics (Bartlett 1995).

The introductory economics course syllabus and textbook are not the only vehicles for communicating economics to students. Instructors "talk" in a variety of ways to students. An instructor communicates both verbally and non-verbally to students enthusiasm about the subject matter, about which students the instructor values, and about which students the instructor expects to succeed. Students who decide to give economics a try may find that the actual day-to-day classroom experience is one that tells them that economics is not a welcoming or supportive classroom for them.

The literature shows that many of the interactions between instructor and student are predicated upon gender- and race-related stereotypes, encouraging preconceived ideas about certain students' abilities and talents. Thus, the classroom dynamics between the instructor and the students, and among the students themselves, play significant roles in determining which students find economics of interest.

Inclusive teaching is about improving lines of communication through printed materials and better student/faculty and student/student interactions. Inclusive teaching is about communicating a realistic picture of our economy, effectively, to all students.

Facing the fears and "What if" questions

Incorporating race and gender issues in the classroom is challenging. A whole array of fears and "What if" questions surface. For example: Where do I find material on race and gender issues without going back to graduate school? When will I find the time to read, understand, and assimilate the new literature on race and gender differentials? Don't race and gender issues belong in an economics of discrimination or labor economics course? I am not a racist, yet race is a "touchy" subject to bring up in class. I have two daughters, so I don't treat female students any differently than I treat male students. If I spend time on race and gender issues, my students will not know the material they need to go on. Key topics have to be covered, so my students are ready for intermediate microeconomics and macroeconomics. If I start discussing "women and minority issues" in introductory economics, my colleagues will think I am being too political. What if I use a politically incorrect term? What if someone wants to talk about sexual orientation? And the "what ifs" go on.

How to proceed

Since introductory economics instructors have a wide range of backgrounds in course development and women's and minorities' studies, this discussion starts with a focus on issues of course design and how race and gender can be introduced with a variety of delivery and evaluative strategies. This section will look at pedagogical strategies for delivering the course content and methodology and for evaluating students' comprehension of the material. Then the McIntosh model of integrating race and gender issues into a discipline will be developed as one way to integrate race and gender issues into the present course content and methodology of introductory economics. This section will present a revised introductory economics course syllabus that more effectively communicates to students the goals, structure, and pedagogy of the course. For some economic instructors, this material will be old hat. For others, the material will be new. For both the initiated and the uninitiated the prospects of reconstructing introductory economics from a race and gender perspective are exciting, challenging, and long overdue. Introductory economics instructors will find that they can use their own experiences and those of their students to reconstruct a more inclusive introductory economics course. Within the following framework, most of the fears and "What ifs" can be alleviated and economics instructors will reach more students and teach them economics more effectively.

COURSE DESIGN

Before outlining a course and thinking about integrating race and gender issues into the introductory economics course, instructors need to think about their goals. What is it that they want to achieve? What are the constraints within which they will try to achieve these goals? Instructors need to think about what concepts they want their students to understand and be able to use when the course is over. The first step of course design is to list your course goals. Select the top three or four goals and notice whether the terms "race" and "gender" appear in any of these goals. If not, think again about what you want students to learn over the course of the term.

In addition, instructors need to know their students, how they learn, and how best to communicate to them. Similarly, instructors need to think about how they learn and what teaching skills they possess. What attitudes, biases, and preconceived notions do they bring to the classroom? Finally, instructors need to think about the role the course plays in the department, the major, and the institution. Introductory economics cannot be all things to all people in all places. The following sections will examine more closely the goals of the introductory economics course, the clientele, the instructors' abilities, and the institutional constraints.

Goals

What do instructors of economics want their students to know, to walk away with? When asked, most introductory economics instructors would say that they want their students to be able to "think like an economist." Surprisingly, Siegfried *et al.* (1990) found that the content of introductory economics courses, as well as of those in the major, and the teaching techniques used in the classroom are very similar. Students are expected to understand the determinants of opportunity costs, demand and supply, market structures, aggregate income, unemployment, and prices. The topics outlined in the introductory economics course syllabus in Figure 1.1 represent the bare minimum. Lecturing is the dominant mode of delivering the material, with occasional clarifying questions asked by students. The material in the textbook serves either as preparation for lectures or as backup for material presented in class. Students generally are tested on their understanding of basic economics with multiple-choice, fill-in-the-blank, or short-answer questions.

Parsimonious mathematical models and graphs are the methods by which students are taught to analyze economic problems. Through the use of optimizing mathematical techniques on hypothetical problem sets, students are supposed to develop problem-solving skills for analyzing economic realities. Paraphrasing W. Lee Hansen (1986), "we only know that our students can answer the questions we ask."

Instructors of economics have a much wider range of secondary goals— goals to be accomplished. Besides developing analytical and mathematical skills, some economics instructors want their students to develop the ability to apply economic theory effectively, to make judgments critically, to calculate measurements accurately, to think creatively, and to communicate effectively.

While few economics instructors explicitly go beyond thinking about primary and secondary goals, some economics instructors want to change student attitudes and get them interested in economics. Race and gender issues usually find themselves connected to tertiary goals. Some economics instructors may want to affirm cultural differences between and among groups of people and demonstrate how these differences add to the richness of the US economy. Or, how these differences block the economic advancement of talented groups of people or stunt the growth of the US economy.

Some instructors may want students to feel the effects of discrimination in order to understand better how people and their behavior are affected in the market. Tertiary goals and activities are often targeted at students' affective rather than cognitive realm of understanding. Feelings explicitly enter the classroom. Many economics instructors feel that feelings have no place in an economics classroom—that economics is a science and without emotional content. Other economists may admit that feelings are present, but feel ill-equipped to deal with them and would rather avoid "touchy" topics. Feelings, however, are in the classroom and are probably the greatest motivating force for students. Discussing race and gender issues in the classroom can be a powerful motivating force for students.

Integrating race and gender issues does not mean that tertiary goals become primary goals and that primary goals get relegated to tertiary status. Instead, integrating race and gender into the introductory economics course means that primary and tertiary goals become one. Every basic economic concept is presented and then examined from the perspectives of race and gender, or is applied to a problem or issue associated with a particular group. For example, the concept of the natural rate of unemployment is presented and then examined from the perspective of race. Does the natural rate of unemployment have a different meaning for African-American than for European-American workers? Is there a different natural rate of unemployment for African-American workers than for European-American workers? If there is, what does that observation say about how "natural" the natural rate of unemployment is?

The public call for educational accountability, the changing demographic characteristics of college-age students, and the declining number of economics majors have forced many economic instructors to rethink their primary goals and methodology in introductory economics. The hierarchy of goals outlined above is exchanged for more inclusive primary goals. In any event, it is prudent to let students know up front what your intentions are.

The three other elements of course design

While developing course goals is important, course design is influenced by several other factors: students' backgrounds, attitudes, and abilities; instructor's attitudes and talents; and the institutional demands upon the course. These factors determine, to some extent, what will be covered and how it will be covered. Designing a course for gifted students would probably be very different than designing a course for ethnically diverse students at a major urban institution. A class comprised predominantly of students of color would warrant different examples and teaching strategies than a class made up predominantly of Euro-American students. Excellent lecturers may find it helpful to add discussion and cooperative learning exercises to their repertoire. Introductory economics courses that are taught in large lecture halls will have a different pedagogy than ones taught in small sections of twenty-five or less students. All of these considerations are important. The next three sections examine how race and gender issues may influence each of these considerations.

Knowledge of students

Novice instructors tend to teach as they were taught, or in ways that are easiest for them to learn. These courses are designed for students very much like themselves—students with an interest in economics, with strong analytical and mathematical skills, and probably with similar cultural heritages—white, male. Many very bright students may be turned off by the focus in introductory economics courses on commodity markets, abstract modeling, and a lecture method of teaching. Many instructors feel that the emphasis on mathematical and analytical techniques at the introductory economics level is appropriate because they feel it screens out the "weak" students and signals the "strong" students. Whether mathematical ability is the best screen for students who will make good economics majors is rarely questioned. Students who may make excellent economics majors, with excellent writing and critical thinking skills, may be discouraged from trying economics because there are few opportunities for them to use their talents. The syllabus rarely outlines writing assignments or details the particulars of how they will be tested on exams. Students learn from the grapevine what to expect. The reliance on this particular method of demonstrating economic principles may inadvertently discourage excellent students from economics.

Other ways of knowing

Mathematical modeling and graphical analysis are one way to develop and demonstrate economic principles. However, other disciplines use a variety of methodologies for illustrating important theoretical concepts. For example, sociologists use flow charts. Philosophers use argument and rhetoric. English majors write stories, develop themes, and read stories. Recently, introductory economics textbooks have turned to more pictorial representation of the economy. In particular, several one-semester introductory economics textbooks have reintroduced the circular flow chart as the basis for understanding macroeconomic activity. No equations or graphs are used. Economics educators who emphasize mathematical modeling as the sole method for understanding economic phenomena ignore a potentially rich array of methodological possibilities that may fit better with some students' way of knowing.

Many nontraditional economics students, women and students of color, may find the abstract modeling of economics not so much daunting as tangential to their primary ways of knowing. Sheila Tobias (1990) has referred to this group of students as the "Otherwise Bright Students" or "OBSs" found outside the sciences. Few economics instructors get to know these students, because their initial contact with economics sends them in a different direction. These students are hurried along their way when it becomes clear that students without well-developed mathematical and ana- lytical skills are at a disadvantage in introductory economics. While studies show that some gender and racial/ethnic differences may exist in verbal and mathematical aptitudes, the observed differences within groups are much larger than the observed differences between groups. Women having a lower aptitude for mathematics, however, cannot explain why economics has a smaller proportion of female majors than does mathematics.

An example of how different methodological approaches affect the pre- sentation of a topic and student understanding of an issue is illustrated with a comparison of the explanation of the observed wage differentials between men and women by Goldin (1990) and that of Amott and Matthaei (1991) in their recent histories of the gender gap. Goldin's presentation uses the human capital model of wage determination and a traditional empirical approach to examine the reasons for the wage gap and its persistence. In contrast, Amott and Matthaei use an alternative feminist-Marxist model within a sociological framework of analysis and descriptive comparisons to determine the reasons for the persistence of the wage gap. Both presenta- tions are effective and come to the same conclusions—that occupational segregation and wage discrimination are the primary causes of the wage gap. Students reading the former book develop a sense of the theoretical and empirical techniques used in the literature. Students reading the second book develop an appreciation for the roles that race/ethnicity, gender, and class play in determining the wage gap. Reading both books gives students a balanced understanding of economics and its methods and a richer under- standing for the persistence of the wage gap.

Connected content

One of the ways to attract students is to apply economic principles to topics in which they have an interest. In the vast majority of undergraduate economics courses, the topics taught, the analysis presented, and the teach- ing techniques employed follow directly from the content in the textbook and its teaching supplements. Unfortunately, as mentioned previously, most textbooks downplay the roles of race and gender in the economy. As a result, the content of introductory economics is more representative of white male economic realities than it is of other economic groups.

Ferber (1989) argues that increasing the female content of introductory economics courses may attract more women. Sports examples, particularly pro baseball and football, engender interest from the male students. And, no doubt, some female students are as up on the latest sports statistics as their male counterparts in the class, but the cultural odds are against it. The economics of child-rearing may be of more interest to some female students than to most male students. The point is that while the economic realities of a particular group are worthy of study, focusing exclusively on one group results in an unbalanced picture of the economic realities.

Which groups should an economics instructor pick for inclusion? The groups will depend upon the students in the class. It is important to know the demographic backgrounds of students in order to develop and use examples that they would find interesting, exciting, and relevant to them. When connections are made between students' economic lives and the models developed in introductory economics, students are motivated to learn whatever techniques are necessary to understand an issues.

How do instructors find out these things about their students? They ask. A series of exercises can facilitate the effort. On the first day, students can form groups and introduce each other. It is best to have a student interview and introduce another student to the group. Students can ask each other why they took introductory economics or what is important to remember about them. In larger classes, one student can report the group's characteristics. In smaller classes, students can do the actual introductions of each other. The result is that the instructor can start getting important information about students and students can start getting important information about each other. Students who feel at the margin hopefully will feel comfortable having someone else introduce them and will be able to identify students with similar interests in the class.

Another way to get to know your students is to ask them to make connections between the material and their own personal lives on exams. For example, students are asked to finish the answer to an essay with a few sentences or a paragraph about how the material or problem relates to their lives. The answer will be graded as usual, but they have the opportunity to gain an additional half of a grade if they make a solid connection with their own life or that of someone they know. Thus, when reading, thinking, or discussing the material with their classmates, students are more likely to go one step further and make the connection to themselves. More importantly, instructors get to know more about their students.

Students could be given multiple-choice/multiple-answer tests. In addition to circling the right answer, they are asked to write a sentence or two about why the other choices are wrong. Students can be asked to pick one of the multiple-choice/multiple-answer questions and relate it to their lives. In addition, students could be asked to keep journals on how they feel about the class. Journals could be periodically and randomly collected for the instructor to get a better sense of his/her students and how they are comprehending the material.

Dependent and independent thinkers

Just as students' interests and backgrounds vary, so do the ways in which they take in information and process it. Some students need a context within which to situate learning. The more an instructor can connect to the student's world, the more the student will connect with the instructor and economics. Belenky *et al.* (1986) found that female students prefer more connected ways of knowing that grow out of their own personal experiences and relationships with others. "Connected" means that the material being covered is directly relevant to some experience that they have had or are having or indirectly relevant to some experience that their friends are having or will experience.

The literature on learning and learning style suggests that some of these differences are innate and some are culturally determined, that males and females may have different ways of knowing, as do people of color. One teaching technique, therefore, is not going to have the same impact on all students. For example, abstract mathematical model building may facilitate learning for some students and terrify other students. Writing assignments may enhance understanding for some students and immobilize other students. A great deal has been written in economics about the learning process (Saunders and Walstad 1990) and economists have addressed issues of male and female differences in the classroom (Bergmann 1987). Thus, economic ideas are best presented within historical, personal, or institutional contexts.

The Instructor

Economics instructors also need to reflect on their own interests and abilities. What biases do they bring to the classroom and what particular pedagogical talents do they possess? Attending a race, gender, or diversity workshop is one way to go about recognizing one's own personal biases and prejudices. One cannot grow up in America without acquiring some racial or ethnic baggage. As a result, instructors may unknowingly engage in a variety of behaviors that reflect these acquired biases and prejudices. Hall and Sandler (1982) document that the classroom can be a "chilly place" for women and show how little behaviors can make a big difference in student performance. Instructors may allow male students to talk more than women students and may also allow male students to interrupt women students. Women students' questions may be taken less seriously or ignored. Male students' answers are generally followed up on. Professors make less eye contact with women students than with male students. Students of color face similar behaviors. The instructor's interaction with a student and with other students communicate his/her expectations and values.

Specializing in one teaching technique can inhibit learning. Lecturing as a teaching technique is the preferred mode of learning for auditory learners. Some of the country's top medical students' interest in a lecture wanes after the first fifteen minutes of the lecture (Meyers and Jones 1993). Points made in the last few minutes of a well formatted lecture are lost on most students. Instructors need to develop new and different teaching techniques. It takes time and effort, however, to learn how to lead a discussion, to invent active learning exercises, and to orchestrate cooperative learning groups.

Institutional demands

Finally, instructors of introductory economics courses must be aware of the context within which their course is being taught. For example, what size are the classes? How does class size limit the delivery and evaluative options of an instructor? It is harder to get to know students in large lecture classes than in smaller classes. Interactive teaching techniques need to be modified for large classes. In addition, the types of tests that can be effectively and efficiently graded need to be thought through. Does the course fulfill a major or general education requirement? The institutional context of introductory economics will affect students' motivations and attitudes toward the course, instructor preparation and level of involvement, and the interaction between the instructor and the students.

For example, in some economics departments, there exists a bias against teaching introductory economics. Upper-level theory courses are preferred. Instructors assigned to introductory economics courses may pay less attention to the course's development and execution. Similarly, students may think that classes that fulfill general education requirements are less challenging than courses for majors and do not come to class prepared to work. The combination of instructor and student attitudes could be deadly. Institutions that require their students to take a course in gender or race/ethnic studies to graduate may find these problems compounded. Introductory economics courses that attempt to incorporate race and gender material for whatever reasons need to be carefully planned, executed, and most importantly, balanced.

Balancing the goals and elements of course design

Instructors need to be very clear about what it is they are trying to do and make their objectives explicit. Moreover, instructors need to understand that very small differences in students' backgrounds, abilities, and interests, in instructor attitudes and skills, and in institutional demands can make a big difference in the classroom and how effectively the course goals are achieved. Therefore, instructors must be equipped with a variety of teaching strategies for delivering the material and for evaluating the effectiveness of these strategies.

Delivery strategies

While lectures are good for some topics and some students, they are not good for all topics and all students. At the other end of the pedagogical continuum is active learning, where students learn by talking and listening, reading, writing, and reflecting on the material (for a summary of active learning, see Meyers and Jones 1993). Computer-assisted instruction, case studies, computer and role-playing simulations, laboratory experiments, cooperative learning groups, and team-learning techniques are teaching techniques situated between these two extremes of only lecturing and hands-on learning.

Combinations of teaching techniques would increase the odds that more students learn more effectively. For example, lectures would be more effective if accompanied by cooperative learning or "hands-on" exercises. Abstract mathematical modeling would be more connected to a student's thought processes if accompanied by reaction papers or diaries.

The connection between in-class and out-of-class activities is important in the learning process. For example, Uri Treisman (1982) developed informal learning environments for African-American students patterned after those developed by Asian-American students at the University of California—Berkeley. His collaborative learning groups emphasized combining academic and social contacts to help students of color to get tutoring from other students and to get the social support they needed to succeed.

The kinds of teaching techniques employed depend upon the instructor's goals and the environmental factors that affect the achievement of those goals. If an instructor wants students to develop skills to discover economic principles on their own, then lecturing in every class will not facilitate that desire. If an instructor wants students to empathize with the plight of an economically disadvantaged group, then a graphical analysis of the effects of minimum wage legislation will probably not develop that feeling. Students may have to go on field trips and talk to the people they are studying to get real answers to their questions (Blinder 1990).

Evaluation strategies

While developing the content and methodology of an introductory economics course has its own problems, evaluating student understanding of the material presents another array of problems. Multiple-choice tests may not be the best instruments for evaluating how much students have achieved your primary and secondary goals, or how their feelings toward particular groups, individuals, or behaviors have changed. The literature shows that female students do worse than male students on multiple-choice questions (Lumsden and Scott 1986). The opposite is true for essays. Not all students are equally adept at writing, speaking, or responding to typical analytical questions in introductory economics courses. Not all students have the same preferred mode of expression. Therefore, it makes sense to use a portfolio or bundle of evaluative procedures in every course whenever possible. In order to determine how well a student understands the material, traditional written exams can be used, along with oral presentations, and written projects. Evaluative techniques can be applied to individuals, to a group, or to a team (Bartlett 1995); each procedure has its advantages and disadvantages. However, an array of evaluative techniques enables most students to feel comfortable with at least one mode of expression and therefore allows them an opportunity to do their best at least once and get positive feedback. Moreover, students who are weak in particular skills will have the opportunity to develop them.

Then the problem of how to weigh each of the activities in a student's final grade is important. Ideally, students would have as many opportunities to answer standard economics type questions as they would to write and to talk about them in a thoughtful manner. The problem with introducing additional opportunities to display economic understanding is that additional grading results. In small classes of twenty-five or less, this is not a problem. However, assigning three or four exams during the term, three or four writing assignments, and giving three or four oral opportunities would be prohibitive in a large introductory economics course. However, using teams (Bartlett 1995) as opposed to groups is one way to make an introductory economics class of 100 into a grading-effective class of twenty-five.

The more diverse the cultural backgrounds of the students in the class the more important it is to have a variety of gradable opportunities that weigh in equally into the student's grade. Students with poor written skills can show their understanding of economics with their ability to solve problems. Students who have poor problem-solving skills will find solace in an opportunity to write about an economic problem. Finally, those students who have advanced oral skills will find oral presentations, role-playing, or discussions to their advantage.

In addition, grades can be individual determined and competitively determined. In the former group, students compete with themselves. If a student gets 90 percent of the questions right or completes 90 percent of the educational tasks, then she/he receives an A. In the latter case, the top 10 percent of students receive an A. The former environment would be more comfortable for those students who feel that they are at the margins. Their grade is more under their control. In the latter situation, students have no control over the ability and amount of time other students study.

Instructors of introductory economics have certain goals they want to achieve over the course of the term. Those goals need to be spelled out and weighed against each other, given the constraints and opportunities presented by the attitudes, backgrounds, and ways of knowing of the students to be served, the attitudes and talents of the instructor, and the institutional demands placed on the course. Given the goals of the instructor, there are several ways to achieve them. A variety of teaching techniques exist and a variety of evaluative techniques are available. An instructor wants to be sure to balance the use of teaching techniques and evaluative techniques so as not to bias the course against or for certain groups of students.

THE MCINTOSH MODEL

Having thought about the issues surrounding goal setting, an instructor can sit down with a calendar and a textbook and begin to map out a course of action. One way to think about integrating differences into the introductory course is to apply McIntosh's (1983, 1990) five-phase model of curriculum development. Greater racial and gender balance is achieved in a course by moving through each of its successive phases. As one does, the realities of women and people of color move from the margins of the course to the center of its inquiry. This model has been productively employed in other sciences.

In the first phase, introductory economics, or any other course, is taught as if race and gender do not matter, as a "Womanless, Raceless Economics." The absence of women and people of color from textbooks and course materials is not seen as a problem because race- and gender-blind economic theory is assumed to be equally descriptive of how women, people of color, and white men go about making economic choices. Moreover, aggregate economic statistics describe the economic well-being of subgroups as well as they describe that of the whole. The course syllabus would look very much like the one initially presented in Figure 1.1.

In stage two, notable female economists and economists of color are recognized to show that people of color and women can succeed if they choose. This phase could be titled "Women and People of Color as Additions to the Curriculum." In this stage, there is still limited, if any, questioning of the underlying assumptions of the models or altering of course content. The contributions of select women and people of color are highlighted in special boxes in the text or special units in the course. The syllabus for this course might look like the one in Figure 1.1, but a textbook would be one that had special boxes or sections highlighting prominent economists—some of whom would happen to be women and people of color.

In the third stage, instructors "Add Women and People of Color and then Stir." Conventional economic theory is used to examine the "special issues" of these select groups. The results of such applications of economic theory, however, often produce findings that differ from those predicted by economic theory. Those behaving in economically perverse ways are seen as "deviant," and the circumstances surrounding such behavior are viewed as "imperfections" in an otherwise perfectly functioning market system. The course syllabus would look like the one in Figure 1.2. The textbook may have special chapters on women and racial issues. The course syllabus would show a day or week devoted to exploring the causes of poverty or discrimination as examples of using economic theory to explain group differences.

In the fourth stage, "Women and People of Color as Anomalies and Deviants," the perverse economic results generated in the previous phase are examined. Instructors either modify existing economic theories or develop alternative explanations for the "deviant" economic behavior. The former instructors attempt to deal with the results by modifying the constraints and adding more explanatory variables. The latter instructors explore other economic models such as Marxism or institutionalism.

The syllabus in Figure 1.2 is a stage three McIntosh model for incorporating race and gender into courses. A quick glance at the text indicates that the words "race" and "gender" appear in the course goals. Every other week a large portion of a class period is devoted to either taking an economic concept and using it to explain a particular group's issue or taking a particular economic concept and examining it from the perspective of race or gender. The race and gender topics found in the syllabus in Figure 1.2 will be discussed in more detail in the next section.

In stage five, instructors draw upon the insights and findings of the race and gender scholarship in economics and other disciplines to produce a reconstructed course. The new introductory economics course would be multidimensional. Introductory economics would have a diverse content and connected to the lives of a diverse student body. Universal explanations designed to fit all people and all economic institutions for all times would be suspect. There would be more interaction between theory and observation. Competing theories and explanations would be weighed against various modes and forms of evidence while observations and conclusions would be checked against the experiences of different groups of people. Instructors would engage in a conversation with their students, acting more as a coach or a guide than as an authority.

AN EXAMINATION OF ECONOMICS 190 R&G: INTRODUCTORY ECONOMICS FROM A RACE AND GENDER PERSPECTIVE

The introductory economics course syllabus in Figure 1.2 is an example of how to take a very traditional course and course syllabus as presented in Figure 1.1 and transform it into a more balanced presentation of introductory economics with a more inclusive range of topics, a broader range of methodologies, and greater mix of teaching and evaluative techniques. Several factors influenced the design of Econ. 190 R&G. First, Denison University is a small residential liberal arts college. The students it attracts have SAT scores above the national average. About 10 percent of the student body are African-American and another 10 percent are international students. One-third of the student body comes from Ohio. Another third comes from the East Coast, and the final third come from across the country. Most of them were born after 1975.

The Department of Economics has a lecture/laboratory curriculum which dictates a class size of twenty-four—the maximum number of students that can fit into the computer lab. Most of the staff would say that their goal is to teach students to "think like economists." The instructors in the department

Figure 1.2 A Syllabus: Economics 190 R&G: Introductory Economics from a race and gender perspective

Economics 190 R&G: Introductory Economics
Department of Economics
Denison University
by
Robin L. Bartlett, Professor of Economics

Welcome to Introductory Economics. According to the *Merriam-Webster Dictionary (New York: Pocket Books, 1974)*, the word "introduce" means: (1) to lead or bring in especially for the first time (2) to bring into practice or use (3) to cause to be acquainted (4) to bring to notice (5) to put in. Introductory Economics will be a course that introduces you to the basic concepts of Economics. Moreover, you will have the opportunity to practise or put into use the basic concepts you learn by examining various personal and political aspects of your lives. For example, we will examine your decision to attend college and whether you made a reasonable economic choice. In addition, we will examine the Administration's recently passed deficit-reduction package and determine the impact it has had on you. Hopefully, after taking this course you will be familiar with the basic tools of economic analysis and able to use them for your own betterment—both personal and professional.

The Course. Your introduction to Economics will begin with several lectures and discussions about terms, definitions, and institutions. Once you have acquired a familiarity with the jargon of the discipline and an understanding of the important institutional frameworks within which the economy operates, we will begin to develop economic models to explain how goods and services are produced, distributed, and consumed in the United States. We will look at the economic behavior of individuals and firms and we will examine the ups and downs of the overall economy. In the process, you will learn to think logically and critically about economic explanations of human behavior and policy actions.

In the end, you will learn how "to think like an economist." What that means is that you will learn to use parsimonious models to explain economic behavior. Economists typically develop graphical or mathematical models to explain economic behavior. We will focus more on graphical representations in this course. More mathematical models await you in upper level courses. However, we will develop other ways of knowing about economics principles. We will rely on your own experiences and those of your classmates to validate the ideas that will be developed. In addition, we will examine each topic from the perspective of race, gender, or class. If there are other groups that are important for you to examine, we can add them. Looking at economic concepts from different perspectives will give us a broader understanding of economic reality.

Procedures. I will use a variety of teaching techniques, from lecturing to cooperative team learning. You will be exposed to a variety of economic models, from abstract mathematical models to textual models. To ensure that everyone finds something of interest in this course, we will try to get to know each other and offer examples or personal experiences that either confirm or challenge an economic idea. As a result, you will be learning about economics from my lectures, from reading your text, and from discussions with your classmates. I will lecture and lead discussions three days a week. You and your classmates (alone or as a team) will solve and present problems for credit one day a week. The problems are the ones found at the end of each chapter. Throughout the semester you will be given handouts that take a closer look at particular economic concepts and examine them from a race and gender perspective. These examples are intended to enrich and expand the coverage of these topics in your text and from our own experiences.

You can do all the course work by yourself or you can form a team with as many of your classmates as you want. Teams will work together to learn the material by teaching it to each other. When it comes time to take a test or to present an explanation of a home work problem in class, a member of the team will be chosen at random to perform the task at hand. Teams can form any time during the term. Teams, however, must stay together once they are formed for the remainder of the term. The final, however, may be taken individually or as a team.

Hourly exams will consist of problems to be solved and short essays. The final exam will be cumulative. While you are expected to give the correct response to questions, you are also expected to make connections between the material and your own experiences. Thus, each answer ends with a few sentences about how the material is relevant to you. This part of your answer adds a half of a grade if the connection is well thought out. Class attendance is a percentage of the classes attended. Finally, you or your group will be randomly selected on Mondays to solve or explain a problem to the rest of the class. You or a randomly selected member of your team will give the analysis or explanation to the class.

The Particulars. While I will be your instructor for the semester, I hope to learn from you. You will find me in Knapp 210. My office hours are 1:30–2:30 MTWR. My office phone is X6574 during the day. My home phone is 587-3813. You may call me at home before 10:00 pm.

Required Texts:
   Bailey, Jennifer L. and Thompson, Judy A. *Understanding Economics Tomorrow*, tenth edition (Granville, OH: Doers, 1996).
   Bartlett, Robin L., *Introductory Economics from a Difference Perspective*. Handouts from text.

Course Outline:
   August 29 to September 2
      Day 1 Introductions by Students and Competitive and Cooperative
         Learning Demonstration
      Day 2 Pretests
      Day 3 The Science of Choice   Chapter 1
      Day 4 Scarcity–Locally and Globally   Chapter 2

   September 5 to September 9
      Day 1 Problems I
      Day 2 The Law of Demand   Chapter 3
      Day 3 Changes in Demand   Chapter 3
         "Market Segmentation: The Role of Race in the Housing Markets"
         by Rosemary Cunningham
      Day 4 The Elasticity of Demand   Chapter 3

   September 12 to September 16
      Day 1 Problems II
      Day 2 The Law of Supply   Chapter 4
      Day 3 Changes in Supply   Chapter 4
      Day 4 The Elasticity of Supply   Chapter 4
         "Protective Labor Legislation and Women's Employment" by Pam
         Nickless and James D. Whitney

September 19 to September 23
    Day 1 Problems III
    Day 2 Supply and Demand   Chapter 4
    Day 3 Market Analysis   Chapter 5
    Day 4 Price Controls   Chapter 5
         "The Economics of Affirmative Action" by Robert L. Moore and
         James D. Whitney

September 26 to September 30
    Day 1 Quantity Controls   Chapter 5
    Day 2 First Hourly Exam
    Day 3 Production   Chapter 6
    Day 4 Profits   Chapter 6

October 3 to October 7
    Day 1 Problems IV
    Day 2 Marginal Analysis   Chapter 6
    Day 3 Marginal Costs   Chapter 6
    Day 4 Marginal Costs and Price   Chapter 6
         "Gender and the Decision to go to College" by Loiuse Laurence and
         Robert L. Moore

October 10 to October 14
    Day 1 Problems V
    Day 2 Monopoly   Chapter 7
    Day 3 Monopoly vs. Competition   Chapter 7
    Day 4 Factor Markets   Chapter 8

October 17 to October 21
    Day 1 Problems VI
    Day 2 Changes in the Demand for Labor   Chapter 8
         "The Labor Supply Decision: Differences between Genders and
         Races" by Margaret Lewis and Janice Peterson
    Day 3 Unions and Wages   Chapter 8
    Day 4 Market Failures   Chapter 9

October 24 to October 28
    Day 1 Government Intervention   Chapter 9
    Day 2 Poverty   Chapter 9
    Day 3 Second Hourly Exam
    Day 4 International Trade   Chapter 10

October 31 to November 2
    Day 1 Free Trade   Chapter 10
    Day 2 Aggregate Economic Activity   Chapter 11
         "A Critique of National Income Accounting" by Rachel
         Nugent
    Day 3 Past Periods of Growth   Chapter 11
    Day 4 No Class

November 7 to November 11
    Day 1 Problems VII
    Day 2 Business Cycles   Chapter 12

"Race and Gender in a Basic Labor Force Model" by Margaret Ray

Day 3	The Circular Flow	Chapter 12
Day 4	Government Policies	Chapter 13

November 14 to November 18

Day 1	Problems VIII	
Day 2	Taxes and Outlays	Chapter 13
Day 3	Money and Interest Rates	Chapter 14
Day 4	The Demand for and Supply of Money	Chapter 14

November 21 to November 25–Thanksgiving Break!

November 28 to December 2

Day 1	Problems IX	
Day 2	The Fed	Chapter 15
Day 3	Monetary Policy	Chapter 15

"General vs. Selective Credit Controls: The Asset Required Reserve Proposal" by William M. Kempey

Day 4 Third Hourly Exam

December 5 to December 9

Day 1	Problems X	
Day 2	Economic Disagreements	Chapter 16
Day 3	Inflation and Unemployment	Chapter 17

"A Disaggregated CPI: The Differential Effects of Inflation" by Irene Powell and Jane Rossetti

Day 4 Posttests and Evaluations

December 12 to December 16

Day 1 Final Exam 9:00–11:00 am (Section 04)
Day 2 Final Exam 9:00–11:00 am (Section 06)

Course Requirements:

A. Three Hourly Exams (100 Points Each)	300
B. A Final Exam (300 Points)	300
C. Class Participation (100 Points)	100
D. Ten In-class Problems (30 Points Each)	300
TOTAL POSSIBLE POINTS	1000

Calculation of Course Grade:

Percent of Total	Minimum Points	Grade
97–100	970+	A+
93–96	920+	A
90–92	900+	A−
87–89	870+	B+
83–86	830+	B
80–82	800+	B−
77–79	770+	C+
73–76	730+	C
70–72	700+	C−
67–69	670+	D+
63–66	630+	D
60–62	600+	D−

are dedicated to teaching and have developed a wide range of teaching techniques from lecturing, to computer and role-playing simulations, to case studies, to laboratory exercises. Introductory economics is the first course in the major and fulfills a general education requirement. Like most dual purpose introductory economics courses many trade-offs are made. The department also uses the introductory economics course to lure students to the major.

The syllabus for Economics 190 R&G first welcomes students and then defines introductory economics, outlines course goals, and spells out the procedures that are going to be used. The textbook chosen for the course presents the bare minimum in terms of economic concepts. The skeletal approach is preferred to offer more opportunity to bring in supplemental race and gender material or to use input from the class. Second, the textbook uses very few equations and the graphical analysis is kept to a minimum. Since the textbook does not integrate race and gender issues into topics, the book is supplemented with examples developed by participants from the National Science Foundation's summer workshops on integrating race and gender into the introductory economics course. Students are encouraged from the beginning to examine the material from a race and gender perspective. In addition, students are asked to use their own experience and that of their classmates to validate the presentation of the material.

The syllabus tries to describe for the students what each day will be like. Lectures one day a week. Problem sets one day a week. Lecture/discussion on the textbook material or of the race and gender examples mentioned in the syllabus on the other days of the week.

On the first day of class, students introduce each other and do two exercises that illustrate the difference between competitive learning and cooperative learning. Students are given the option of doing the work of the course by themselves or forming teams. If a student wants to do all the work by himself or herself, that is perfectly acceptable. A team is a cooperative learning group where one member of the group is randomly selected to take a test or make a presentation for the entire group (Bartlett 1995). Teams are voluntary. The grade this student earns is the grade given to every member of the group. The random selection of a group member eliminates the free-rider problem that haunts most group efforts. Marginal students get the tutoring and support they need and better students get to teach and improve their understanding of the subject.

Students know that they will have a great deal of input into the course and that they will have a variety of ways of letting the instructor know if they know the material. Problem sets and exams are the main instruments of evaluation. The problem sets done once a week prepare students for the kinds of questions found on the exams. While students are given numerous multiple-choice questions and problems to solve over the weekend, only a few are actually discussed in class. The practice, however, gives students a good idea of what will be on the exam, lots of practice doing exam-type questions in a graded situation, and some confidence about how to answer questions on the test.

Tests are slightly different from those in the course outlined in the first syllabus. The exams have three sections. The first section is multiple-choice questions, but they are different than those found in the first course outline. The multiple-choice questions are now multiple-choice/multiple-answer questions. Students are to indicate the correct answer and then explain in a sentence or two why all the other answers are wrong. Each component of the question is worth points. The short essay part of the exam usually deals with a particular problem often found in principles text. The final section of each exam, unlike originally described in the syllabus, asks students to pick any question on the exam and relate it to their life or to someone they know. They are given an additional five points if they make a good connection.

Having explained to students how the material will be covered, how they will be tested on it, and grading procedures is the next item. Team work accounts for 60–90 percent of the final grade and individual work accounts for 10–40 percent of the final grade. The difference in these percentages is a result of students deciding to take the final by themselves or as a member of a team. Furthermore, grades will be individualistic in the sense that students who get 90 percent of the test correct will receive an "A," and so on. Competitive grading where only the top 10 percent get "A"s is not used, so students know that hard work could pay off.

SUMMARY

In order to begin thinking about how to integrate race and gender into the introductory economics course, the necessary elements of course design were discussed and models of inclusion and balancing the curriculum were introduced. The course syllabus found in Figure 1.2 is an example of how to begin the process. The changes that need to be made may seem overwhelming at first, but instructors can start with one change at a time. Drastic change is not necessary, and probably not helpful. Instructors should teach within their comfort zone. Including one new example, new exercise, or exam question will help instructors to learn and grow with the process of reconstructing their courses.

The way that each of the examples in Parts II and III of the book were used in the course will be discussed at the beginning of each section.

BIBLIOGRAPHY

Amott, T. L. and Matthaei, J. A. (1991) *Race, Gender, and Work: A Multicultural History of Women in the United States*, Boston: South End Press.

Bartlett, R. L. (1995) "A Flip of the Coin–a Roll of the Die: An Answer to the Free-rider Problem in Economic Instruction," *Journal of Economic Education* 26, 2 (spring): 137–9.

Bartlett, R. L. and Becker, W. E. (1991) "Special Issue on Undergraduate Economic Education," *Journal of Economic Education* 22, 3 (summer): 195-6.

Belenky, M. F., Clinchy, B. M., Goldberger, N. R. and Tarule, J. M. (1986) *Women's Ways of Knowing: The Development of Self, Voice, and Mind*, New York: Basic Books.

Bergmann, B. R. (1983) "Feminism and Economics," *Academe*, (September–October) 69, 5: 22-5.

—— (1986) *The Economic Emergence of Women*, New York: Basic Books.

—— (1987) "Women's Roles in the Economy: Teaching the Issues," *Journal of Economic Education* 18, 4 (fall): 393– 407.

—— (1990) "Women's Studies in Economics," *Women's Studies Quarterly* 18, 3 and 4 (fall/winter): 6–86.

Blau, F. D. and Ferber, M. A. (1986) *The Economics of Women, Men, and Work*, Englewood Cliffs, NJ: Prentice-Hall.

Blinder, A. S. (1990) "Learning by Asking Those Who are Doing," *Eastern Economic Journal* 16, 4 (October–December): 297– 306.

Feiner, S. F. (1993) "Introductory Economics Textbooks and the Treatment of Issues related to Women and Minorities, 1984 and 1991," *Journal of Economic Education* 24, 2 (spring): 145– 62.

Feiner, S. F. and Morgan, B. A. (1987) "Women and Minorities in Introductory Economics Textbooks: 1974–1984," *Journal of Economic Education* 18, 4 (fall): 376–92.

Ferber, M. A. (1989) "Gender and the Study of Economics," in P. Saunders and W. Walstad (eds) *The Principles of Economics Course: A Handbook for Instructors*, New York: McGraw-Hill.

Goldin, C. (1990) *Understanding the Gender Gap: An Economic History of American Women*, New York: Oxford University Press.

Hansen, W. L. (1986.) "What Knowledge is Most Worth Knowing— for Economics Majors?" *American Economic Review* 76, 2 (May): 149–52.

Hall, R. M. and Sandler, B. R. (1982) "The Classroom Climate: A Chilly one for Women?" Washington, DC: Project for the Status and Education of Women, Association of American Colleges.

Johnson, D. W., Johnson, R. T., and Smith, K. A. (1991) *Cooperative Learning: Increased College Faculty Instructional Productivity*, ASHE-ERIC Higher Education Report No. 4, Washington, DC: The George Washington University, School of Education and Human Development.

Lumsden, K. G. and Scott, A. (1986) "Gender and the Economics Student Reexamined," *Journal of Economic Education* 18, 4 (fall): 365–75.

McIntosh, P. (1983) "Interactive Phases of the Curricular Re-vision: A Feminist Perspective," Wellesley, MA: Wellesley College, Center for Research on Women, Working Paper No. 124.

—— (1990) "Interactive Phases of Curricular and Personal Re-vision with Regard to Race," Wellesley, MA: Wellesley College, Center for Research on Women, Working Paper No. 219.

Meyers, C. and Jones, T. B. (1993) *Promoting Active Learning: Strategies for the Classroom*. San Francisco: Jossey-Bass.

Musil, C. M. (1992) "Collaborative Learning and Women's Ways of Knowing," *Students at the Center: Feminist Assessment*, Washington, DC: Association of American Colleges.

Rosser, S. V. (1990) *Female-friendly Science: Applying Women's Studies Methods and Theories to Attract Students*, The Athene Series, New York: Pergamon Press.

Saunders, P. and Walstad, W. B. (1990) *The Principles of Economics Course: A Handbook for Instructors*, New York: McGraw-Hill.

Siegfried, J. J., Bartlett, R. L., Hansen, W. L., Kelley, A. C., McCloskey, D. N., and Tietenberg, T. H. (1990) "Economics," *Liberal Learning and the Arts and Sciences Major, Reports from the Field*, Washington, DC: Association of American Colleges: 25–42.

Tobias, S. (1990) *They're Not Dumb, They're Different: Stalking the Second Tier*, Tucson, AZ: Research Corporation.

Treisman, U. (1992) "Studying Students Studying Calculus: A Look at the Lives of Minority Mathematics Students in College," *College Mathematics Journal* 23, 5 (November): 362–72.

Part II

Integrating race and gender topics into introductory microeconomics

Part II provides the microeconomics examples that can be used to reconstruct the microeconomic portions of an introductory economics course. In this section of the book, six examples are presented that incorporate race and gender into particular microeconomic topics. Each example provides the necessary background information or context within which the example is to be used, the necessary data, and suggestions for classroom activities.

The syllabus in Chapter 1 uses five of the six examples to help illustrate several basic economic concepts: property rights through protective legislation; segmented markets as a result of the income distribution, government, and bank regulations policies; price ceilings and floors with affirmative action policies, marginal analysis and the choice of whether to attend college; and opportunity costs with male and female labor supply trends.

Pam Nickless and James Whitney, in "Protective Legislation and Women's Employment," develop a case study of protective legislation and the minimum wage. The case is a good historical example of the importance of property rights and the necessity of the freedom to make contracts and have equal access to the labor market. They also develop the context within which this legislation was taking place by providing excerpts from early American and French suffragists.

Rosemary Cunningham, in "Market Segmentation: The Role of Race in the Housing Market," illustrates how markets can get segmented as a result of the income distribution, governmental policies, social and personal assumptions. While many of the market interventions were done with good intentions, the effect is to isolate buyers and sellers.

Louise Laurence and Robert Moore, in "Gender and Race and the Decision to Go to College," present an example that develops the notion of comparing costs and benefits from various options. They explore gender differences by asking students to examine relevant data and to make observations about why women's decisions to invest in human capital may be different from those of men. Then the same questions are asked, but information on race is also included.

Margaret Lewis and Janice Peterson's chapter on "The Labor Supply Decision—Differences between Genders and Races" is an in-depth exploration of the definitions of work and leisure. What activities constitute work and leisure and are they easily separable? How do work and leisure activities vary by race and gender? Their market versus non-market discussion is an excellent race and gender balanced introduction to the topic of labor supply. Their annotated selection of readings is an excellent resource for exploring ethnic and racial differences.

Robert Moore and James Whitney's chapter on "The Economics of Affirmative Action" could be placed in several sections of a course. In the syllabus in Chapter 1, this example is used as an example of restricting quantity and the impact such restrictions have on market outcomes. This example offers some excellent pedagogical exercises that can be used with other examples. Finally, Kathy Parkison delves into the construction of societal cost and benefit curves to evaluate environmental, technological, and public health risks. She does a nice job dealing the problems of defining risk.

All of these examples give students an opportunity to apply the economic principles they have learned from the traditional course content found in a standard textbook to issues of race and gender. In addition, the nontraditional student of economics may find that economics is relevant to understanding their world and may be motivated to develop the analytical skills necessary to work successfully with the traditional methodology of economics.

2 Protective labor legislation and women's employment

Pamela J. Nickless and James D. Whitney

By the 1960s, protective labor legislation that applied only to women had the effect of limiting the ability of women to compete in the labor market. In the context of the post-World War II economy, it seemed as if that legislation was surely passed by men to limit women's work and to benefit male workers at the expense of women. Most undergraduates will assume that this was the case, and yet much of the protective legislation in Europe and the United States was passed by a coalition of women reformers, women workers, male reformers, and labor leaders of both genders. Opposition came, as one might expect, from employers and classical economists and, one might be surprised to learn, from suffragists and women's rights advocates. In the United States after 1920, the women's rights movement split over this very issue. Advocates of the Equal Rights Amendment opposed protective legislation for women while proponents of special legislation for women opposed the Equal Rights Amendment.

Since many of the arguments on both sides of the protective legislation issue rested on differing economic interpretations of how the labor market worked, the controversy can be used to illustrate a variety of key economic concepts. The topic is suitable for courses on labor economics, economics of race and gender, women's studies, or as a detailed application in a principles or intermediate microeconomics course. The second and third sections of this chapter offer two alternative lesson plans for covering protective legislation. Lesson Plan 1 deals with the treatment of protective legislation in US case law and lays out the basic economic analysis at issue. The material for Lesson Plan 1 is adapted from Professor Richard Burkhauser's Vanderbilt University course "Economics/Women's Studies Gender Issues in the Marketplace: The Nexus of Law and Economics." Lesson Plan 2 provides a broader context for the past and continuing history of protective legislation and draws on material utilized in Professor Pamela Nickless's University of North Carolina at Asheville course, "Introduction to Women's Studies and US Economic History." The material in Lesson Plan 2 was in turn suggested by Dr. Kathleen Nilan's coverage of the topic in *Women in Modern Europe*.

LESSON PLAN 1: PROTECTIVE LEGISLATION IN US CASE LAW

The two Supreme Court rulings compared in this lesson give students an opportunity to apply a number of basic economic concepts in evaluating the effects on women of protective labor legislation: gains from trade, supply and demand, equilibrium, efficiency, complements and substitutes, rational actors, externalities, and equal power.

Background and preparation

Students should prepare for class by reading the decisions reached in the two relevant Supreme Court cases, Lochner vs. New York (1905) and Muller vs. Oregon (1908). Baer (1978: chapters 1 and 2) serves as a useful additional reference for the instructor.

Lochner vs. New York (1905) was the high water mark of institutional *laissez-faire*. The New York state legislature had passed a law limiting workers in the baking industry to a maximum of sixty labor hours per week. In a five-to-four decision, the court struck down the law, ruling that it was an unconstitutional infringement of the Fourteenth Amendment's protection of individuals' freedom to contract.

One Supreme Court justice died between 1905 and 1908. Muller vs. Oregon (1908) was the first case related to Lochner to reach the Supreme Court after his death. The Oregon state legislature had passed a maximum hours law that restricted only women from working more than sixty hours per week in hotels. Reversing for women the effects of Lochner vs. New York, the US Supreme Court ruled unanimously that the Oregon law was constitutional.

Class discussion: questions and responses

Protective hours legislation

Concerning Lochner vs. New York which concerned maximum hours legislation for bakers. Review (or prompt students to review) the facts of the case, and proceed to the following questions and responses:

Question: What are the economic underpinnings of "freedom to contract?" That is, how does freedom of contract promote the general good?

The key is gains from trade. Voluntary trades are mutually beneficial, and, if no third party is worse off, society gains from permitting them.

Question: What are the limits of freedom to contract even in 1905 as discussed in Lochner (i.e. when is it in society's interest to limit trade)?

Five exceptions are noted in the decision:

1 absence of "rational actors" (minors, for example, can't sign contracts);
2 health risks to others, such as with immunizations (externalities);

3 unequal power, as in the case of a firm giving "script" to buy goods at the company store (monopsony);
4 immoral acts (prostitution, blue laws, etc., examples again of externalities in the sense of offending third parties); and
5 "rule of reason" limitations (acceptable pursuant to the separation of legislative and judicial powers; the restriction in this case was deemed unreasonable in the opinion of the majority).

Question: What was the reasoning underlying the court's majority opinion?

The court found there was no compelling reason to interfere with freedom of contract—in other words that there were gains to unregulated trade. Justice Peckham's opinion for the court:

> The question of whether this act is valid as a labor law, pure and simple, may be dismissed in a few words. There is no reasonable ground for interfering with the liberty of the person or the right of free contract, by determining the hours of labor, in the occupation of a baker. There is no contention that bakers as a class are not equal in intelligence and capacity to men in other trades or manual occupations, or that they are not able to assert their rights and care for themselves without the protecting arm of the state interfering with their independence of judgment and of action. They are in no sense wards of the state. Viewed in the light of a purely labor law, with no reference whatever to the question of health, we think that a law like the one before us involves neither the safety, the morals, nor the welfare, of the public, and that the interest of the public is not in the slightest degree affected by such an act.
>
> We think the limit of the police power has been reached and passed in this case. There is, in our judgment, no reasonable foundation for holding this to be necessary and appropriate as a health law to safeguard the public health. . . .
>
> We think that there can be no fair doubt that the trade of baker, in and of itself, is not an unhealthy one to that degree which would authorize the legislature to interfere with the right to labor, and with the right of free contract on the part of the individual, either as employer or employee;. . . There must be more than the mere fact of the possible existence of some small amount of unhealthiness to warrant legislative interference with liberty. . . .
>
> The act is not, within any fair meaning of the term, a health law, but is an illegal interference with the rights of individuals, both employers and employees, to make contracts regarding labor upon such terms as they may think best, or which they may agree upon with the other parties to such contracts. Statutes of the nature of that under review limiting the hours in which grown and intelligent men may earn their living, are mere meddlesome interferences with the rights of the individual, and they are

not saved from condemnation by the claim that they are passed in the exercise of the police power and upon the subject of the health of the individual whose rights are interfered with, unless there be some fair ground, reasonable in and of itself, to say that there is a material danger to the public health, or to the health of the employees, if the hours of labor are not curtailed.

(Baer 1978: 49–50)

From this brief excerpt, students can see the court looking for the conditions under which gains from unregulated trade will be forthcoming.

In dissent, Justice Oliver Wendell Holmes wrote: "Court is not in the business of determining whether *laissez-faire* is the best economic philosophy or some other philosophy is best. To be constitutional, court only must decide if reasonable legislators could believe that this law was not an unconstitutional limitation on liberty."

Proceeding to Muller vs. Oregon (1908), which upheld maximum hours legislation for women. Review the facts of the case, and turn to the following question/response:

Question: Which of the exceptions to freedom of contract did the Court use in letting Muller stand?

Two of the exceptions played a prominent part in the decision. One, women were considered to be like minors who must be protected by public policy. And two, externalities are involved in that women must be protected for the survival of the race. Women have different roles to play in society. Consider the following key paragraphs from the Muller decision:

That woman's physical structure and the performance of maternal functions place her at a disadvantage in the struggle for existence is obvious. This is especially true when the burdens of motherhood are upon her. Even when they are not, by abundant testimony of the medical fraternity, continuance for a long time on her feet at work, repeating this from day to day, tends to [have] injurious effects upon the body, and, as healthy mothers are essential to vigorous offspring, the physical well-being of women becomes an object of public interest and care in order to preserve the strength and vigor of the race. Still again, history discloses the fact that woman has always been dependent upon man. He established his control at the outset by superior physical strength, and this control in various forms, and with diminishing intensity, has continued to the present. As minors, though not to the same extent, she has been looked upon in the courts as needing especial care that her rights be preserved. Education was long denied her, and while now the doors of the schoolroom are opened and her opportunities for acquiring knowledge are great, yet even with that and the consequent increase of capacity for business affairs, it is still true that in the struggle for subsistence she is not an equal competitor with her brother. Though limitations upon personal and contractual rights may be removed by legislation, there is that in her disposition and habits of life which will operate against a full assertion of those rights. She will still be where some legislation to protect her seems necessary to secure a real equality of rights...looking at it from the viewpoint of the effort to maintain an independent position in life, she is not upon an equality. Differentiated by these matters from the other sex, she is properly placed in a class by herself, and legislation designed for her protection may be sustained, even when like legislation is not necessary for men, and could not be sustained. It is impossible to close one's eyes to the fact that she still looks to her brother and depends upon him. Even if all restrictions on political, personal, and contractual rights were taken away, and she stood, so far as statutes are concerned, upon an absolutely equal plane with him, it would still be true that she will rest upon and look to him for protection; that her physical structure and a proper discharge of her maternal functions—having in view not merely her own health, but the well-being of the race—justify legislation to protect her from the greed as well as the passion of man. The limitations which this statute places upon her contractual powers, upon her right to agree with her employer as to the time she shall labor, are imposed not only for her benefit, but also largely for the benefit of all.... The two sexes differ in structure of the body, in the amount of physical strength, in the capacity for long-continued labor, the influence of vigorous health upon the future well-being of the race, the self-reliance which enables one to assert full rights, and in the capacity to maintain the struggle for subsistence. This difference justifies a difference in legislation.

(Baer 1978: 62–3)

So note that here the court finds that women do need special protection and freedom of contract is not upheld. Students should easily find the externalities that would limit gains to trade as well as the court's doubts about women possessing equal power.

The minimum wage

The minimum wage started out as another example of protective legislation. Like maximum hours legislation, minimum wage legislation was rejected as unconstitutional under the Fourteenth Amendment in the early part of the twentieth century. The first minimum wage legislation that was upheld as constitutional applied only to women (West Coast Hotel Co. vs. Parrish [1936]).

Question: Does gender-based minimum wage legislation help or hurt women?

Develop the answer with two separate labor-market supply and demand diagrams, one for women and one for men. Depending on the level of the course, a few scenarios are possible. Consider first the simple case of competitive labor markets for women and men in which workers of both sexes are perfect substitutes in the production of goods and services. Illustrate how a minimum wage applied only to women decreases women's employment and increases the demand for men's employment.

If students are familiar with the concept of derived demand, work through an example of completely segmented labor markets for men and women in which no substitution in production is allowed. The results are the same, since the demand for labor is a derived demand. Even if men and women are *not* substitutes in the production of a given product, goods produced by women laborers will still increase in price relative to goods produced by men laborers, and the output effect will still cause the same result as before.

Finally, if the students are familiar with complements and substitutes in production (or, more precisely with respect to resource markets, complementary and anticomplementary inputs), consider a case in which women and men are complementary inputs in production. In that case, a minimum wage for women reduces the demand for men workers. Men workers do experience economic losses or gains in this case. Moreover, reduced employment of men reduces the marginal productivity of women; the derived demand for women therefore decreases, further reducing their employment.

Current examples of protective legislation

Despite the civil rights revolution of the 1960s which fundamentally restated the legal rights of women, gender-based legislation continues to affect women.

Question: Can you think of examples of such legislation? Is it "good" or "bad" social policy?

Illustrative examples for discussion which include mandatory pregnancy leave and parental leave policies are in the bibliography.

LESSON PLAN 2: THE POLITICAL ECONOMY CONTEXT OF PROTECTIVE LEGISLATION

Many of the women and men who argued for protective legislation for women did not base their arguments on the special maternal function of women. Many reformers at the end of the nineteenth century wanted regulation of hours and conditions of work for all workers, but knew that the legislatures were hostile to regulating male labor.

Many of them saw protective legislation for women as a first step, leading the way to legislation for all workers. Many reformers also believed that, in industries that employed men and women, limiting women's hours would limit men's hours. They were assuming, of course, that men and women are complementary workers rather than substitutes in the labor market.

Background and preparation

Students can readily grasp the underlying issues by reading two short pieces by Beatrice Webb and Maria Pognon. The same basic tools used in Lesson Plan 1 can be used in this example. These short pieces are available in Bell and Offen (1983: 205–13).

Beatrice Webb's piece is particularly informative from the point of view of an economist, since she is directly responding to the arguments of the British suffragists who oppose special legislation for women. In Britain, Millicent Fawcett was one of the leaders of the suffrage movement and was also an economist who wrote on the topic of equal pay for women. (See Fawcett 1918.) Consequently, the argument is phrased in economic terms.

Class coverage of the material

Relevant passages useful for focusing class discussion

Consider beginning with the following brief excerpt from Beatrice Webb (1896):

It is frequently asserted as self-evident that any special limitation of women's labor must militate against their employment. If employers are not allowed to make their women work overtime, or during the night, they will, it is said, inevitably prefer to have men. Thus, it is urged, any extension of factory legislation to trades, at present unregulated, must diminish the demand for women's labor. But this conclusion, which seems so obvious, really rests on a series of assumptions which are not borne out by facts.

The first assumption is, that in British industry today, men and women are actively competing for the same employment. I doubt whether any one here has any conception of the infinitesimal extent to which this is true. We are so accustomed, in the middle class, to see men and women engaged in identical work, as teachers, journalists, authors, painters, sculptors, comedians, singers, musicians, medical practitioners, clerks, or what not, that we almost inevitably assume the same state of things to exist in manual labor and manufacturing industry. But this is very far from being the case. To begin with, in over nine-tenths of the industrial field there is no such thing as competition between men and women: the men do one thing, and the women do another. There is no more chance of our having our houses built by women than of our getting our floors scrubbed by men. And even in those industries which employ both men and women, we find them sharply divided in different departments, working at different processes, and performing different operations. In the tailoring trade, for instance, it is often assumed that men and women are competitors. But in a detailed investigation of that trade, I discovered that men were working at entirely separate branches to those pursued by the women. And when my husband, as an economist, lately tried to demonstrate the oft-repeated statement that women are paid at a lower rate than men, he found it very difficult to discover any trade whatever in which men and women did the same work. As a matter of fact, the employment of men or women in any particular industry is almost always determined by the character of the process. In many cases the physical strength or endurance required, or the exposure involved, puts the work absolutely out of the power of the average woman. No law has hindered employers from engaging women as blacksmiths, steel-smelters, masons, or omnibus-drivers. The great mass of extractive, constructive, and transport industries must always fall to men. On the other hand, the women of the wage-earning class have hitherto been distinguished by certain qualities not possessed by the average working man. For good or for evil they eat little, despise tobacco, and seldom get drunk; they rarely strike or disobey orders; and they are in many other ways easier for an employer to deal with. Hence, where women can really perform a given task with anything like the efficiency of a man, they have, owing to their lower standard of expenditure, a far better chance than the man of getting work. The men, in short, enjoy what may be called a "rent" of superior strength and endurance; the women, on their side, in this preference for certain employments, what may be called a "rent" of abstemiousness.

I do not wish to imply that there are absolutely no cases in British industry in which men and women are really competing with each other. It is, I believe, easy to pick out an instance here and there in which it might be prophesied that the removal of an existing legal restriction might, in the first instance, lead to some women being taken on in place of men. In the book and printing trade of London, for instance, it has been said that if women were allowed by law to work all through the night, a certain number of exceptionally strong women might oust some men in book-folding and even in compositors' work. We must not overlook these cases; but we must learn to view them in their proper proportion to the whole field of industry. It would clearly be a calamity to the cause of women's advancement if we were to sacrifice the personal liberty and economic independence of three or four millions of wage-earning women in order to enable a few hundreds or a few thousands to supplant men in certain minor spheres of industry.

Maria Pognon's piece was written in response to a French law limiting the right to work for women. Pognon was the President of the Ligue Française pour le Droit des Femmes (French League for Women's Rights) and her piece was published in *La Fronde*, a Parisian women's daily newspaper. The newspaper had challenged the law in court and lost. Since the newspaper had an entirely female staff that had to work at night to get a daily paper out, the tone of Pognon's article is understandable.

On this very day that unfortunate law of so-called protection is returning to the Chamber of Deputies from the Senate. It is so badly written that it is impossible to apply, and on behalf of women we have a duty to protest against it.

On the pretext of protecting women against exploitation by their employers, on the pretext of safeguarding the future of the race through the women, our legislators decided that all night work should be prohibited and that the number of working hours of a female worker should be limited to eleven hours a day.

In practice it was quickly realized that, on the one hand, the mixed workshops [i.e. sexually integrated] could not function without shared work and that with the departure of the women who ran a machine, for instance, the men could not continue with their own tasks. On the other hand, it appeared that there were certain types of work such as folding newspapers, binding periodical reviews, lighting lamps in the mines, which were so badly paid that no man wanted the jobs. Now, however lowly certain tasks may seem, they are nonetheless indispensable and pressure was brought on the law to allow night work at these newspapers, journals, and mines.

A decree issued on July 15, 1893, authorized the employment of women on a permanent basis in these types of work for seven hours per night.

In addition to the newspaper folders, who are now authorized to wear themselves out for very little gain, it was noted that certain morning newspapers employed female compositors and that these women were well able to support themselves and their children.

At that point came an about-face! Women folders could be permitted, but not women compositors. The inspectors received strict orders, and everywhere the women compositors were replaced by men. In the meantime, one printer in the provinces resisted; on the basis of the law that prohibited night work by minor girls and married women, he alleged that adult single women were not included under this prohibition. In consequence he dismissed the married women he had employed and replaced them with single women who were of age, affirming that this put him right with the law. The court found against him; he lost his appeal and was obliged to dismiss the adult single women along with the others.

Are we supposed to believe that this law was made in the interest of women? Quite the contrary: it is protection in reverse. What? For seven years we have witnessed new decrees authorizing night work in certain industries, such as pouring and drying starch: in the glassworks women are permitted to sort and arrange bottles—in a word, to execute such tasks as men refuse because they are not sufficiently lucrative.

The 1892 law was made by antifeminists, who were concerned with reserving all the well-paying work for their constituents: this is the real truth!

We have nothing against the protection of children. But we find the law much too harsh for them; they are not allowed to work in factories or workshops more than six hours per day before the age of sixteen, and are supposed to use the remaining hours for their instruction and their physical development. As for a woman, she is an adult being who should be free to govern herself just as much as a man. If the end result is to limit the workday to a certain number of hours for all workers, so be it, but there should be no unfavorable exceptions for one sex to the profit of the other. In all the industries such as the cotton spinneries of the Vosges, the wool-combing establishments of the Nord, the 1892 law had the effect of opening up jobs for men, whose hours were not restricted. The poor children were plunged into utmost misery as a result of the forced unemployment of their mothers.

Since then many, many exemptions have been granted, on the demand of employers who said they could not do without their female workers. The hat makers, the *couturières* have all arranged a certain number of authorized night-work sessions.

But wherever the night work is well paid, someone has found it too tiring for women, or unhygienic, or even dangerous!

Many thanks for your protection, *Messieurs les députés*. From now on leave women free to work or to rest as they see fit, according to the circumstances. Get used to considering them as responsible beings, capable of directing their own lives and of taking responsibility for their own actions; do not confuse them with their children, whose reasoning powers are not yet fully developed, and, if you want to protect the little ones, let their mothers work in their places.

Help these women to unionize so that they can themselves arrange their terms of work with the employers, but do not deprive them of their jobs on the pretext of safeguarding their health. If the father's health is not good, the children will not be much to brag about either.

We can improve the race by requiring of workers only a reasonable expenditure of physical strength. But since both sexes are called upon to procreate, we must be prudent and kind to both; otherwise it is lost labor.

Class assignment

For a class assignment, consider asking students to write an essay on whether or not the labor market for women and that for men are competitive. What evidence would they need to decide whether men and women were competing for jobs at the end of the last century? What about now?

Current examples of protective legislation

As with Lesson Plan 1, it is easy to convince students that these issues are not merely of historical interest. A recent article in *The Margin* argued that the Parental Leave Bill passed by Congress and signed by President Clinton in 1993 would, in fact, disadvantage women in the labor market since employers would have to provide maternity leave for women workers. The arguments were identical to the ones used by Millicent Fawcett in opposing special legislation for women. A recent Supreme Court case involving Johnson Controls also took up the question of women's special role as mothers. Johnson Controls had sought to ban fertile women from jobs where there was exposure to lead. The court ruled Johnson Controls were discriminatory in their policy.

BIBLIOGRAPHY

Baer, J. A. (1978) *The Chains of Protection: The Judicial Response to Women's Protective Legislation*, Westport, CT: Greenwood Press.

Bell, Susan Groaf, and Offen, Karen M. (eds) (1983) *Women, the Family and Freedom: The Debate in Documents* II, *1880–1950*, Stanford, CA: Stanford University Press.

Fawcett, Millicent (1918) "Equal Pay for Equal Work," *Economic Journal*, 28 March, pp. 1–6.

Goldin, C. (1988) "Maximum Hours Legislation and Female Employment in the 1920s: A Reassessment," *Journal of Political Economy* 96 (February): 108–205.

—— (1990) *Understanding the Gender Gap: An Economic History of American Women*, New York: Oxford University Press.

Lehrer, S. (1987) *Origins of Protective Labor Legislation for Women, 1905–1925*, SUNY Series on Women and Work, New York: SUNY Press.

Lochner vs. New York (1905) 198 US 45, 61.

Lundahl, M. and Wadensjo, E. (1984) *Unequal Treatment: A Study in The Neoclassical Theory of Discrimination*, New York: New York University Press.

Muller vs. Oregon (1908) 28 Supreme Court Reporter 324, 327.

Sklar, K. K. (1985) "Hull House in the 1890s: A Community of Women Reformers," *Signs* 10 (Summer). Reprinted in E. C. DuBois and V. L. Ruiz (eds) *Unequal Sisters: A Multicultural Reader in US Women's History*, New York: Routledge (1990).

West Coast Hotel Co. vs. Parrish (1936) 300 US 379, 414.

3 Market segmentation: the role of race in housing markets

Rosemary T. Cunningham

In introductory economics, we introduce the idea of markets from a rather abstract perspective. We define a market as any place or space in which buyers and sellers come together to exchange a good or service. Without government intervention, any time there is excess supply in a market, we explain that the price will fall until the market clears and, conversely, if there is excess demand, the price will rise. If the government intervenes in a market with either price ceilings or price floors, then a shortage or surplus of the good may persist with the possibility of a black market or discrimination in the market developing.

When discussing specific markets, however, we frequently overlook the differences among market segments and focus on the overall market for the good. This may be easier for instructional purposes, but it may mislead students attempting to connect the discussion in the classroom with their everyday experiences. It is important to identify the buyers, sellers, and goods relevant to a particular market segment.

When introducing the idea of market segments to my students, I begin with a fairly benign example of market segmentation, the market for hair services (i.e. haircuts, permanents, straightening, coloring, shaves). I explain that, frequently, there are separate markets for men's and women's hair care. Although today it is common to see both men and women in the same hair salon, there are still traditional barber shops that provide service essentially for men only and beauty parlors for women. Very often, hair shops specialize in styling the hair of white or African Americans. There is some overlap among the different market segments but for the most part these segments comprise markets distinct from other hair markets.

After introducing the idea of market segments, I present the housing market as one worthy of special attention. By focusing on segmentation rather than segregation, I hope to avoid any previous conceived notions regarding housing. In addition to providing one of the basics of life, the housing market may influence the quality of educational and other public services to which an individual has access. Owning your home is central to the "American dream" and, according to the Economic Report of the President, owner-occupied real estate is the source of more than one-third of the total net wealth in the United States. Although there are many forms of segmentation in the housing market in the United States, I focus here on segmentation by race and discuss possible causes, effects, and solutions.

INCOME DISTRIBUTION

Beginning with the most benign perspective, I note how the existing distribution of income influences the housing market. Persons with little disposable income and no car have little choice but to seek low-income apartments near public transportation. Given that few substitutes to such apartments exist, landlords can exploit some of their monopoly power in the form of higher rents. With no build-up of equity, the chance of amassing the necessary down payment for a home is very small or nil. Therefore, we see that these market segments tend to perpetuate the type of housing markets in which individuals can participate.

In the United States, African-American families are overrepresented in the lower income classes. Table 3.1 shows the distribution of income in the United States by race for the year 1990. Given that 50 percent of all black families earn less than $21,423, compared with $36,915 for white families, it will be particularly difficult for black families to amass the down payment needed to purchase a single-family home. Therefore, many African-American families have no option but to rent and primarily in multi-family dwellings. A survey by the Board of Governors of the Federal Reserve System in 1989 found that, although almost two-thirds of all American families owned their homes, only 42.8 percent of minority families owned their home (Brimmer 1992: 43).

It is also important to explain to students that, inasmuch as the segments of the housing market equilibrate, the equilibrium price will allow all those willing and able to purchase housing services and all those willing and able to provide such services at the equilibrium price to do so. However, there are those who, for whatever reasons, cannot afford to purchase housing services, but at a lower price would demand housing. These individuals may

Table 3.1   Percent distribution of families, by income level, in 1990

Income	All	White	Black	Hispanic
Under median $10,000	9.4	7.2	25.6	18.6
$10,000–$14,999	7.5	7.0	11.3	12.6
$15,000–$24,999	16.4	16.0	19.5	21.7
$25,000–$34,999	16.2	16.5	14.0	16.6
$35,000–$49,999	20.1	20.8	15.0	15.7
$50,000–$74,999	18.2	19.3	9.8	10.0
$75,000 and over	12.3	13.2	4.7	4.8
	$35,353	$36,915	$21,423	$23,431

Source: Statistical Abstract of the United States (1992), Table 702, p. 449.

live with family, friends, or on the street. Federal, state, and local government agencies try to intervene in the market for low-income housing to help provide these very needed housing services.

GOVERNMENT POLICIES

We must remember that the traditional-age college student was born well after the civil rights movement. During his or her lifetime, the government has tried to eliminate discrimination rather than create or maintain racial or ethnic barriers. However, the segmentation of the housing market by race may in part be the result of government lending policies. In the early years of the Federal Housing Administration, in particular, the FHA actively discriminated against non-white families. In its 1938 *Underwriting Manual*, it advised banks to avoid areas that might be surrounded by "incompatible racial and social groups" because they might contribute to instability in the neighborhood and a fall in property values. This type of government lending preference continued into the late 1950s: "between 1946 and 1959, less than 2 percent of all the housing financed with the assistance of federal mortgage insurance was made available to blacks" (Judd 1991: 740). At the same time, the 1949 Housing Act reinforced the racial segmentation of markets by tearing down low-income housing and building high-rise housing projects in primarily black areas.

The Fair Housing Act of 1968 outlawed discrimination in housing. Yet, previous government policy had already reinforced the idea that when African-American families move into a neighborhood, it is a sign of neighborhood decline. Some studies have shown that when the proportion of black families increases beyond 8 percent of the neighborhood, white families become nervous and white flight begins (*Economist*, July 10, 1993, p. 17).

DISCRIMINATION IN LENDING PRACTICES

Another problem confronting African-American families is that they do not always have the same access to mortgages as white Americans. It surprises me that some of my students have never heard of the term "redlining." They are unaware that banks may illegally limit or refuse to lend in certain neighborhoods because of the ethnic or racial composition. One study of "redlining" that received substantial attention was the 1988 Pulitzer Prize-winning series, "The Color of Money," in *The Atlanta Journal/Constitution* that uncovered alleged instances of the practice by Atlanta banks. The series indicated that whites received home loans five times as often as blacks. It is helpful to have students read and comment on some of the articles from this series.

The difficulty of obtaining loans might explain a portion of why proportionately fewer black families own their homes and fewer black families have outstanding mortgages. According to a 1989 Federal Reserve Board survey, although approximately 38.7 percent of US families have mortgages outstanding on their homes, a breakdown on racial lines shows that while 40.9 percent of white families have outstanding mortgages, only 23.7 percent of minority families do.

Although the practice of redlining is illegal under the Fair Housing Act of 1968, suspicion that it continued led Congress to pass the Home Mortgage Disclosure Act (HMDA) in 1976 and amendments to the act in 1989. HMDA requires most mortgage-lending institutions to publicly disclose the geographic distribution of home mortgage and home improvement loans that they originate and purchase, as well as the race or national origin, gender, and annual income of loan applicants and borrowers. It may surprise students that studies of the HMDA data still indicate wide differences in mortgage approval and rejection rates for minorities and whites. Table 3.2 highlights some of the disparities in both government-backed (loans insured or guaranteed by FHA, the Veterans' Administration, or the Farmers' Home Administration) and conventional mortgage approvals and denials for individuals of different ethnic backgrounds but of similar income groups from the 1991 HMDA data. The data are divided into individuals having less than 80 percent, 80–99 percent, 100–120 percent, and more than 120 percent of the median family income for their metropolitan statistical area (MSA).

Table 3.2 Mortgage approvals and denials, by race, 1991 (%)

	Government-backed mortgages		Conventional mortgages	
	Approved	*Denied*	*Approved*	*Denied*
Less than 80%				
Black	58.8	30.1	44.9	48.2
Hispanic	64.6	23.9	54.0	37.1
White	67.3	25.2	61.7	31.5
80%–99%				
Black	66.8	22.1	60.7	30.0
Hispanic	70.8	17.1	64.9	25.3
White	79.5	12.5	77.0	15.3
100%–120%				
Black	66.9	22.1	63.9	26.1
Hispanic	71.2	16.0	67.0	22.3
White	81.0	10.9	79.9	12.2
More than 120%				
Black	69.3	19.5	66.0	23.2
Hispanic	75.7	13.3	68.5	19.8
White	81.8	9.7	81.0	9.7

Source: G. B. Canner and D. S. Smith, "Expanded HMDA Data on Residential Lending," *Federal Reserve Bulletin*, November 1992, p. 812.

Table 3.2 indicates that, regardless of income group, white applicants are more likely to have their mortgages approved and black applicants to have theirs denied. Figure 3.1 shows the percentage point differential between white and black approval rates by income groups, while Figure 3.2 shows the differential between black and white denial rates. Although the differentials in both approval and denial rates are smaller for government-backed mortgages than for conventional mortgages, with the exception of families with less than 80 percent of the median family income in the MSA, the differential approval and denial rates are close to or exceed ten percentage points.

When discussing HMDA data with students, it is necessary to emphasize that the HMDA data do not provide information on the credit history or financial position of the loan applicants, nor on the property they wish to purchase. However, major studies have examined the influence of such factors on the approval and denial of mortgages in three cities: Atlanta, Boston, and New York. Two of the three studies find evidence of racial discrimination on the part of mortgage lenders.

1 The Department of Justice investigated the lending practices of Decatur Federal Savings and Loan Association in Atlanta, GA. After reviewing more than 4,000 mortgage application files, the Department of Justice found that, after controlling for other financial factors, Decatur Federal rejected significantly more black applicants than white applicants. (Canner and Smith 1992: 808.)
2 Concerned about the pattern of racial lending in Boston, the Federal Reserve Bank of Boston examined data from 131 financial institutions concerning the financial and other economic circumstances of typical

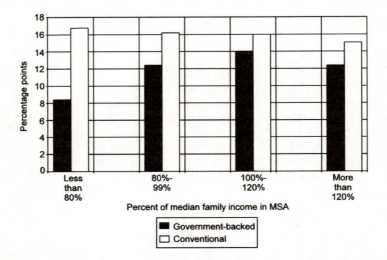

Figure 3.1   Differential in mortgage approval rates

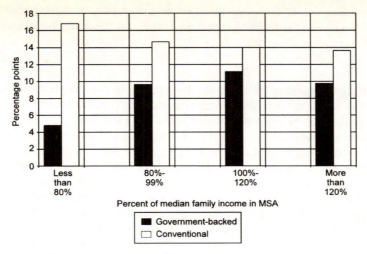

Figure 3.2 Differential in mortgage denial rates

loan applicants. Although they found that minority applicants on average had weaker credit histories, fewer liquid assets, and lower net worths than white applicants, after controlling for these factors, they found that loan denial rates for minority applicants would have been 20 percent rather than the actual rate of 28 percent if race had not been a factor. (Canner and Smith 1992: 809–10.)

3 The New York State Banking Department reviewed the mortgage under-writing criteria and the applicant of the criteria of ten savings banks in the metropolitan New York City area. They concluded that the banks did not discriminate on the basis of either race or gender in their mortgage-lending practices. (Canner and Smith 1992: 810–11.)

Banks have a responsibility to service the area from which they draw their deposits. This responsibility was codified in 1977 by the Community Reinvestment Act (CRA), which requires banks to meet the borrowing needs of the communities in which they operate. Using HMDA data, community groups could challenge any bank application to open or close branches, acquire or merge with other banks, etc., based on the CRA. Unfortunately, the regulators charged with enforcing the CRA, the Federal Reserve Board, the Federal Deposit Insurance Corporation, the Comptroller of the Currency, and the Office of Thrift Supervision, had not used HMDA data to evaluate bank CRA performance. From 1977 to 1989, no major bank's application was turned down based on the CRA. However, after the highly publicized "The Color of Money" series, a similar series in the Detroit *Free Press*, and Senate Banking Committee hearings reviewing the effectiveness of regulators in enforcing CRA, the Federal Reserve Board clarified the importance of CRA and denied Continental Illinois's application to acquire a bank based on CRA grounds (Dreier 1991: 16–18). In light of that Federal Reserve Board action, CRA has taken on increased importance.

THE EFFECT OF STEERING

In addition to redlining by mortgage lending institutions, real estate agents often reinforce housing market segmentation by a practice known as "steering." Agents steer prospective buyers or renters to areas where members of their racial or ethnic group already live. Rather than listen to the characteristics their clients are looking for in a neighborhood, they automatically show black clients apartments and homes in black areas and whites neighborhoods that are primarily white. Analysis of census bureau data by Knight-Ridder Newspapers reveals that more than 30 percent of blacks and 66 percent of whites live in "racially isolated" communities (Baskerville 1992: 45). Should white clients ask to see something in the "wrong" neighborhood, real estate agents will explain that it is not a good neighborhood either because of criminal activity or the quality of schools. Similarly, black clients asking about housing in white areas will be told that the neighborhood is overpriced. In many instances, the clients are unaware that they are being steered to particular neighborhoods.

Another method of steering concerns where advertisements for homes or apartments are placed. Again, there is a pattern of advertising properties and vacancies that reinforces segmentation of the housing market. Homes or apartments for rent or sale in predominantly white areas are advertised in publications that white persons are likely to read, whereas in publications read by the black community, only advertisements for property in predominantly black areas appear.

The practice of steering can be more overtly discriminatory where advertisements of rentals and sales are concerned. Housing advocates frequently use auditors, or testers, to unmask patently illegal steering practices. To do this, a black tester and a white tester both answer an advertisement for a rental or sale. Frequently, the testers receive vastly different treatment. For example, the black tester may be told that the house or apartment has already been rented or sold. Or they may be treated indifferently and no attempt is made to hide the property's disadvantages. The white tester may be shown the property with great fanfare and discussion of its advantages. Different security deposits or down payments may be required, depending upon the tester's racial background.

One major study of housing discrimination was conducted by the Urban Institute and Syracuse University for the US Department of Housing and Urban Development's Office of Policy Development and Research (Turner *et al.* 1991). This study focused on the interaction between an agent and homeseeker from the time a homeseeker responds to an advertisement until he or she commits to renting or purchasing the unit. The Urban Institute and Syracuse University conducted a total of 3,800 audits in twenty-five

Table 3.3 Incidence of discrimination (%)

Probability of discrimination on:	Rentals		Sales	
	Blacks	*Hispanics*	*Blacks*	*Hispanics*
Denial of access to any unit	13	7	6	5
Availability of advertised unit	6	8	5	4
Number of units shown and recommended	45	35	41	45
Availability index	47	29	34	42
Contributions to completing transaction	53	52	51	53
Overall index	56	50	59	56

Source: M. A. Turner *et al.*, *Housing Discrimination Study*, p. 36.

metropolitan areas during the late spring and early summer of 1989. They selected real estate and rental agents randomly from newspaper advertisements.

They identified three different potential problem areas of the homeseeker–agent encounter: housing availability disclosures, contributions to completing a transaction, and steering. Unfavorable treatment was defined as when minority customers are denied information available to white customers concerning the availability of housing units; when agents constrain minority access to housing through the level of "sales effort" invested in the transaction; the rental terms and conditions offered, or assistance provided to home buyers in obtaining financing; and when minority customers are shown houses in different neighborhoods than white customers. Table 3.3 reports the results of the Housing Discrimination Study. The numbers in the table reflect the best estimates of discrimination in favor of the white homeseeker. The overall index indicates that black and Hispanic homeseekers experience discrimination more than half the times they visit a rental or sales agent in response to a newspaper advertisement. Although the table indicates that there is little systematic discrimination with respect to minority homeseekers being denied access to advertised housing units, more than one-third of minority clients are denied information about units shown or recommended to white households; the availability index indicates that discrimination ranges from a low of 29 percent for Hispanic renters to 47 percent of black renters. The incidence of discrimination is greatest for minority clients attempting to complete a transaction. While negotiating the terms and conditions, financing assistance, and general sales effort, more than half of minority clients encounter discrimination.

PROSPECTS FOR THE FUTURE

Although it will be discouraging to students that housing markets are still segmented to such a large degree by race, we can report some positive developments. In particular, federal, state, and local governments are increasing their efforts to eliminate discrimination in housing. The Clinton administration is committed to strengthening the Community Reinvestment Act (Hansell 1993: C1). In late 1993, the Comptroller of the Currency announced new guidelines for determining whether banks discriminate against minority mortgage applicants by reviewing files to detect patterns of disparate treatment (Bacon and Kansas 1993: A2, A7). On the state level, New York State attempted to tighten CRA by designing a formula for rating a bank's compliance with CRA (Hansell 1993: C1).

Some, such as Judd in *The Nation*, argue that to level the playing field in housing we need to redress past discrimination by affirmative action. Judd argues that affirmative action is necessary not only because of a history of discrimination, but because over the last fifty years the federal government helped create the present pattern of racial housing segmentation, and therefore it is obligated to reverse the effects of these policies (Judd 1991: 742). Similar to affirmative action in employment, the government should commit itself to substantial change in housing through an affirmative action program. Certainly, the nation could consider subsidies to minority families seeking to purchase a home or to move to a predominantly white neighborhood. When the students think about housing subsidies, they frequently think about direct subsidies to tenants in public housing projects or recipients of "Section 8" housing. Yet it is important to point out that the recipients of housing subsidies are overwhelmingly affluent homeowners, who receive subsidy in the form of mortgage interest and local property tax deductions on their federal income taxes. In 1988, these subsidies amounted to almost $44 billion, while the budget authority for public housing was $8.6 billion (Judd 1991: 742).

BIBLIOGRAPHY

Anderson, G. (1990) "Housing Discrimination: A White Collar Crime," *America*, March 31: 322–5.
Bacon, K. H. and Kansas, D. (1993) "Comptroller's Office to Use Stricter Test in Probing Mortgage Discrimination," *Wall Street Journal*, November 8: A2 and A7.
Baskerville, D. M. (1992) "Separate and Unequal," *Black Enterprise*, April: 45.
Brimmer, A. F. (1992) "The Cost of Bank Bias," *Black Enterprise*, July: 43.
Canner, G. B. and Smith, D. S. (1992) "Expanded HMDA Data on Residential Lending: One Year Later," *Federal Reserve Bulletin*, November: 801–24.
Dedman, W. "The Color of Money" (1988) *Atlanta Journal/Constitution*, May 1–16.
Dreier, P. (1991) "Redlining Cities: How Banks Color Community Development," *Challenge*, November–December: 15–23.
Economic Report of the President (1993) January, Washington, DC: Government Printing Office.
Economist (1993) "The Other America," *The Economist*, July 10: 17–18.
Hansell, P. (1993) "New York Tightens Law on Community Lending," *New York Times*, October 8: C1 and C11.
Judd, D. R. (1991) "Segregation Forever?" *The Nation*, December 9: 740–4.

Turner, M. A., Struyk, R. J., and Yinger, J. (1991) *Housing Discrimination Study: Synthesis*, Washington, DC: US Department of Housing and Urban Development.

US Bureau of the Census (1992) *Statistical Abstract of the United States 1992*, Washington, DC: Government Printing Office.

4 Gender and race and the decision to go to college

Louise Laurence and Robert L. Moore

The economic way of thinking postulates that individuals make decisions by comparing the costs and benefits of various choices. One choice of particular interest to students in the principles class is the decision to go to college. This issue is usually included at some point in the standard principles class. Some instructors introduce it early on as an application of opportunity cost since students often overlook forgone earnings in calculating the cost of attending college. Other instructors wait until factor markets when the discussion turns to earnings differences and human capital. In this context, the decision to attend college can be compared conceptually to the decision to invest in physical capital. Still others use the decision to go to college as an application of the concept of present value since many of the benefits accrue in the future and must be discounted.

This chapter illustrates several different ways to incorporate issues of gender and race when the decision to go to college is introduced. The next two sections apply when the decision to go to college is discussed in the factor market portion of the course under the topic of human capital. In the next section—on gender differences in the decision to go to college—the students are asked to apply the basic human capital model to explain the dramatic increase in the percentage of women attending college from 1950 to 1988. Data on the increasing labor market experience of women are also provided for this purpose. Students are first asked to evaluate how the model would be adjusted to account for those taking the more traditional path of childbearing and child-rearing. They are then asked to use the human capital model and the changes in the labor market experience of women during the last forty years to explain the dramatic increase of women attending college. In the following section students are asked to apply the model to the decision of the typical African-American male. Limited data are provided on college attendance and earnings by race and gender.

For those who use the decision to go to college very early in the course as an application of opportunity cost, the final section provides a case study based on a *Los Angeles Times* newspaper article. In the case itself, Janet Sullivan, the wife, filed for a divorce after working for ten years while her husband, Mark, completed a degree, internship, and residency in urology. As part of the divorce settlement, Janet sought compensation for her investment in Mark's medical training/degree. The court had to decide two key issues: (1) whether Mark's degree was "community property," and (2), if so, what was the value of that degree. (Under California community property law, Janet would receive one half of all property.)

The instructor asks the class to read the newspaper article and then provide answers to the two key issues above. It turns out that conventional economic analysis does not really help much in answering the first question, although it generates a lot of heated discussion about gender roles and other issues. But conventional economic analysis does provide an answer to the second question, and that answer turns out to be quite different from the judge's decision, or from the "Sullivan Law," which the California legislature passed after the case. A detailed discussion of what to expect when you use this case study and suggested questions are included in this section.

We end this chapter with a brief discussion of some of the problems an instructor might anticipate when using this material in their principles course.

GENDER DIFFERENCES IN THE DECISION TO INVEST IN EDUCATION

Women made up 54 percent of all college students in 1988. This represents a 22 percent increase since 1950.[1] Why is the enrollment of women in colleges and universities increasing? It's instructive to examine the decision to attend college.

Income is earned by investing not only in physical capital, but also in human capital. Some occupations, such as medicine, law, and nuclear physics, require many years of training. The fact that wages in these skilled professions are higher than the wages of unskilled labor is not coincidental. Before people are willing to endure the years of training to become highly skilled professionals, they must be reasonably sure that their investment of time and other resources will pay off in the long run. While a person is going to college, attending a trade school, or gaining on-the-job training, he or she is building human capital.

Gaining human capital requires an investment period, such as four years of college. What is the cost of going to college? Many students incur two types of costs—the direct costs of tuition, fees, books, etc., and the indirect or opportunity costs of the income they could have earned if working. The gross benefit of attending college is depicted by the difference in the two earnings profiles of Figure 4.1. After graduating from high school at the age of eighteen, the high school graduate has a choice. He or she may enter the labor force immediately and earn an income stream of Y_H from that time until retirement at the age of sixty-five. Note how this income increases

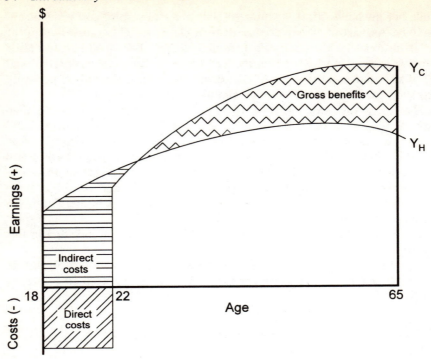

Figure 4.1   The education investment decision

through the years as the individual acquires job-related skills. Or this high school graduate could choose to attend college from the age of eighteen to twenty-two. Here the student forgoes a steady full-time income for four years, but after graduation the earnings profile, Y_C, is higher. The student must then weigh the present value of the gross benefits against both the direct and indirect costs.

Group Project 1

In this exercise, the class or discussion section, if this is a large lecture, forms groups of three or four students. Each group is asked to adjust the human capital model for women who have taken the traditional path of childbearing and child-rearing. The group must make sure that each student can explain the answer because the identity of the student who will be called upon to make the group presentation is unknown. Given the time constraints, one could ask different questions of each group rather than several similar questions. The following information is provided to each group.

Women who follow the traditional path of childbearing and child-rearing spend some years out of the labor force. This model needs to be adjusted to reflect years out of the labor force.

In this case, the woman enters the labor market at age twenty-two and remains until the birth of her first child at age twenty-six, remaining out of the labor force until age thirty-six. When the woman reenters the labor force, she will not be able to obtain a wage equal to her past income if her skills have deteriorated or the employer is unsure of her abilities given the ten-year layoff from formal employment.

Questions and answers

1 On the graph, with benefits and costs on the vertical axis and age on the horizontal axis, show the income stream for both the female college and high school graduate, plus the costs of attending college, given that the woman remains out of the labor force between the ages of twenty-six to thirty-six.

2 What has happened to her gross benefits of increased education compared to a woman who remained in the labor market?
   Her earnings profile is interrupted, reducing the gross benefits of increased education.

3 Has the incentive to attend college increased or decreased in this case?
   The incentive to attend college has diminished as the gross benefits may not exceed the costs.

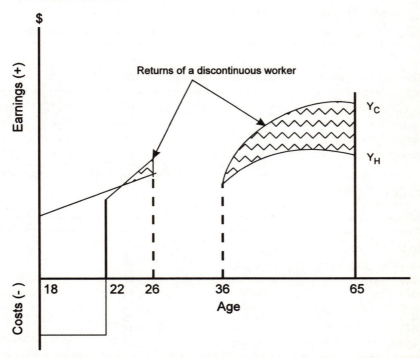

Figure 4.2 The impact of childbearing and child-rearing

If the woman does decide to attend college, she may make additional decisions that would affect her lifestyle.

4 First, what type of occupation would she train for?

She would choose an occupation where her skills would not deteriorate over time. It would be more difficult to reenter if she were an engineer, nurse, or computer specialist given the technological changes in those fields than if she were a teacher or real estate agent.

5 Second, what decision might she make towards childbearing and child-rearing?

She may decide to delay childbirth and/or have fewer children in a shorter time span to minimize her time out of the labor force.

In the last two decades, women's labor force attachment has increased as seen in Table 4.1. In each age group, the average number of years in the labor force has increased with a marked increase occurring since the 1970s. In addition, Table 4.2 shows a 22 percent increase in the college enrollment of women since 1950.

6 Explain how the human capital model can account for this change.

Instead of having children and exiting the labor force, the woman may take a short maternity leave. In this case, then, the gross benefits increase causing the rising enrollment in higher education. (Note: Here you could discuss the feedback effect—is it increased labor force attachment that leads to rising enrollment or vice versa.)

Table 4.1   Estimated years of labor market experience of working women, 1950–86

Year	Age				
	25	30	35	40	45
1950	5.87	7.97	10.57	13.99	16.43
1960	5.76	8.48	11.83	13.68	16.58
1970	5.69	8.68	11.21	14.24	17.21
1980	6.23	9.50	11.7	14.39	16.97
1986	6.52	10.45	13.51	15.47	18.31

Source: F. Blau and M. Ferber, *The Economics of Women, Men, and Work*, p. 163, Englewood Cliffs, NS: Prentice-Hall, 1986.

Table 4.2   College enrollment of women, 1950–88

Year	Enrollment of women	Percent of total enrollment
1988	7,044,914	54
1985	6,378,366	52
1980	6,222,521	51
1975	5,035,862	45
1970	3,537,245	41
1965	2,290,844	39
1955	919,850	35
1950	720,906	32

Source: US Department of Education, *Digest of Educational Statistics 1990*, Table 157.

RACE AND THE DECISION TO GO TO COLLEGE

Group Project 2

In this exercise, the class or discussion section, if this is a large lecture, again forms groups of three or four students. Each group is asked to use the human capital model to analyze the decision of whether to go to college from the perspective of an African-American male. The same ground rules hold for each member in the group being able to answer the questions. The information is provided in Table 4.3.

Figure 4.3 represents the earnings profile and both direct and indirect costs of the typical white male. Show how the graph is modified to represent the choice faced by the typical African-American male.

Answer the following questions

1 Have you modified the direct costs? Why or why not?

No, the costs of tuition, books, and fees are identical.

2 Have you modified the opportunity costs? Why or why not?

Yes, the forgone income is lower for African-American males who face discrimination in the labor market.

3 Have you modified the earnings profiles? Why or why not?

Yes, the earnings profile of both the college and high school graduate is lower. This is supported by the information in Table 4.3.

4 Do the results of your analysis support the data in Table 4.4?

Table 4.4 shows a rising number of African-American males enrolled in college. However, the human capital model as presented yields an ambiguous result. Both the indirect cost as well as the earnings profiles for college and high school graduates are lower. This implies a lower opportunity cost of attending college, but also lower gross benefits. Thus, whether gross benefits are greater than costs is unknown for certain.

Table 4.3 Median annual earnings of full-time year-round workers by sex, race, and education, 1991

Type of worker	High school grad	College grad
All	20,675	31,674
Males	24,148	36,733
Females	16,892	26,241
White males	25,200	37,227
White females	17,023	26,184
African-American males	18,845	30,371
African-American females	15,928	26,439
Hispanic males	19,665	32,408
Hispanic females	15,670	22,235

Source: US Department of Commerce, *Educational Attainment in the United States: March 1991 and 1990*, Table 9.

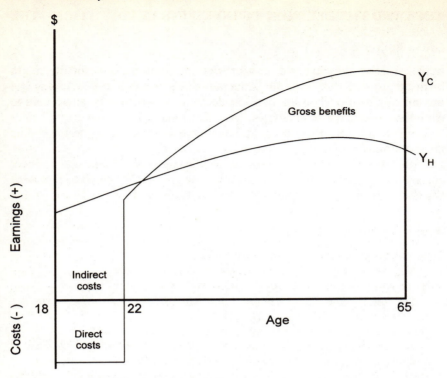

Figure 4.3   Sample graph for group project

5 Can you think of any shortcomings of this model? Does it consider all the variables that go into this decision? If not, what might they be?

   Here you could expect answers such as financial constraints, past discrimination in education, etc.

Table 4.4   College enrollment by sex, race, gender and ethnicity 1965–89 (1,000)

	1965	1970	1975	1980	1985	1989
White	5,137	6,759	8,514	8,875	9,334	9,376
Men	3,326	4,066	4,771	4,438	4,633	4,513
Women	1,991	2,693	3,743	4,437	4,701	4,863
Black	274	522	948	1,007	1,049	1,141
Men	126	253	442	437	458	433
Women	148	269	506	570	591	708
Hispanic	–	–	411	443	579	640
Men	–	–	219	222	280	311
Women	–	–	192	221	299	330

Source: US Department of Commerce, Bureau of the Census, *Current Population Reports*, Series P-20, No. 403.

THE OPPORTUNITY COST OF INVESTING IN EDUCATION—THE JANET SULLIVAN CASE[2]

Those who introduce the decision to go to college very early on as an application of opportunity cost and the economic way of thinking might want to consider the following case study. It also has the advantage of introducing gender issues early in the course and provides an alternative to the more standard lecture format.

The instructor asks the students to prepare for the case study by reading the newspaper article (see Appendix 4.1) from the *Los Angeles Times*, entitled "A Divorced Spouse's Professional Degree: Is it Community Property?" and to answer the questions that accompany the article. Normally this assignment would be given and completed before the actual case study discussion that follows.

The opportunity cost of education and training plays a controversial role in this article about divorce. The wife, Janet Sullivan, filed for a divorce after working for ten years while her husband, Mark, completed a degree, internship, and residency in urology. As part of the divorce settlement, Janet decided to seek compensation for her investment in Mark's medical training.

1 Start by asking someone in the class to briefly outline the basic facts of the case. Limit this to one minute or so.
2 Divide the class into groups of three or four to discuss whether Mark's degree is indeed community property. After the groups have had a chance to discuss their answers, call on one person in each group to explain what consensus, if any, was reached by their group.
   It turns out that economic analysis cannot decide this issue, and this provides an important point. Economic analysis does not provide answers to a lot of questions.
3 Now tell the class to assume that it has been decided that Mark's degree is indeed community property. Under California community property law, Janet Sullivan would receive one half of all property, including the value of Mark's degree. Passage [A] suggests two ways of determining compensation. One method awards Janet half of the difference between expected earnings over the lifetime of such a degree holder and over the lifetime of a non-degree holder. The other method awards Janet half of Mark's income when he begins his professional career for a period equal to the time it took to earn the degree. At this point you should ask them to break into groups and discuss how they would determine the benefits and costs (Questions 1 and 2 of Appendix 4.1).
4 Ask the groups for their various answers.
5 Now ask the groups to discuss their answers to the question they prepared that dealt with Passage [A] of the article (Question 3 of Appendix 4.1).

(a) *There are two main differences: (i) the first formula is based on the average earnings of an individual with Mark's degree, and the second is based on Mark's actual earnings; (ii) the first formula is applied to Mark's entire career, and the second is applied to the first ten years of Mark's career.*

(b) *The first formula is more accurate. The cost of an investment precedes the return from the investment. At the time the investment is made, the expected return equals the gross enhancement in earnings minus the costs (both direct and opportunity costs) and spans the entire subsequent career.*

6 Lastly, ask the groups to compare their answers to the judge's decision, which is included as an informational note to the article. Also ask them to compare their answer to the "Sullivan Law," which was passed by the state of California after the case, and which specified that awards for education investments should not exceed total expenditures on tuition and books.

The judge has chosen the wrong alternative from Passage [A]—note the answer above. The "Sullivan Law" ignores the opportunity cost of forgone income in determining the "cost" of education. This serves to demonstrate to students that the economic way of thinking may very well change the way they approach issues, and that judges and lawmakers may reach different answers than those suggested by economic analysis.

PROBLEMS TO ANTICIPATE IN USING THIS MATERIAL

The material in the first and second sections is fairly difficult. It is one thing to understand the basic human capital model but another to be able to apply it. Since issues of race and gender are involved, it is necessary to spend some time trying to create a "safe" discussion environment where students feel free to voice their views without fear of reprisal, and where each student's view will be considered on its own merits.

One thing you might want to experiment with when the students are working in groups, is to announce that you will be calling on a "random" student in the group to explain the "group's answer." This necessitates that the better students teach the weaker students using whatever language makes sense to them.

For the case study, we have always had extremely lively discussions about whether Mark's degree is indeed community property. You should antici- pate some heated discussions and statements involving gender stereotypes. Again, it is important that you spend some time trying to create a "safe" discussion environment where every student's view will be respected and considered on its own merits. Our experience also indicates that the students will very often miss the answer in step 5. They also find it instructive that the judge and legislatures do not use the concept of opportunity cost in their analysis and judgments.

Appedix 4.1

A DIVORCED SPOUSE'S PROFESSIONAL DEGREE: IS IT COMMUNITY PROPERTY?

by Roxane Arnold[3]

After ten years working as an accountant while husband Mark completed medical school, an internship and residency in urology, Janet Sullivan decided their marriage was over. She walked out, taking their young daughter with her.

When the couple filed for divorce two years later in Santa Ana, there wasn't much to divide in the way of community property—some used furniture and two cars that weren't paid for.

Janet decided to try for more—a share of Mark's earnings as a doctor.

On Tuesday, the California Supreme Court is scheduled to take up the Sullivan case, which centers on Janet's claim that she should be compensated for putting her ex-husband through medical school. It is a contention that has jolted medical and professional groups and unleashed a storm of clashing views.

The case has become a *cause célèbre* among those who see it as the "most important women's issue of the day," and has prompted at least one California assemblyman to draft so-called Sullivan legislation to take care of former spouses like Janet.

It also has spurred Mark's fellow doctors in Orange County to establish a legal defense fund to battle what they call a "threat to all people who have a degree," and has convinced the powerful California Medical Assn. to enter the fray on behalf of its members.

"The ramifications of the case are shocking for some," said UCLA law professor Grace Blumberg. "It means that people could be paying through their noses for the rest of their professional lives."

Although a rash of cases involving professional degrees have been heard in courtrooms across the country in the last two years, few have been heard in state high courts and none is likely to have the national impact of a Sullivan decision, since the California Supreme Court is regarded as a trendsetter in family law.

Unlike most other states, where judges have discretion in dividing marital assets, California is bound by a no-fault divorce law that requires an even distribution of property accumulated during a marriage regardless of who wanted to end the marriage. The state definition of community property includes furniture, real estate, and other tangible assets as well as intangibles such as pensions and professional reputations that have recognized value.

"California doesn't have the flexibility of other states," said Blumberg, the co-author of a friend-of-the-court brief on Janet's behalf. "The

California Supreme Court is not going to be able to fudge the issue. In other states, courts can give her something without giving her too much. In California, it has got to be an all-or-nothing proposition. The future earnings represented by her husband's degree is either property or it isn't, and she gets half or she gets nothing."

The court actually faces two decisions. Justices must first determine whether Mark's medical degree is community property and if so, how to measure its future value.

Ultimately, however, the court's decision will affect not only physicians but those who earn professional degrees while married.

Some argue that a degree-is-property ruling could apply to every faltering marriage, creating nightmares for the courts and never-ending entanglements for couples who just want to split. Others predict it will produce a booming market for pre-nuptial agreements and bring romance to an end.

"It's not going to be very good for the couple," said Sacramento attorney Fred J. Hiestand, who filed a brief for the California Medical Association. Hiestand said that the association decided to become involved in the case when its members agreed they didn't want their degrees to become a target for a vindictive spouse or a potential future creditor.

Hiestand said that "when you start considering a degree property, you open a potential floodgate.... I don't see how you can distinguish between a medical degree and any other kind of degree—a college degree, a junior college degree. There is going to be a burgeoning business in evaluating degrees... it will take a lot more time to unwind a marriage."

When the Sullivans were divorced, there was no indication that theirs would become a landmark case. As Janet's attorney, Patricia Herzog, explains it, there was just a nagging feeling that something wasn't fair.

The judge who handled the Sullivan divorce trial decided not to consider the medical degree in the divorce settlement, based on then-existent case law. Janet, who earns enough to support herself, was not eligible for alimony. She was, however, awarded $250 a month in child support payments even though the couple was awarded joint custody of their child.

In January, 1981, the 4th District Court of Appeal took Janet's side and sent the case back to the trial court to determine what was due to her.

Eight months later, the appellate court reversed itself, finding that professional training is not part of the marital kitty because it does not fit traditional concepts of property. The justices who changed their minds said that the unusual reversal resulted from a closer review of the case.

By the time the California Supreme Court agreed to hear the Sullivan case, more than a dozen other states were grappling with the same issue and a handful of high courts had rendered opinions. Most of the cases involved medical and legal degrees. In one state, though, it was a master's in business administration; in another, a doctorate of philosophy. Apparently the degree holders in these cases have been men.

Although few courts have ruled that a degree is property, most have tried to give the woman some reimbursement for her time and trouble. But the disparity in the judgments has resulted mostly in confusion.

Very confusing

'Everyone is doing their own thing trying to fit in with traditional definitions of property...to try to achieve equity in one way or another," said New York divorce lawyer Doris Free. "It's very confusing and it's wrong...you can get so hung up on terminology that you come up with zilch."

Two cases heard in New York last summer illustrate the chaos. One trial court judge, calling a husband's medical license the only valuable asset of the nine-year marriage, awarded the schoolteacher wife almost $190,000. Weeks later, an appellate court considering another case held that a medical license was not property and gave the wife nothing.

The record is just as muddled in other states. In Minnesota, one wife received $11,400 after a court determined she was due reimbursement for the amount she contributed to her husband's education. In a similar case in Kentucky, the spouse was awarded $11,600. In Illinois and Arizona, two wives came away empty-handed. In Oklahoma, a doctor's wife was awarded an extra $39,000 in alimony based on the husband's increased earning ability.

A few states have tried to legislate consistency. Lawmakers in Wisconsin added a statute providing for some compensation for spouses who have contributed to their mates' education. In Indiana, legislators enacted a provision calling for reimbursement of tuition, books, or other fees if there is little else to divide.

If the California Supreme Court decides to classify degrees as property, some legal experts believe there would be a great impact on other states.

"It would be such an extreme, unusual step," said University of Missouri law professor Joan Krauskopf. "It would be highly significant because it would be the first Supreme Court in the country to classify a degree as property. It would highlight for the whole country how important this issue is."

Krauskopf acknowledged that the ramifications of legally recognizing one spouse's role in the education of the other are staggering, but she said it is "one of the most important women's issues in the country."

"It is still the woman who is putting the man through professional school, the woman who doesn't develop her own earning capacity...the MDs around the country are scared to death they might have to give some reimbursement to that woman who put them through medical school, who suffered through an internship with them—the woman they then walked out on."

"The whole principle of community property in California is that all assets, all property belongs to both," said Stanford sociologist Lenore Weitzman. "Our courts are making a mockery of that...by letting the husband hide his gold behind his back. The educational degree is the jewelry of the marriage."

"The notion of a professional education kind of piggybacks on these earlier rulings," Blumberg said. "A professional degree is just another intangible, something you can't package, but it is still property."

To those who would argue that the value of a professional degree defies calculation, Blumberg answered, "it is a little complicated, but it is doable."

But California Medical Assn. Attorney Hiestand predicts evaluating degrees will "open a real Pandora's box. It will be a fight of the experts, a great boon to economists...and a step backward."

Southwestern University law professor Max Goodman predicted that a court-ordered payoff to Janet will mean "you won't be able to settle any case...in every marriage, there is enhanced earning of some sort, either by way of education or more experience or promotions. If Mrs. Sullivan's theory is accepted by the court, you're going to have these problems of enhanced earning ability in every single dissolution case."

Economists and lawyers already have been working to come up with ways to value degrees and divide the earnings.

[A] One formula projects what an average degree holder would earn over a lifetime with the degree and subtracts projected earnings without it. The difference is reduced through a series of equations to its value in current dollars. A former spouse would get half that amount through installments with interest.

A second formula depends on the professional's actual work. The supporting spouse would be entitled to half of what is earned during a time span comparable to the period it took to earn the degree.

To make such formulas work, Blumberg says, the degree must be worth something. What sets professional degrees apart from job promotions earned during marriage or courses taken for fun is what she called the "opportunity cost."

"For Dr. Sullivan, the real cost of his education was not books, it was not tuition: it was being absent from the labor force for ten years doing whatever he could have done as a bachelor of science," Blumberg said. "These people would have had lots of money if one of the spouses hadn't undertaken ten years of self-enhancement."

Attorney Goodman, who will help argue Mark Sullivan's case before the Supreme Court, admits it is that kind of "perceived injustice" that has him worried as the court date nears.

"It's the gut-level reaction," Goodman said. "He walks out instant doctor and she walks out with a baby...and so she should get paid somehow." In the Sullivans' case, Mark is now a urologist in Laguna Hills and Janet is a medical accountant and living in a rented house in Laguna Beach.

Marriage is risk

Goodman argues that marriage is a risk under any circumstances. To deal with it otherwise would be unjust to Dr. Sullivan.

"Implicit in her [Janet's] theory is there is an obligation to work while you are married, and if you don't work, you can be sued for damages," he said. "That's not true ... there is the expectation that the marriage will last. But if it doesn't, that is the risk she took. That's the way the cookie crumbled, that's the way the marriage crumbled ... there is no injustice in this."

The California legislature already has reached that same conclusion, Goodman said.

Lawmakers recently amended community property laws by making educational debts an exception to the 50–50 distribution rule. The spouse receiving the education must pay its costs as part of a divorce settlement.

"The legislature could have said that education is an asset, but they didn't," Goodman said. "The courts should respect that."

Not all legislators agree.

Assemblyman Alister McAlister (D-Milpitas) is drafting a measure that includes earning capacity in community property.

[B] "The most important property that most couples have when they separate is the earning capacity of the husband," McAlister said. "The wife should not be left high and dry ... there is a need to protect her."

What sociologist Weitzman calls a "blueprint for marriage"—the pre-nuptial agreement—also would protect warring spouses.

Although many believe signing contracts does not make for a good marriage, others say the pacts simplify the ending of a relationship. Whether pre-nuptial agreements will be used widely is another question.

"Marriage contracts are one way of handling things, but they're not used that often and I don't think that's likely to change," attorney Herzog said. "People marry when their eyes are filled with stars and their hearts with love. They don't consider divorce."

Blumberg countered that a Supreme Court ruling that puts professional degrees up for grabs could change that.

"I suppose if people keep doing this," Blumberg predicted, "there will come a time when your indoctrination packet going into medical school will have information on how to write contracts. It will be there along with your Blue Cross card."

Informational note

The judge in this case awarded Janet Sullivan half of Mark's earnings for the first ten years of his medical practice. After the case, the state of California passed the "Sullivan Law," which specified that awards for education investments should not exceed total expenditures on tuition and books.

Questions

1 Suppose the court decided to award Janet a "refund" equal to half the investment the couple had made in Mark's medical training. What items should be included in determining the amount of this refund? In other words, what items make up the economic (opportunity) cost of Mark's medical training?
2 If you had been the judge hearing the Janet Sullivan case, what would you have awarded Janet? Briefly support your decision.
3 Passage [A] of the article covers two options for measuring the value of a degree:
   (a) How do the two options differ?
   (b) Which option more accurately measures the expected return on an investment in education (including your own)?
4 For each of the two sentences in passage [B] of the article, decide whether the sentence constitutes a positive or a normative statement, and briefly explain your decision in each case.

NOTES

1 US Department of Education, *Digest of Educational Statistics 1990*, Table 157.
2 This case study and material was developed by Jim Whitney for use in the principles of economics course at Occidental College. One of the authors, Robert L. Moore, has used Professor Whitney's material in his own principles class and incorporated Professor Whitney's materials for inclusion in this chapter.
3 *Los Angeles Times*, February 7, 1983. Copyright, 1983, *Los Angeles Times*. Reprinted by permission.

5 The labor supply decision—differences between genders and races

Margaret Lewis and Janice Peterson

One of the most important economic and social developments in the United States this century has been the tremendous influx of women into the labor market. This development has significantly affected the family (e.g. the acknowledgment of the second shift), the workplace (e.g. the recognition by business of the need for family-friendly work policies to improve worker productivity), and the economy (e.g. the impact on GDP as a result of the changing mix of home-provided and market-produced goods and services demanded). This development is also visible to many students in their own labor supply decisions and in changes observed in their own families. Thus, a discussion of the labor supply decisions by different gender and race-ethnic groups in our society addresses an important current economic issue that is relevant to our students' lives.

This chapter illustrates how the labor supply decision, as explained by neoclassical economic theory, can be incorporated into a course emphasizing gender and race differences. Depending on the text used, this example can be used as an introduction to or as a reinforcement of the neoclassical concepts of constrained maximization, "rational" choice, and opportunity costs. The example will also introduce students to the neoclassical model of individual labor supply decision-making as part of the discussion of factor markets. In addition, this example will provide students with a link between theory and current economic issues: by using the labor supply model presented here, students will gain understanding of recent trends in women's labor force participation. This application will also introduce students to two statistical concepts, the labor force and the labor force participation rate, and will offer students the opportunity to increase their economic literacy by encouraging them to move between economic models and empirical data. Finally, if an instructor wishes to emphasize the relation between economics and public policy, the trends identified could serve as a catalyst for discussing such policies as education, parental leave, child care, and recent incentive changes in the federal tax structure to reduce the marriage penalty.

The chapter is organized as follows. The next section (pp. 000–00) presents the theoretical frameworks used to examine changes in labor force participation rates, beginning with the neoclassical labor–leisure model; included here is a discussion of the concept of leisure and a critique of the model which emphasizes gender and race differences in the meaning of leisure. Next, the basic model is extended to account more fully for these differences by analyzing decisions based on the value of market time relative to the value of non-market time. Also included in this section are suggested teaching techniques for presenting the theoretical material.

In the following section, the extended model discussed above is used to examine trends in labor force participation, with the emphasis on women by race, marital status, and presence of children. Data for identifying these trends are provided for this discussion, and again, pedagogical strategies are suggested. In the final section of the chapter, we discuss some problems instructors may encounter when using this material in an introductory course, and offer suggested readings for more in-depth study and policy analysis.

The material in the first two sections can be presented in the order indicated above, where the theoretical models are presented first and then applied to a real-world example. In a course where economic developments are used as a "hook" for seeing how economic theory can enhance understanding, instructors may wish to begin by examining labor force participation data and then move to the theoretical models for understanding why women's rates have increased so significantly in recent years.

Finally, we would like to stress the importance of covering the labor market in the micro principles or introductory economics course. There is a tendency in many economics texts to place the discussion of labor markets *after* discussions of consumer choice, firm decision-making, and market structures. This placement, along with the time constraints many of us encounter, often leads us either to discuss only briefly or to omit entirely labor markets from our courses. However, de-emphasizing the individual's role as worker not only disappoints students, it also limits their complete understanding of economic relationships and obscures one of the most important sources of gender and race differences in the economy. We would thus encourage all instructors, especially those interested in examining these differences, to structure their courses to include an extensive discussion of labor markets so that students are more fully cognizant of key economic relationships and how these relationships may differ by gender and race.

TWO NEOCLASSICAL MODELS OF INDIVIDUAL LABOR SUPPLY

The basic labor–leisure model

A good place to start this discussion is to point out to students that the neoclassical model of labor supply is very similar to the model of consumer choice—a model they have probably seen in some form earlier in the class.

Students can be reminded that, in the neoclassical model of consumer choice, the consumer is faced with the problem of allocating limited income to different goods and services with the goal of maximizing utility. Consumers are assumed to know their preferences with respect to the different goods and to have perfect information about the goods and their alternatives.

This is an example of a constrained maximization problem: the consumer wishes to maximize the satisfaction from consumption but is constrained by his/her income and the prices of the goods and services in question. Thus, the consumer makes "rational choices;" taking into consideration all of the information available, he/she compares the costs and benefits of the different consumption alternatives, and finds the optimal combination of goods and services.

In the neoclassical labor supply model, the individual is once again faced with the problem of constrained utility maximization. Here the scarce "resource" to be allocated is time. Time is "scarce" because there are "only twenty-four hours in a day." (This is something students can relate to! The problem of time allocation is probably something that was discussed earlier in the class when introducing the concept of opportunity cost.)

In this model, the utility-maximizing individual is faced with a choice of allocating time between "labor" (work in the paid labor market) and "leisure." Again, it is assumed that the individual has all of the information necessary to make rational choices between these two activities. Because time is scarce, the individual must weigh the costs and benefits of each activity to find the optimal combination. The benefit of allocating time to labor is obtaining income, which allows for the consumption of market goods, which provides satisfaction. The cost (opportunity cost) of labor is the value of the leisure time which must be given up. The benefit of allocating time to "leisure" is the satisfaction derived from these activities; the cost (opportunity cost) of leisure is the wage income forgone.

The number of hours allocated to "labor" determines the individual's labor supply. This decision is seen to reflect the individual's rational choice between these two activities and is determined by preferences toward work and leisure, the prevailing wage rate and availability of non-wage income. (*Note*: Indifference curve analysis can be used here to go through the theory in more detail.)

Assignment 1—What constitutes "leisure"?

Questions for discussion

1 List five activities that you consider to be part of your "leisure time."
2 Choose a family member (e.g. a parent or spouse) and list five of their leisure-time activities. Do they differ from yours? Explain the reasons for these differences.

Assignment 1 can be done in small groups of three to five students, with individual students, or the entire group, generating lists of their top five leisure activities. If the class is heterogeneous, this exercise will generate interesting differences; if it is homogeneous, the next step is more crucial. The group is then asked if their lists look like those for chosen family members or specific groups in society (e.g. single mothers or the working poor) to point out potential differences in "leisure" by race, gender, age, marital status, class, etc.

An alternative exercise is to ask students to list individually their top five leisure activities. Responses solicited from the class are recorded on the board, and the class is asked to discuss how their list differs from lists that might be generated by different family members or social groups.

Discussion 1

Assignment 1 can provide the basis for discussing how the time/activities classified by the basic model as "leisure" may mean very different things to different people, depending on their life circumstances (as well as individual preferences, etc.). This can also lead to a discussion on the meaning and role of "rational choice" in neoclassical models. Students can be asked to consider how different circumstances and constraints have important implications for the choices made by different individuals.

As part of this discussion, students could be asked whether or not they make "rational" time allocation decisions in their own lives. This is also a good place to stress the perfect information assumption of the model—how realistic is this assumption, and how could imperfect information affect the ability to make time allocation choices?

The extended model of labor supply

The labor supply discussion can be developed further by defining the choices in terms of "market" versus "non-market" time. The class discussion on the meaning of "leisure" can provide a nice transition here. After establishing that the choices are more complex than simple "labor" versus "leisure," the class can be asked to list the type of activities that comprise "market time" and "non-market time." After this, a version of the extended labor supply model could be presented. (For a complete discussion of this version of the extended model, see Blau and Ferber (1992: chapter 4.)

In this version of the labor supply model, the individual decides whether or not to participate in the labor force by comparing the value of time in the market (w) to the value placed on non-market activities, most particularly time spent in the home (w*). This model assumes that all income earned is spent on market goods, that all non-market time is spent on producing commodities (which can include a clean house or a healthy child), and that the labor supply of other family members is taken as given and is not influenced by the individual's labor supply choices.

If the value of market time is greater than the value placed on non-market time (w > w*), the individual will choose to participate in market activities; i.e. enter the labor force. If the value of market time is less than the value placed on non-market time (w < w*), the individual does not enter the labor force. In this context, the value of non-market time (w*) can be interpreted as the "reservation wage," the value the individual places on non-market time. Thus the market wage must be greater than the reservation wage to induce individuals to enter the labor force.

The value of non-market time (w*) is determined by a variety of factors—individual preferences, demands put on non-market time (e.g. child care responsibilities), and availability of non-wage income (e.g. transfer payments or spouse's income). The value of market time (w) is the prevailing wage rate and is determined by such factors as education and changes in labor demand. If the value of market or non-market time changes as a result of a determinant changing, we would expect to see a change in labor force participation. For example, a higher wage rate (due to more education) increases the benefits of market time and the costs (opportunity costs) of non-market time, thereby increasing the likelihood of labor force participation. Alternatively, increased participation could result from a decline in the value of non-market time, or a combination of changes in the two values.

After establishing how labor force participation depends on changes in the values of market time and non-market time, the instructor can then use this model to examine reasons for increased labor force participation rates among women in the United States.

APPLYING THE EXTENDED MODEL—FEMALE LABOR FORCE PARTICIPATION RATES

Many textbooks stress that one of the most important trends in the US labor market has been the increased participation of women, particularly married women with children. A good place to start this discussion is with the official definition of the "labor force" and what the "labor force participation rate" (LFPR) means. Then the statistics on female labor force participation over time, disaggregated for different racial-ethnic groups, can be examined.

Assignment 2—Identifying trends in LFPR by gender and race

For this assignment, students form groups of three to five to identify trends in labor force participation rates by gender, race, and marital and family status using the data and questions in Appendix 5.1. Depending on class size and time available, each group might analyze the data in all tables or focus on a specific table or an element of a specific table.

There are at least two methods students can use to analyze the data. One is to graph LFPR trends, using either graph paper or computer spreadsheets. This approach is effective for developing quantitative reasoning skills as students move between tables, graphs, and words. A second method is to calculate index numbers. This approach is especially effective for indicating large changes over time, such as those changes in women's LFPRs.

After trends are identified, the groups present their findings to the class; this may be desirable if each group examines only some of the data. Alternatively, each group might submit its findings in writing for evaluation.

Discussion 2—Reasons for observed trends in women's LFPRs

Assignment 2 can be the basis for discussing some specific factors contributing to the identified LFPR trends. Students are asked to list two to three reasons they believe are the most important for increasing the labor force participation of women. These reasons can then be discussed in terms of the extended model of labor supply; that is, does each factor change the value of market time or the value of non-market time for women? This discussion can be done in small groups or by soliciting responses from the class.

After the students have looked at trends in the data and offered their own explanations, the instructor can provide an overview of reasons mentioned in the economics literature for the increased labor force participation of women. Relating the discussion back to the theoretical model, these reasons can be classified as factors influencing the value of market time and those influencing the value of non-market time. For more detailed discussions of these factors, instructors should refer to Blau and Ferber (1992) and Spitze (1988).

Factors influencing the value of market time (w) of women

Increased educational attainment

Some analysts argue that increased education has changed women's preferences and attitudes towards work, causing them to choose careers outside the home. In addition, it is argued that increased education has allowed women to earn higher wages and get better jobs. This has increased the opportunity cost of staying out of the paid labor market.

Increased demand for female labor

Some analysts argue that there has been an increase in the demand for female labor which has increased women's wages, thereby bringing more women into the paid labor market. The expanding service sector has increased the number of "women's jobs" available. (This may provide an opportunity to discuss occupational segregation and the "pink collar ghetto.") In addition, anti-discrimination legislation and changing social attitudes have likely increased the demand for women in traditionally male occupations.

Factors influencing the value of non-market time (w*) for women

The Availability of market substitutes for housework

Some analysts argue that the availability of labor or time-saving home technology (e.g. microwaves and dishwashers) and the ability to purchase goods and services (e.g. restaurant meals and child care) previously produced in the home have reduced the demands on non-market time for women. These changes have reduced the value of women's non-market time.

Demographic trends

Several demographic trends are frequently cited as reducing the value of women's non-market time. The declining birth (or fertility) rate is typically mentioned as a major reason for reduced demands on non-market time for many women. The increase in the divorce rate and growth in the number of female-headed families are often mentioned here as well. As more and more women are financially responsible for their families, the value they place on non-market time decreases.

Changes in "tastes and preferences"

Some analysts argue that the increased labor force participation of women reflects the consumerism of the "me generation": increased preference for purchased consumer goods has reduced the value placed on non-market time. It is also argued that changing social-cultural views on women's roles has reduced that value many women place on non-market activities.

Changes in non-wage income

For married women, the husband's income is an important source of non-wage income. Many analysts focus on the issue of economic need, stressing how the weak economy of the 1970s and 1980s pushed many wives into the work force as their husband's real wages declined; this decline in income has been particularly apparent for younger workers.

Urbanization

Growing urbanization in the United States reduces the opportunity for producing non-market goods and increases the availability and desirability of market-produced goods. Some analysts cite this factor as reducing the value of non-market time and increasing the need for income derived from time spent in the labor market.

Summary

This discussion can be summed up with a discussion of "pull factors" and "push factors." Some of the increase in female labor force participation is due to women being pulled into the paid labor force owing to increased opportunities, thus increasing the opportunity cost of not participating in the paid labor force. Others have been pushed into the labor force by economic need.

After discussing these determinants, instructors should note that the factors often cited in the economics literature may best explain LFPR trends for *white* women. However, as the students may bring up, the experience of white women may not reflect the experiences of women of color. Consequently, it is crucial to examine if the above factors adequately explain LFPR trends for non-white women. (Some instructors may also want students to examine how well the model works for explaining male LFPRs.)

Assignment 3—How does the extended model explain LFPR trends for women of color?

As noted in Tables 5.2 and 5.3, women of color have not faced LFPR trends identical to those of white women. This assignment, which can be done in small groups or individually for presentation and/or written evaluation, is designed to examine if the extended model explains the trends for women of color.

To enable students to do this analysis, instructors may wish to provide students with the data presented in Appendix 5.2. These data will allow students to identify several determinants of w and w* for whites and blacks, and some determinants for Hispanics. Because the data are limited for Hispanics and almost non-existent for other race-ethnic groups, the instructor may also want to provide students with the following readings.

1 Amott, T. L. and Matthaei, J. A. (1991) *Race, Gender, and Work: A Multicultural Economic History of Women in the United States*, Boston: South End Press. This book contains chapters on the following groups of women: American-Indian, Chicana, European-American, African-American, Asian-American, and Puerto Rican. Each chapter contains considerable relevant material on each group. Because of each chapter's length, instructors may only want to assign this material if considerable time is devoted to Assignment 3.

2 Blau, F. and Ferber, M. (1992) "Black and White Participation Differentials: An Analysis" in *The Economics of Women, Men and Work*, second edition, Englewood Cliffs, NJ: Prentice-Hall: 110–13. This short section

discusses some of the reasons for black and white LFPR differentials for men and women. We would caution instructors, if this reading is used, to be aware of potential black stereotype problems with the last paragraph, which discusses AFDC as a disincentive to labor force participation.

3 Bonilla-Santiago, G. (1990) "A Portrait of Hispanic Women in the United States," in S. Rix (ed.) *The American Woman 1990–91: A Status Report*, New York: W. W. Norton: 249–57. This article points out the diversity among Hispanic women; for example, women of Cuban and Central and South American origin have LFPRs similar to those of white women, while Mexican and Puerto Rican women's rates have been lower. Bonilla-Santiago also mentions several factors that may account for the overall trends for Hispanics (such as low education attainment and high unemployment rates resulting from little job tenure and low-wage jobs vulnerable to layoffs) as well as the differences among Hispanics (such as large numbers of Mexican-American women doing migrant work in agricultural industries and a high percentage of Puerto Rican women as heads of households.

4 Burgess, N. J. and Horton, H. D. (1993) "African-American Women and Work: A Socio-historical Perspective," *Journal of Family History* 18, 1: 53–63. This article discusses reasons for the historically high labor force participation rates for black married women and focuses on the influences of black married women's history (especially the institution of slavery, which forced black women to work) and cultural backgrounds and attitudes (e.g. toward women working). The authors also indicate that discriminatory practices, especially against black men, and social policies growing out of slavery encouraged black women to enter paid employment earlier and at higher rates than white women.

5 Jones, B. (1987) "Black Women and Labor Force Participation: An Analysis of Sluggish Growth Rates," in M. Simms and J. Malveaux (eds) *Slipping through the Cracks: The Status of Black Women*, New Brunswick, NJ: Transaction Books: 11–31. This article focuses on the declining gap between the LFPRs of white and black women. It examines why the LFPR of black women has not grown as rapidly as that of white women despite the fact that black women have many of the characteristics associated with increased labor force participation—increased relative earnings, decline in average family size, and increased educational attainment. According to Jones, the key factor that might explain the above is the demand side of the labor market. More specifically, she concludes that the lack of employment opportunities for black women with limited educations, and the lower returns to education for more highly educated black women, might hold the key to understanding recent trends in LFPRs for black women.

6 Lott, J. T. (1990) "A Portrait of Asian and Pacific-American Women," in S. Rix (ed.) *The American Woman 1990–91: A Status Report*, New York: W. W. Norton: 258–64. This article discusses factors that may account

for the relative high LFPRs of Asian and Pacific-American (APA) women: high educational attainment, above average median income, cultural values of a strong work ethic and self-reliance, and more multiple wage earners (suggesting the need for APA women to contribute to the economic support of their families). Lott also points out the diversity among Asian and Pacific-American women. For example, for Korean and Asian-Indian families, small family businesses are an important source of income, and women and girls often work in such businesses as unpaid help. (This may cause their economic contribution to be over-looked in the official labor force statistics. Students could be reminded of the official definition of the labor force and asked to consider how it may undercount APA women's economic contribution.)

7 Smith, S. and Tienda, M. (1988) "The Doubly Disadvantaged: Women of Color in the US Labor Force," in A. Stromberg and S. Harkess (eds) *Women Working: Theories and Facts in Perspective* second edition, Mountain View, CA: Mayfield Publishing: 61–80. Instructors may find this article useful for more background on the economic status (labor force participation, employment and earnings) for black, Hispanic, and American-Indian women.

8 Snipp, C. M. (1990) "A Portrait of American-Indian Women and their Labor Force Experiences," in S. Rix (ed.) *The American Woman 1990–91: A Status Report*, New York: W. W. Norton: 265–71. This article discusses reasons for the historically low LFPR for American Indian women (although this gap has narrowed in recent years). As Snipp discusses, geographic isolation and concentration in rural areas are major factors limiting the labor force options for American Indian women. (Instructors could note that rural areas often have significant "informal economies" where women's economic activities go unmea-sured.) Snipp also notes that American-Indian women married to men with higher incomes were *more* likely to be in the labor force than those with lower incomes, and concludes that while many American-Indian women seek employment to augment family income, many of those who need it the most cannot find it.

9 Spitze, G. (1988) "The Data on Women's Labor Force Participation," in A. Stromberg and S. Harkess (eds) *Women Working: Theories and Facts in Perspective*, second edition, Mountain View, CA: Mayfield Publishing: 42–60. Instructors may find this article useful for more background on female labor force participation, unemployment, and underemployment, occupational distribution, and earnings.

Using the data and readings, students are asked to address the following:

1 Discuss if the factors cited by economists "explain" the trends in women's LFPR for blacks, Hispanics, Asian and Pacific Americans (APAs), and American Indians.

2 Discuss if the differences in black women's labor force experiences help explain the relatively (compared to white women) higher LFPR for black women.
3 Discuss if the differences in Hispanic women's labor force experiences help explain the relatively (compared to white women) lower LFPR for black women.
4 Discuss if the differences in APA women's labor force experiences help explain the relatively (compared to white women) higher LFPR for APA women.
5 Discuss if the differences in American-Indian women's labor force experiences help explain the relatively (compared to white women) lower LFPR for American-Indian women.
6 Discuss if all Hispanic and APA women have had the same labor force experiences. (This last point will bring out the lack of homogeneity within race-ethnic groups.)

After Assignment 3 is completed, the instructor can summarize the class's findings about the applicability of the extended model to women of color. As the students will discover, this economic model (like most) may best explain the experiences of only part of society. Recognizing gender and race differences thus not only means examining disaggregated data but also reevaluating the models we use to describe "the" economy.

POTENTIAL PROBLEMS

One potential problem to anticipate is students' unwillingness to rely explicitly on the extended model for explaining changes in LFPRs. While students will easily identify and understand the determinants affecting LFPR via changes in the value of market or non-market time, they often omit the effect of these determinants on the values of time in their analysis. In other words, they often do not articulate that it is the *relative changes in the value of time* (market and/or non-market) which affect the decision to participate in the labor market. Students thus may need encouragement to use the language of the model in their analysis.

As mentioned in Tables 5.2 and 5.3, gender, racial and ethnic stereotypes may become an issue when discussing labor force participation rates. One way to handle this problem is to be prepared to provide a more in-depth discussion of the labor force experiences of the different groups by using the articles mentioned in Assignment 3. Information on earnings, occupational distribution, geographic location (rural–urban), unemployment rates, and educational attainment gives students a more detailed picture of the factors affecting the labor supply decision of women in different situations. It may help show students that the picture is far more complex than the usual stereotypes would have us believe.

It may also be helpful to stress that *within* each of the race-ethnic groups identified there may be substantial differences in labor force experiences that are concealed by the overall labor force participation figures. Again, this reinforces the notion that the world is a complex place and what "everybody knows" about particular groups is likely to be untrue.

The articles listed in Assignment 3 could also contribute to a discussion of policy alternatives. An interesting theme that arises throughout these articles is the role of education. Some analysts would argue that increased educational attainment increases labor force participation and economic status. Others, particularly Jones, argue that education alone is not enough; in fact, it is possible that lack of employment opportunities and limited returns to education limit the impact of increased education on labor force participation and status. The extent to which education affects labor force participation (as the model suggests it should) and its value as a policy variable could be introduced as a discussion question.

Other policies that may be mentioned when discussing women's increased labor force participation are child care and parental leave policies and changes in the federal tax system. Interested instructors may wish to discuss these policies in general or by focusing on specific pieces of legislation, such as the ABC Child Care Bill, the Family and Medical Leave Act, and the Tax Reform Act of 1986. For background on child care and parental leave policies, we recommend: Blau and Ferber (1992: 181–3, 278–85) (which needs to be updated to reflect Clinton's signing of the Family and Medical Leave Act). In addition, Marx and Seligson (1990: 132–69), offer a thorough (although a bit dated) discussion of issues surrounding child care. Discussion of the incentive effects in the federal tax system can be found in Blau and Ferber (1992: 95). In addition to class discussion of these policies, instructors may wish to have students do short research projects on these policy alternatives and present their findings to the class.

Appendix 5.1
LABOR FORCE PARTICIPATION RATES—DATA BY SEX, RACE, MARITAL STATUS, AND AGE AND PRESENCE OF CHILDREN

The following data are provided so students can see the tremendous increase in women's labor force participation rates, especially among married women with children. For each table, we have indicated what the data illustrate. At the end, we have suggested exercises for using the tables in which students analyze actual data. As students identify the trends, they will also develop quantitative reasoning skills as they move between data tables, graphs, and words.

Note: These tables are intended to provide a complete picture of labor force participation by gender and race. However, instructors may wish to focus on only some groups presented here, such as married women or married women with children.

Table 5.1 illustrates the significant increase in women's labor force participation rates and the slight decline in men's participation over the last 100 years.

Questions for Table 5.1

Describe the trends in women's and men's labor force participation that you've identified, and explain how each compares to the trend in total worker labor force participation.
Note: Amott and Matthaei's data was calculated from decennial censuses and may not be strictly comparable to data obtained from other sources.

Tables 5.2 and 5.3 illustrate similar *trends* in labor force participation rates for women and men. They also point out the different *levels* in participation, e.g. black women have had historically higher participation in the labor force than white women, which may be explained, in part, by more black female-headed households and better job opportunities for black women than for black men. These differences in levels can be explored by placing the data in an historical and cultural context and are likely to generate interesting discussion; Amott and Matthaei offer an excellent source of background on these historical and cultural differences. However, if this discussion is undertaken, the instructor would want to be careful that the discussion does not disintegrate into racial and gendered stereotypes.

Questions for Table 5.2

Describe the similarities and differences between racial groups for women and for men. Indicate two reasons which you believe might account for the observed similarities and/or differences for women and for men.

Table 5.1 Labor force participation rates, actual and projected, by sex, 1890–2005[a]

Year	Total	Men	Women	Year	Total	Men	Women
1890	52.2	84.3	18.2	1970	60.4	79.7	43.3
1900	53.7	85.7	20.0	1975	61.2	77.9	46.3
1920	54.3	84.6	22.7	1980	63.8	77.4	51.5
1930	53.2	82.1	23.6	1985	64.8	76.3	54.5
1940	55.2	82.5	27.9	1990	66.4	76.1	57.5
1945	61.6	87.6	35.8	1991	66.0	75.5	57.3
1950	59.9	86.8	33.9	1992	66.3	75.6	57.8
1955	60.4	86.2	35.7	2000	68.7	76.0	62.0
1960	60.2	84.0	37.8	2005	69.0	75.4	63.0
1965	59.7	81.5	39.3				

Sources: US Department of Commerce, *Historical Statistics of the United States: Colonial Times to 1970*, Bicentennial Edition, Part I, 1975, pp. 131–2; US Department of Labor, Bureau of Labor Statistics, *Employment and Earnings*, January 1993, pp. 172–3; US Department of Commerce, *Statistical Abstract of the United States 1992*, No. 609.
Note: a For ages fourteen and above, 1890–1946; ages sixteen and above, 1947–2005.

Table 5.2 Civilian labor force participation rates by sex and race, 1955–2005

	Women			Men		
Year	White	Black	Hispanic	White	Black	Hispanic
1955	34.5	46.1	n.a.	85.4	85.0	n.a.
1960	36.5	n.a.	n.a.	83.4	n.a.	n.a.
1965	38.1	48.6	n.a.	80.8	79.6	n.a.
1970	42.6	n.a.	n.a.	80.0	76.5	n.a.
1975	45.9	48.8	43.1	78.7	70.9	80.7
1980	51.2	53.1	47.4	78.2	70.3	81.4
1985	54.1	56.5	49.3	77.0	70.8	80.3
1990	57.5	57.8	53.0	76.9	70.1	81.2
1991	57.4	57.0	52.3	76.4	69.5	80.1
2000	62.3	61.2	56.6	76.7	71.0	81.8
2005	63.5	61.7	58.0	76.2	70.2	81.6

Sources: Blau, Francine D. and Ferber, Marianne A., *The Economics of Women, Men, and Work*, second edition, p. 76; Ries, Paula and Stone, Anne J., eds, *The American Woman 1992–93* (1994), table 6–1, p. 308; US Department of Commerce, *Statistical Abstract of the United States 1992*, No. 609.

Table 5.3 Women's labor force participation rates by race, 1900–80

Race	1900	1910	1920	1930	1940	1950	1960	1970	1980
American-Indian	13.8	15.0	11.5	15.4	17.9	17.0	25.5	35.3	47.7
Chicana				14.8		21.9	28.8	36.4	49.0
European-American	16.0	17.8	19.5	20.3	24.5	28.1	33.6	40.6	49.4
African-American	40.7	39.8	38.9	38.9	37.8	37.4	42.2	47.5	53.3
Chinese-American	10.4	11.5	12.5	16.3	29.0	33.7	44.2	49.5	58.3
Japanese-American	30.1	28.0	25.9	19.0	38.7	41.6	44.1	49.4	58.3
Filipina-American			11.6	13.0	15.1	28.0	36.2	55.2	68.1
Island P. Rican	13.9	16.4	18.9	22.9	25.0	21.3	20.0	22.9	29.1
US Puerto Rican						38.9	36.3	31.6	40.1

Source: Teresa L. Amott and Julie A. Matthaie, *Race, Gender, and Work*, Table C-1.

Questions for Table 5.3

Describe the similarities and differences between racial groups. Which group has experienced the largest increase in labor force participation rates? Which group the lowest?

The importance of disaggregating the data by marital status as well as gender and race becomes very apparent in Table 5.4. As can be seen in either graphs or index numbers, the data in Table 5.4 indicate the significant increases in labor force participation rates for single and married white and black women, lesser increases for single white and black men, other white women and black women and men, and declines for married black and white men and other white men.

Questions for Table 5.4

The graphs for Table 5.4 could focus on several variables but probably the most interesting here is marital status by gender and race; each of the four graphs would have data for single adults, married adults with spouse present, and adults who are widowed, divorced, or separated. For each graph, identify for which marital status labor force participation rates have increased the most and the least since 1960. Discuss the similarities and differences in trends between men and women, and between blacks and whites.

Tables 5.5 and 5.6 illustrate the tremendous increases in labor force participation rates for married women with children still at home (under eighteen years of age), especially for those women with children under six years of age. The data for married women with children under fourteen years of age also reflect the level differences noted above between whites and blacks.

Questions for Table 5.5

Identify which group has experienced the largest increase in labor force participation rates. Discuss how the trends for women with no children under eighteen, women with children between six and seventeen years of

Table 5.4 Labor force participation rates by sex, race, and marital status, 1960–88

	White men			*White women*		
Year	*Single*	*Married*[a]	*Other*[b]	*Single*	*Married*	*Other*
1960	55.6	89.0	57.5	45.5	29.6	38.6
1965	50.9	87.6	54.6	41.8	33.6	36.9
1970	61.2	86.9	53.6	54.5	39.7	37.8
1975	68.8	83.2	65.9	59.4	43.5	39.7
1980	72.8	81.3	68.0	64.2	49.3	43.4
1985	72.7	78.9	70.6	67.9	53.3	44.7
1988	76.5	78.5	68.4	70.5	55.9	45.4
	Black and other[c] *men*			*Black and other women*		
Year	*Single*	*Married*	*Other*	*Single*	*Married*	*Other*
1960	55.0	87.9	67.7	33.6	40.8	47.2
1965	46.4	88.3	60.9	31.1	46.7	48.6
1970	57.5	86.9	56.6	43.6	52.5	45.9
1975	56.9	80.8	61.7	43.5	54.2	45.8
1980	60.6	78.7	60.5	49.4	59.0	47.4
1985	62.6	77.8	61.8	55.4	63.8	49.2
1988	66.6	78.8	61.5	58.1	65.6	50.3

Sources: US Department of Labor, Labor Force Statistics Derived from the Current Population Survey, 1948–87, August 1988, Bulletin 2307, C-11, pp. 798–800; Blau and Ferber, table 4–6, p. 111.
Notes: a Spouse present. *b* Widowed, divorced, separated. *c* Blacks only after 1975.

age, and women with children under six compare with the trend for all married women's labor force participation rates. How might you explain these results?

Questions for Table 5.6

List, in order of largest to smallest, the increase in labor force participation rates for white married women by age of own youngest child. List, in order of largest to smallest, the increase in labor force participation rates for black married women by age of own youngest child. Discuss the similarities and differences you observe between white and black married women.

Table 5.5   Married (spouse present) women's labor force participation rates, by age and presence of children, 1948–91

Year	Total	No children under 18	With children 6 to 17	With children under 6
1948	22.0	28.4	26.0	10.8
1950	23.8	30.3	28.3	11.9
1955	27.7	32.7	34.7	16.2
1960	30.5	34.7	39.0	18.6
1965	34.7	38.3	42.7	25.2
1970	40.8	42.2	49.2	30.3
1975	44.4	43.8	52.2	36.7
1980	50.1	46.0	61.7	45.1
1985	54.2	48.2	67.8	53.4
1987	55.8	48.4	70.6	56.8
1990	58.2	51.1	73.6	58.9
1991	58.5	51.2	73.6	59.9

Sources: US Department of Labor, *Labor Force Statistics Derived from the Current Population Survey, 1948–87*, August 1988, Bulletin 2307, C-12, p. 801; US Department of Commerce, *Statistical Abstract of the United States 1992*, No. 621.

Table 5.6   Married (spouse present) women's labor force participation rates, by race and age of own youngest child, 1975–91

Year	Total	No child under 18	Child under 18	1 year or under	Under 3 years	3–5 years	6–13 years	14–17 years
White women								
1975	43.6	43.6	43.6	29.2	30.7	40.1	50.7	53.4
1985	53.3	47.5	59.9	48.6	49.4	56.6	67.7	66.6
1990	57.6	50.8	65.6	53.3	54.9	62.5	72.6	74.9
1991	57.9	50.9	66.2	54.9	55.9	64.0	72.4	76.0
Black women								
1975	54.1	47.6	58.4	50.0	50.1	61.2	65.7	52.3
1985	63.8	55.2	71.7	63.7	66.2	73.8	73.3	74.4
1990	64.7	52.9	75.6	64.4	67.5	80.4	77.6	78.8
1991	66.1	54.8	76.5	66.9	70.3	77.3	80.1	77.6

Source: US Department of Commerce, *Statistical Abstract of the United States 1992*, No. 621.

Appendix 5.2
DATA TO SUPPORT CHANGES IN DETERMINANTS OF W AND W*

Increased educational attainment

Table 5.7 High school graduation rates, age twenty-five and over, for women

Year	White	Black	Hispanic
1970	55.0	32.6	30.9
1980	68.0	51.5	42.6
1989	78.2	65.0	50.8

Source: The American Woman 1992–93: 278.

Table 5.8 High school graduates completing at least four years of college

	Women				Men			
Year	All races	White	Black	Hispanic	All races	White	Black	Hispanic
1966	15.9	15.8	13.6	n.a.	23.7	24.4	11.0	n.a.
1976	24.1	24.3	18.4	8.2	32.0	32.9	16.5	17.9
1987	25.2	26.2	13.6	13.7	26.1	27.2	13.7	15.7

Source: The American Woman 1992–93: 280.

Table 5.9 Postsecondary degree attainment by gender (1,000)

	Women			Men		
Year	Bachelor's	Master's	Doctoral	Bachelor's	Master's	Doctoral
1959–60	138	24	1	254	51	9
1969–70	341	83	4	451	125	25
1979–80	456	147	10	474	151	23
1988–89	534	160	13	482	148	23

Source: The American Woman 1992–93: 288.

Table 5.10 Undergraduate degree attainment in various fields (%)

Field	White non-Hispanic	Black non-Hispanic	Hispanic	Asian/ Pacific islander	Native American/ Alaskan Native
Arts/humanities	14.8	9.7	16.9	12.7	14.4
Biological sciences	3.2	3.5	3.8	7.9	3.4
Business/management	21.0	25.3	22.1	23.4	20.4
Education	15.3	8.7	10.8	4.6	16.1
Engineering	1.6	1.9	2.1	6.2	1.6
Physical sciences	2.2	2.1	1.4	4.3	1.4
Professional[a]	13.1	12.6	9.6	10.7	11.2
Protective services	0.9	3.0	1.8	0.3	1.7

Social sciences	19.2	22.6	23.9	20.7	22.7
Other[b]	8.6	10.7	7.6	9.3	7.1
Total percent	100.0	100.0	100.0	100.0	100.0
Total number	451,530	35,651	15,880	18,682	2,278

Source: The American Woman 1992–93: 294.
Notes: a Includes architecture, health care, home economics, and library sciences. *b* Includes agriculture, communications, computer science, military sciences, and parks and recreation.

Increased demand for female labour

Table 5.11   Occupational distribution of workers by sex, 1975 and 1990

	1975		1990	
	Women	*Men*	*Women*	*Men*
Executive, administrative, and managerial	5.2	12.2	11.1	13.8
Professional specialty	13.2	10.4	15.1	12.0
Technicians and related support	2.7	2.5	3.5	3.0
Sales	11.3	10.2	13.1	11.2
Administrative support (including clerical)	31.6	6.1	27.8	5.9
Private household	3.4	0.1	1.4	0.1
Other service	17.4	8.6	16.3	9.7
Precision production craft, and repair	1.7	19.3	2.2	19.4
Machine operators, assemblers, and inspectors	9.2	9.5	6.0	7.5
Transportation and material moving	0.6	7.6	0.8	6.8
Handlers, laborers, and equipment cleaners	2.2	7.1	1.6	6.2
Farming, forestry, and fishing	1.6	6.3	1.0	4.4

Source: The American Woman 1992–93: 334.

Table 5.12   Occupational distribution of workers by race, 1983 and 1990

	1983			1990		
	White	*Black*	*Hispanic*	*White*	*Black*	*Hispanic*
Executive, administrative, and professional	22.6	16.1	12.2	27.2	18.7	12.6
Technicians, sales, and administrative support (including clerical)	47.3	36.3	25.5	45.3	39.1	24.1
Private household and other service	17.5	30.6	18.2	16.4	27.3	20.1
Precision production, craft, and repair	2.2	2.1	13.3	2.1	2.3	13.2
Machine operators, transportation, and handlers	9.0	14.3	26.1	7.8	12.2	24.6
Farming, forestry, and fishing	1.4	0.6	4.7	1.1	0.3	5.5

Sources: Black and white data–*The American Woman 1992–93*: 338; Hispanic data–US Department of Commerce, *Statistical Abstract of the United States 1986*, No. 670 and US Department of Commerce, *Statistical Abstract of the United States 1992*, No. 610.

Table 5.13 Occupational distribution of black and white women, 1940 and 1988

	1940		1988	
	Black women	White women	Black women	White women
Managerial, professional, and technical	4.9	17.6	19.6	28.6
Clerical	1.5	26.9	30.1	33.3
Sales	0.4	6.2	5.0	9.6
Domestic service	57.4	11.0	3.2	1.4
Other service	10.0	11.7	25.1	15.3
Farming, forestry, and fishing	16.1	2.4	0.2	1.1
Craftworkers, operatives, and laborers	9.7	24.3	16.8	10.7

Source: Mary C. King, "Occupational segregation by race and sex, 1940–88," *Monthly Labor Review*, April 1992: 32.

Availability of market substitutes

While not broken out by gender and race, Figures 5.1 and 5.2 illustrate the increase in the percentage of households in the United States with selected household appliances, cars, radios, and televisions in the last century. Increases in these factors are often cited as instances of time-saving home technology.

The increased use (and social acceptability) of child care provided outside the home is another factor associated with increased availability of market substitutes. As Table 5.14 indicates, there has been a significant decline in care provided in the child's home and a significant increase in group care since 1965.

Table 5.14 Child care arrangements used by employed mothers with children five years or younger (percent distribution)

	1965	1982	1988
Care in child's home	47.2	25.7	29.1
By father	10.3	10.3	12.9
By others	36.9	15.4	16.2
Care in another home	37.3	43.8	32.6
Group care[a]	8.2	18.8	31.2
Under 2 years	n.a.	n.a.	11.8
2–3 years	n.a.	n.a.	32.6
4–5 years, not in school	n.a.	n.a.	52.4
4–5 years, in school	n.a.	n.a.	25.7
All other arrangements	7.3	11.7	7.3

Source: F. Blau and M. Ferber, *The Economics of Women, Men, and Work*, p. 289.
Note: a Includes day-care center, nursery or preschool, kindergarten, extended day care and day camp.

Demographic trends

Table 5.15   Birth rates for women by race (live births per 1,000 women)

Year	All races	White	Black
1960	118.0	113.2	153.5
1970	87.9	84.1	115.4
1980	68.4	64.7	88.1
1988	67.2	63.0	86.6

Source: The American Woman 1992–93: 217.

Table 5.16   Divorce ratio[a] by sex and race

	Women				Men			
Year	All races	White	Black	Hispanic	All races	White	Black	Hispanic
1960	42	38	78	n.a.	28	27	45	n.a.
1970	60	56	104	81	35	32	62	40
1980	120	110	258	132	79	74	149	79
1990	166	153	358	155	118	112	208	103

Source: The American Woman 1992–93: 252.
Note: a Divorce ratio is the number of currently divorced persons per 1,000 currently married persons with spouse present. This ratio differs from the divorce rate, which is the number of divorces per 1,000 population.

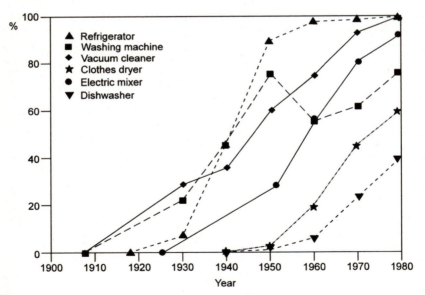

Figure 5.1   Percentage of households with selected household appliances.
Source: Julie A. Matthaei, *An Economic History of Women in America*, pp. 239, 241, Boston, MA: South End Press, 1991.

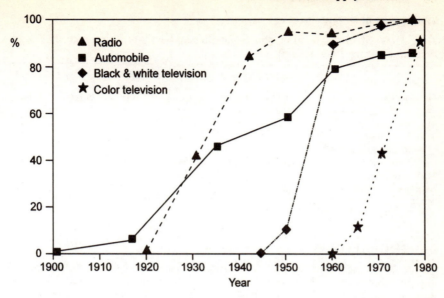

Figure 5.2 Percentage of households with automobiles, radios, and televisions.
Source: Julie A. Matthaei, *An Economic History of Women in America*, pp. 239, 241

Table 5.17 Percent distribution of family households by family type and race

Year	White	Black	Asian/Pacific islander	Hispanic
Married Couple				
1970	89	68	n.a.	81
1980	86	56	84	75
1985	84	51	n.a.	72
1990	83	50	82	70
1991	83	48	80	69
Male householder				
1970	2	4	n.a.	4
1980	3	4	5	5
1985	3	5	n.a.	5
1990	4	6	6	7
1991	4	6	7	7
Female householder				
1970	9	28	n.a.	15
1980	12	40	11	20
1985	13	44	n.a.	23
1990	13	44	12	23
1991	13	46	13	24

Source: US Department of Commerce, *Statistical Abstract of the United States 1992*, No. 57.

Changes in non-wage income

Table 5.18   Median annual income of families by family type and race, 1979 and 1989 (in constant 1989 dollars)

Family type	1979			1989		
	White	*Black*	*Hispanic*	*White*	*Black*	*Hispanic*
Married couple	37,275	28,843	28,756	39,208	30,650	27,382
Wife in paid labor force	43,234	35,364	35,034	45,803	37,787	34,821
Wife not in paid labor force	31,092	19,818	22,349	29,689	18,727	20,717
Male householder	30,231	21,335	24,879	30,487	18,395	25,176
Female householder	19,560	11,795	11,339	18,946	11,630	11,745

Source: The American Woman 1992–93: 391.

BIBLIOGRAPHY

Amott, T. L. and Matthaei, J. A. (1991) *Race, Gender, and Work: A Multicultural Economic History of Women in the United States*, Boston, MA: South End Press.
Blau, F. and Ferber, M. (1992) "Black and White Participation Differentials: An Analysis," in F. Blau and M. Ferber (eds) *The Economics of Women, Men, and Work*, second edition, Englewood Cliffs, NJ: Prentice Hall, pp. 110–13.
Bonilla-Santiago, G. (1990) "A Portrait of Hispanic Women in the United States," in S. Rix (ed.) *The American Woman, 1990–91: A Status Report*, New York: W. W. Norton, pp. 249–57.
Burgess, N. J. and Horton, H. D. (1992) "African-American Women and Work: A Socio-historical Perspective," *Journal of Family History* 18, 1: 53–63.
Jones, B. (1987) "Black Women and Labour Force Participation: An Analysis of Sluggish Growth Rates," in M. Simms and J. Malveaux (eds) *Slipping through the Cracks: The Status of Black Women*, New Brunswick, NJ: Transaction Books, pp. 11–31.
King, Mary C. (1992) "Occupational Segregation by Race and Sex, 1940–88," *Monthly Labour Review*, April: 32.
Lott, J. T. (1990) "A Portrait of Asian and Pacific-American Women," in S. Rix (ed.) *The American Woman 1990–91: A Status Report*, New York: W. W. Norton, pp. 258–64.
Marx, Fern and Seligson, Michelle (1990) "Child Care in the United States," in S. Rix (ed.) *The American Women 1990–91: A Status Report*, New York: W. W. Norton, pp. 132–69.
Ries, Paula and Stone, Anne J., eds (1992) *The American Woman 1992–93*, New York: W. W. Norton.
Smith, S. and Tienda, M. (1988) "The Doubly Disadvantaged: Women of Color in the US Labor Force," in A. Stromberg and S. Harkness (eds) *Women Working: Theories and Facts in Perspective*, second edition, Mountain View, CA: Mayfield Publishing, pp. 61–80.
Snipp, C. M. (1990) "A Portrait of American-Indian Women and their Labour Force Experiences," in S. Rix (ed.) *The American Woman 1990–91: A Status Report*, New York: W. W. Norton, pp. 265–71.
Spitze, G. (1988) "The Data on Women's Labour Force Participation," in A. Stromberg and S. Harkness (eds) *Women Working: Theories and Facts in Perspective*, second edition, Mountain View, CA: Mayfield Publishing.

6 The economics of affirmative action

Robert L. Moore and James D. Whitney

Affirmative action with respect to employment and college applicants is clearly a "hot-button" topic. Principles of economics instructors may be tempted to omit or gloss over the subject for fear of mishandling it by, for example, sparking unresolved tensions, reinforcing student misconceptions, being misinterpreted by students or revealing one's own biases. However, the issue of affirmative action offers principles instructors a compelling opportunity to illustrate the importance and relevance of economic analysis. As a legitimate controversy about which economists themselves are sharply divided, affirmative action gives instructors a chance to improve students' analytical skills without shoe-horning them into a predetermined final opinion. And affirmative action can also serve as a magnet for a diverse group of students who might find that many of the conventional applications in economics do not speak to the issues that concern them most.

Our purpose here is to offer a variety of options for introducing and dealing with the topic of affirmative action in principles of economics courses. Many of the options were suggested by fellow participants in the May 1993 Conference on Improving Introductory Economics by Integrating the Latest Scholarship on the Economics of Race and Gender. Particularly valuable suggestions were offered by Denise Janha in her conference presentation on addressing ethnicity issues, May 25, 1993.

The next section of this chapter starts with suggestions about the placement of this topic in the principles course and then provides a brief *economic* perspective on affirmative action by providing a "checklist" of key points (from economic analysis) that bear on this issue. The following section presents a more detailed description of teaching options, divided into the basic categories of preparation options, in-class activity options, and reaction options. The final section discusses some problems to anticipate, based partly on the authors' actual experiences using some of the suggested options.

AN ECONOMIC PERSPECTIVE ON AFFIRMATIVE ACTION

Because of the controversial nature of affirmative action, it is convenient that the subject fits most appropriately into a microeconomic principles course near the end of the term when the course typically turns to resource market issues. The timing is advantageous since it allows students most of the term to get acquainted with each other and gives instructors time to develop a mutually respectful classroom atmosphere.

A typical sequence of coverage begins with the basics of resource market supply and demand, followed by an examination of actual earnings differentials. After some initial attempts to account for these differentials using the resource market supply and demand discussion, theories and evidence concerning economic discrimination are often introduced. The introductory coverage of discrimination affords a number of opportunities to apply the economic perspective in ways that can challenge students' initial perceptions:

1 Highlighting the role of compensating differentials and various human capital variables (experience, education, etc.) in accounting for earnings differences.
2 Contrasting the potential roles of choice versus entry barriers and other constraints in accounting for observed occupational distributions.
3 Illustrating the possible role market forces can play in reducing the wage-differential effects of certain types of discrimination, particularly discrimination on the part of employers and employees.

The bridge to anti-discrimination policies generally consists of the empirical evidence of unexplained residual earnings differentials and the theoretical possibilities of persistent consumer discrimination and/or barriers to entry which result in segmented labor markets. Affirmative action can then be introduced and covered as a potential policy response to the inefficiency and inequity of the entry barriers implicit in segmented labor markets.

Two logical places to first elicit student opinions about affirmative action are:

1 After the basic coverage of supply and demand in labor markets and immediately before any specific analysis of discrimination.
2 After the theory and evidence of economic discrimination, as a way to introduce the analysis of anti-discrimination policies.

The first option allows students to share initial views uninfluenced by any coverage of the economic perspective on discrimination; the second option maintains the logical flow of the subject matter.

The next section details a number of specific options for introducing and dealing with affirmative action in economics principles classes. Regardless of the approach, the following checklist of key points can help challenge students' initial opinions and sharpen their views on affirmative action:

1 Without appropriate anti-discrimination policies, it is possible for economic discrimination to persist despite its inefficiency because of the benefits it engenders for privileged groups at a greater cost to the rest of society.

2 Broadly defined, affirmative action implies a wide range of strategies to encourage a more inclusive employment or admissions process, such as assembling a more diverse initial applicant pool, offering supplementary preparation for promising disadvantaged applicants, etc. It does not necessarily imply employment or admission quotas.

3 If there are efficiency-reducing barriers to entry, affirmative action has the potential to reverse the effects of the entry barriers and thereby result in a more efficient allocation of resources.

4 The "quality" of individual job or college applicants is generally a multi-dimensional mix of desirable attributes. One-dimensional measures such as test scores can help create an initial pool of qualified applicants, but within that pool the ranking of candidates often varies according to the attribute under consideration. As with jury decisions, the final choices between competing applicants can be difficult to interpret from a distance, based strictly on easily quantifiable criteria.

5 In some situations, there are material externalities involved in employment or admission decisions. Role models in high-profile positions, for example, can have beneficial long-term effects. Diverse representation can enhance democratic processes, judicial decision-making and educational experiences.

6 The externalities associated with affirmative action can be negative as well as positive. If, for example, affirmative action results in the acceptance of systematically less competitive applicants from disadvantaged groups, it risks reinforcing stereotypes and engendering hostility.

7 Affirmative action can erode the self-esteem of accepted applicants by making them less confident of their own individual comparative merits.

8 With specific respect to higher education, a popular barometer of an institution's academic reputation is the perceived quality of its incoming applicants. From an economic perspective, a preferable measure of institutional quality is the institution's value added: the difference the institution makes in the potential achievements of the students who attend.

DETAILED MENU OF TEACHING OPTIONS FOR AFFIRMATIVE ACTION

Because of the controversy of affirmative action, a spur-of-the-moment presentation approach is unlikely to be very successful. For that reason, this section is divided into three subsections: preparation options, activity options, and reaction options.

Preparation options

Option 1: Readings

1 "Is Affirmative Action Reverse Discrimination?" Kurt Finsterbusch and George McKenna (eds) *Taking Sides: Clashing Views on Controversial Political Issues*, second edition, pp. 206–21, Guilford, CT: Dushkin Publishing Group, 1982. (The "yes" view by Nathan Glazer is adapted from *Affirmative Action: Ethnic Inequality and Public Policy* (1975), New York: Basic Books. The "no" view is excerpted from Justice Thurgood Marshall's dissenting opinion, Regents of the University of California vs. Allan Bakke, 1978. Glazer argues against "affirmative action," contending that even well-intentioned forms of racial discrimination are unwise. Marshall emphasizes the need to remedy past injustices.)

2 D'Souza, Dinesh, "Sins of Admission," *New Republic* 18 (February 1991). (D'Souza critically examines the effects of college admissions policies based on proportional representation, arguing that it devalues the merit criteria and is partly responsible for the recent increases in racial tensions on college campuses.)

3 Larew, John, "Why are Droves of Unqualified, Unprepared Kids Getting into our Top Colleges?" *Washington Monthly* (June 1991). (In this examination of the admissions policies of Ivy League colleges, the author finds favoritism to children of alumni. The consequences of legacy privilege are also explored.)

4 Williams, Walter, "Race, Scholarship, and Affirmative Action," *National Review*, May 5, 1989. (This article explores the relationship between college admissions policies and recent increases in racial and ethnic intolerance on college campuses. Details of the African-American educational deficit are also given.)

(These three articles are reprinted in Susan F. Feiner, (ed.) *Women and Minorities in the U.S. Economy: Views from across the Spectrum*, Englewood Cliffs, NJ: Prentice-Hall, 1994.

Option 2: Video

Media and society seminars of the Columbia University Graduate School of Journalism in association with WNET/New York and WTTW. "The Constitution, that Delicate Balance, part 12: Affirmative Action versus Reverse Discrimination." New York: Media and society seminars, video recording, 1984. (This video offers conflicting views on affirmative action by a group of distinguished analysts; though not economists, the speakers do raise a number of relevant concerns.)

Option 3: Student exercises

Reaction paper: Require students to prepare a one-to-two page position paper in advance. Variations:

1 If supplementary material has been assigned, require them to respond to the material, including the leading arguments advanced by those opposed to their point of view.
2 Some time before covering the topic, have students briefly record their pro or con position concerning affirmative action and the main reason(s) for their position. For the reaction paper, require them to argue the opposite position, including specifically addressing the reason(s) they gave for their own initial position.

Self-focusing exercise: As suggested by Janha, it can be very helpful to students to begin a discussion of ethnicity issues by having them draw on their own experiences. Janha suggests that students prepare their answers to the following questions:

1 What is your racial or ethnic identify?
2 How did you first become aware of your racial or ethnic identify? (Try to be specific—for example, was there an event or incident that you remember?)
3 Describe a time in your life when your racial or ethnic identify was advantageous to you.
4 Describe a time in your life when your racial or ethnic identify was a disadvantage to you.
5 Describe a time when you felt different as a student: What did the teacher do or not do? What did other students do or not do?

Before discussing affirmative action itself, encourage individual students to share their responses to these questions in class, which can serve as an effective ice breaker. Often, students will report their race or ethnicity in greater detail than the few categories which appear on application forms. It will also become evident that race or ethnicity has never seemed to matter much to some students, while it has been of crucial importance in the lives of others. This simple recognition can help engender sensitivity and respect during the subsequent discussion of affirmative action.

Activity options

Option 1: Directed discussion

Directed discussion of a situation in which the traditionally dominant group benefits from affirmative action. For example, one of the authors used in his class the exaggerated version below of a true-life situation faced by a

Midwest college whose female applicants typically have higher average SAT scores than its male applicants.

1 Announce: "The head admissions officer announces to the admissions committee that they have ranked their applications by a combined measure of SAT scores and high school grades. The head admissions officer indicates that if they simply proceed down this list until they have accepted enough applications to fill the class, they can expect that the entering class of 1,000 would be composed of 700 women and 300 men."
2 Solicit responses to the following questions:
   (a) What are some of the disadvantages you see in using this approach? Ideally, some of the responses will address concerns about a less appealing social life for students, possibly less stimulating classroom discussions, a college population not representative of the population graduates will face, etc.
   (b) Should the committee take gender explicitly into account? For example, should they lower the acceptable cutoff for males so that it is now below the previous one, and raise the cutoff for females so that it is above the previous one?
   (c) Would your answers above be any different if the issue was not between men and women, but between students of different ethnicities?

Responses to the last two sets of questions are likely to be more divided and can lead into a more general discussion of pros and cons.

Option 2: Role playing

Assign students gender/ethnicity roles different from their own. Then work through an example and discussion with each student presenting views from their own role perspective. Since students are not directly putting their own views on the line, they may be more willing to contribute ideas or make stereotypical statements.

Option 3: Randomized feedback

Have students write down one or two persuasive arguments for or against affirmative action. Instruct them to fold their papers and begin passing them around the room. Then have students report the arguments they end up with. This allows students to share controversial views without necessarily claiming them as their own.

Option 4: Affirmative action "Boggle"

Give students three minutes to write down as many distinct pro and con arguments concerning affirmative action as they can think of. Then randomly select students to read their lists, and record the arguments on the board. Award points to students who mention an argument that no one else in the class has on their list.

Option 5: Classroom debate

To defuse the tension that can arise with a debate, consider assigning students randomly, or force some to argue a position counter to their own. Allow students to opt out of participating if they are uncomfortable with the format or topic. And avoid having the class decide who "won" the debate.

Reaction options

Option 1: Journal

Consider having students maintain a journal of responses to class discussions and activities throughout the term. They can then use the journal to record their own responses to the assignments and classroom coverage of affirmative action.

Option 2: Reaction paper

Particularly if a reaction paper was not used to prepare for in-class coverage of affirmative action, consider assigning one based on the in-class coverage. For example, consider the following assignment:

Write a one- to two-page reaction paper in which you explain whether or not gender and race/ethnicity should be taken into account in college admissions decisions. If your answer is yes, explain how these factors should be taken into account. If your answer is no, explain why not. In explaining and defending your answer, you *must* explicitly take into account the arguments that were made in the class discussions by students who disagreed with the position you are now taking.

PROBLEMS TO ANTICIPATE

Because of the controversial nature of affirmation action, instructors are likely to experience discomfort themselves in covering the topic. Janha suggests a number of reasons for this:

1 Fear of making mistakes, using stereotypical labels, being paternalistic, showing insensitivity or anger, revealing bias and ignorance.
2 Uncertainty about how to handle student anger, guilt and anxiety.
3 Fear of reinforcing what students thought before.
4 Fear of being dismissed or criticized by students.

Janha also offers some advice for addressing these obstacles:

1 Use a self-conscious focus exercise for students at the start of the discussion (for example, the five-question exercise covered above under preparation options).
2 Make a self-disclosure, acknowledging your own limitations.
3 Establish ground rules for frank but respectful discussion.
4 Avoid using classmates to teach each other (avoid "life stories" as lessons for others).
5 Be supportive to make sure everyone's humanity is dignified.
6 Anticipate student initial positions to be prepared to challenge students' assumptions, misconceptions and possible racism.

Student discomfort can make it difficult to get past classroom silence in order to start and maintain discussion of student views on affirmative action. Many feel uncomfortable in general when called on to state opinions instead of facts, and, in the case of topics like affirmative action, many feel the pressure to appear "politically correct" and are therefore unwilling to speak freely. Some of the class activity options listed above are designed to get around this reluctance and get some of the key arguments on the table. Our own experience in this regard may be instructive. One of the authors actually had students report their answers to the exercise about their ethnicity/racial background at the start of the class on affirmative action while the other did not. The ensuing discussion was more heated and forthcoming in the class where they did spend some time talking about their racial/ethnic backgrounds.

A related key issue is trying to move the instructor off center-stage in order to encourage students to speak to each other. Strategies that might help in this respect include:

1 If possible, arrange desks in a circle and take a seat yourself.
2 Do not respond to each individual comment.
3 Consider explicitly instructing students that you'd like them to respond to each other and ignore your presence.
4 If confrontations do arise, try to let students work them out. (There is a delicate balance here; Janha suggests trying to steer arguments to an intellectual and respectful level, but interceding too early can stifle discussion.)

Successful discussion will spark a number of common statements on the part of students. As Janha suggested, it is helpful to anticipate these statements in order to be prepared to respond to them and challenge students to rethink their arguments. The frequently repeated statements include:

1 "Affirmative action means quotas."

Response: This is a common perception, but it is not generally true. Affirmative action encompasses a wide range of policies designed to increase occupational or educational participation of targeted groups.

2 "Affirmative action means lower quality."

Response: Quality is rarely one-dimensional, especially in complicated cases of employment and education. College admissions decisions, for example, typically factor in test scores, grades, class rank, letters of recommendation, personal essays, extracurricular activities and personal characteristics—applicants never rank equally high in each of these respects. Also, employment and education decisions focus not just on the quality of each individual separately, but the quality of the enterprise as a whole, and different applicants can contribute to that overall quality in a variety of ways.

3 "Affirmative action is reverse discrimination. Two wrongs don't make a right."

Response: The implication of a second wrong is that it would move society further away from a more desirable initial position. But the aim of affirmative action is to undo the effects of an initial wrong, in this case, offsetting the inefficiency and inequity of pre-existing discrimination and thereby approximately restoring the outcome which would have occurred if there had been no discrimination in the first place. However, affirmative action is a second-best solution to the elimination of discrimination itself, so it may not work out as well in practise as in principle.

4 "It's not my fault; affirmative action corrects group wrongs at the expense of the individual."

Response: The fact that affirmative action creates highly visible winners and losers is undoubtedly what makes it so controversial. However, the initial discrimination created winners and losers too, and the inefficiency inherent in discrimination suggests that the winners from affirmative action stand to gain more than the losers stand to lose. Lots of other economic events and policies do the same thing, from technological change to defense cutbacks to trade liberalization. Societies face many tough trade-offs involving not just benefits and costs, but winners and losers as well.

5 "Affirmative action devalues the accomplishments of members of 'favored' groups."

Response: A potentially costly risk of affirmative action is that it might end up hurting the individuals it is intended to help. In practice, affirmative action can result in accepting applicants who end up failing due to lack of follow-up support or not being sufficiently well qualified to succeed. It can also lead to an impression that members of favored groups are less qualified, stigmatizing those individuals and/or reducing their own self-esteem. Costs like these underlie the ongoing intellectual debates about the overall net benefits of affirmative action.

7 Risk analysis: do current methods account for diversity?

Kathy Parkison

Most introductory economics textbooks discuss pollution in the context of externalities and then discuss correcting for externalities using marginal costs and marginal benefits. While the concepts of social costs and benefits may be explored, few textbooks delve into exactly how these societal curves are determined or even if there is a single social cost or social benefit curve. If one of the goals of an introductory economics course is economic literacy, then a solid understanding of how marginal costs and benefits are to be used in determining governmental policy is appropriate.

Society has chosen to utilize a wide variety of methods to convey information to consumers about goods and services. These range from mandatory informational labels to owner's manuals. The information level chosen is often a function of how risky society views the good. If the product or service is assumed to carry only a moderate risk, then simple product warning labels are assumed to be sufficient. These are precautionary warning labels indicating potential problems with the product or with its misuse and have no quantified data or statistical information. If society wants to explore risk and benefit tradeoffs, then more information is needed and more quantitative methods must be utilized. These quantitative methods include the risk assessment method discussed below.

The National Academy of Science has made an effort to distinguish between "risk assessment" as outlined in the five-step methodology later in this chapter, "risk management," and "risk communication" (NAS, 1983). These are ever-expanding topics encompassing economics, ethics, and governmental policy issues. Since students are most familiar with the published reports of risk, the discussion starts with the issues in risk communication. Students are familiar with the general concept of risk in that every day they are exposed to news releases touting the benefits or risks of a product. Unfortunately, these risk numbers, while widely circulated, do not adequately convey what risk actually is and how it affects students' lives. In the risk assessment literature, the term "risk" has generally been defined as the potential for adverse consequences arising from an event or activity. In the popular literature, risk is often defined as the certain probability of an adverse consequence, with the adverse consequence being defined in one of two ways. An adverse consequence may be narrowly defined as death or disease. Or, in the broader sense, an adverse consequence may be defined in terms of societal costs or losses. Defining a risk in the narrow sense of consequences may seriously underestimate the true losses or costs. The broader definitions of an event's consequences may be difficult to measure, calculate, and compare.

During an introductory economics course is an ideal time for discussion of how the current risk assessment and risk management methods may be flawed in that they do not take into account differences in age, race, and gender. This exercise also shows the dangers of basing governmental policy on aggregated and extrapolated data. This example would fit toward the end of the semester after the students have been exposed to externalities and governmental issues in microeconomics. This material could be presented as a lecture with class involvement in finding current risk assessments for the next period discussion. Estimates of risk are found daily in the popular news media, the trade journals, or the medical press. In the popular news media, risk numbers are usually presented as absolutes while the trade and medical journals will have a more complete presentation of the confidence ranges and the procedures involved in the experiments.

Students have many misconceptions about the scientific approach to risk identification and assessment, so the lecture begins by discussing what risk is and how it is estimated. Tables of risk estimates are available in resources such as *Technology Review* or *The Practical Journal for the Environment*. Querying students as to which is the riskier behavior: eating forty tablespoons of peanut butter or smoking 1.4 cigarettes usually elicits the opinion that "of course, the cigarette." The reality is that the estimates of risk of both behaviors are the same and this surprises students. Table 7.1 is a sample risk table.

This table surprises students in that many behaviors are more or less risky than they originally thought. This can lead to a discussion of perceived and actual risk. The lay population differs systematically from the experts in the meaning assigned to the term risk, leading to a large difference between the

Table 7.1 Risks that increase the annual death risk by one in one million

Activity	Cause of death
Smoking 1.4 cigarettes	Cancer, heart disease
Spending 1 hour in a coal mine	Black lung disease
Traveling 10 miles by bicycle	Accident
Traveling 150 miles by car	Accident
One chest X-ray at a good hospital	Radiation cancer
Eating 40 tablespoons of peanut butter	Liver cancer caused by aflotoxin B
Living 150 years within 20 miles of a nuclear reactor	Radiation cancer

Source: Richard Wilson, "Analyzing the Daily Risks for Life," *Technology Review* 81 (1979): 40–6.

public's perceived risk and the actual calculated risk. There have been a wide variety of studies that indicate that the public defines "risk" using a broader set of factors than the set considered by the experts (e.g. Slovic *et al.* 1978; Vlek and Keren 1991; Vlek and Stallen 1981). Many studies (Beach 1990; Fischhoff 1983; Martin 1989; Miller 1983; Nelkin 1989; Russell 1990; Stern *et al.* 1986; Tversky and Kahneman 1981) have shown that the factors that can affect the public's perception of risk include the following:

1 Synthetic is viewed as more risky than natural.
2 Unfamiliar is viewed as more risky than familiar.
3 Involuntary risk is viewed as more risky than voluntary risk.
4 Uncontrollable risk is viewed as more risky than controllable risk.
5 If it affects children, it is viewed as more risky than if it affects adults.
6 Untrusted institutions are viewed as more risky than trusted institutions.
7 Uncertain risk is viewed as more risky than certain risk.

Implicit in the entire process of risk assessment and management is the crucial role of communication. Risk communication, informing the public about risk, in also a public issue. In presenting aggregate risk estimates to lay individuals, the commonly asked question is, "What does this mean for me or my family?" (Sharlin 1986). The non-expert may reframe the numbers in terms of personal risk (Plough and Krimsky 1987)—an issue not addressed by the aggregate numbers released. Another complicating factor is that risk descriptions/probabilities may not be completely neutral. Reporting authorities may have their own agendas behind model assumptions made, numbers calculated or reported, and how they are presented. This is easily seen in the differing reports on the risks of cigarette smoking.

The ideal risk communication system would tailor the information to the consumer's level of knowledge and include a discussion of all the factors involved in the process. Risks do not seem to be communicated in this fashion since the public receives only bits and pieces from the news media. The public presentation often ignores the technical and qualifying details, and emphasizes the sensational parts.

In summation, risk communications are likely to evoke responses depending on the perceived personal relevance of the situation. Individuals may overestimate the risks that are out of personal control and under-estimate the risks that they can control. This is not meant to imply that individuals are acting irrationally. So an individual may not be best judge of risk due to perception problems, and society may not make optimum decisions due to pressure from individuals or due to publicity problems. Addressing the public's fear about a risk may alter the perception of that risk and encourage a more informed discussion.

Beyond the issues of risk communication, the processes of risk assessment and risk management are not understood by the general public. The starting point is that of risk assessment. By quantifying risks, assessors try to rationalize the debate on what to do about them. Risk assessment methods can range from "empirical" methods based on data and experiences, to "model-based" methods which use predictive models, to "qualitative" methods which use the judgmental reasoning of a panel of experts. The qualitative method is primarily used when there is limited empirical evidence or no predictive model available. The qualitative models, while just as useful as the other two models, do not strive for any mathematical precision. The empirical or mathematical models follow a five step assessment methodology as developed by the National Science Foundation (Covello and Hadlock 1985):

1 *Risk identification*. This includes designating the nature of the risk, its source, mechanism of action (if known), and potential adverse consequences. The first step in assessing a risk is to pinpoint the source of the adverse consequences. In the case of clearly identified links between a substance and an outcome, such as lead and the symptoms of lead poisoning, this step may include analyzing what are the potential sources of lead such as leaded gasoline or leaded paint. In the case of an adverse consequence with no clearly identified hazard, additional detective work may be needed to locate and determine the hazard.
2 *Risk-source characterization*. This step includes a description of the characteristics of the sources of risk that have the potential for creating the risk. What is there in the substance/behavior that makes it risky? How does it affect the body? This step could include monitoring of the environment or equipment, accident investigation, statistical methods for sampling, computer simulation models, etc.
3 *Exposure calculation*. This includes measurement (or estimation) of the intensity, frequency, and duration of human exposure to the risk source. This step can also include many of the items listed in the previous step. The goals of this step are to describe the sources of risk; how this risk is dispersed through the affected population (e.g. air pollution); and to categorize what is the affected population.
4 *Dose–response assessment*. This step includes the estimation of the relationship between the dose of the risk source received and the body's response to the source. This assessment is done using tests on animals; tests on humans; long-term case studies of individuals; and computer models.
5 *Risk estimation*. This final step establishes an overall summary measurement indicating the levels of health, safety, or environment risk being assessed. Determining a final number for the risk involved requires complex mathematical models and assumptions on human behavior and health. Formally, this step combines the quantitative predictions of the exposure step with the quantitative dose–response step. This formulation assumes that hazard and exposure can be separated experimentally and mathematically.

These five steps provide a general framework to analyze a wide variety of risk types. It may be used to model both the chronic risks of ongoing exposure to hazards such as radiation as well as the acute risk associated with events such as a nuclear reactor accident. Done correctly, a comprehensive risk assessment should also include a description of the range of uncertainty in these numbers. This is expressed as a confidence interval. This uncertainty range encompasses both the degree of variability in the real world and the degree to which the model assumptions differ from the real world. These uncertainty ranges are seldom reported in the popular press.

From there, the discussion proceeds to this general risk assessment methodology and how it is implemented in reality. The first two steps are often lumped together in a generalized risk source and exposure analysis. These two steps are attempting to determine what the sources of risk are and which population groups may be affected. To determine if a substance has harmful properties, it is usually tested for harmful effects on animals. One question that is often raised during these first two stages is whether all hazards have actually been identified.

The third step involves examining how people (or any other group such as animals, fish, birds, etc.) are exposed to the risk. The exposure portion requires the identification of the affected population as well as its size and spatial distribution. While other groups may be considered, the emphasis is on the risks to human health. There are additional data collection and aggregation problems in this step. Certain subpopulations (the elderly, the infirm, minority groups, etc.) may be more at risk than others, but the traditional medical studies are performed on white males. The data may therefore be skewed by ignoring these other groups.

The goal is to determine whether or not a substance or behavior is risky for humans. This is the question of how much of the substance (the dose) is needed to see adverse reactions (the response). In general, higher doses are assumed to result in a higher probability of an effect, a faster effect, a more severe effect, or some combination of the above. There may even be a threshold below which there is no hazard, though this threshold may differ by individuals. Since time and money are scarce, animal studies are used. These animal studies attempt to mimic human response to low doses over long periods of time by exposing the animals to extremely high doses of the chemicals, much higher than normally encountered by humans. A common example that students are familiar with is the testing of cosmetics on animals. Various firms, for example the Body Shop, have used in their advertising the fact that they do not test their products on animals. Animal testing of cosmetics involves painting potential cosmetics onto the animal's skin and their resulting effects noted. This, of course, raises ethical questions concerning animal welfare as well as the question of whether animals are appropriate proxies for humans.

In the fourth step, attempts are made to actually quantify the risk to humans based on actual dosages received by humans. To assess the risk of a particular hazard quantitatively, an understanding of the mathematical relationship between the dose and the response is necessary. Therefore, some methodology for dose–response extrapolation is necessary. The need to use some model for extrapolation creates uncertainty because different models can yield different estimates of risk. There are three common methodologies used in dose–response work.

In the first method, because of moral and ethical considerations against testing on humans, animals again serve as proxies. Human risk is estimated from the animal studies by using the same ratio of substance mass to body mass. If a rat which weighs 200 grams shows harmful effects when fed 2 milligrams/day of a substance for a year, then this data is extrapolated up to a 90 kilogram (200 pound) man exposed to 100 milligrams/day of the substance for a year. Since the rats used are traditionally male, the extrapolation has been to men. The differing effects that substances may have on children, women, the elderly, and minorities have traditionally been ignored. There are few studies that even attempt to see if the same extrapolation rates hold for men and women.

A second potential methodology in the fourth step uses collective data based on subject recollection of their own behavior. For example, when studying a risky behavior such as smoking, subjects are asked to estimate their own cigarette consumption. Since cigarette smoking has been receiving a great deal of bad publicity lately, there may be incentives for subjects to either lie or underestimate their consumption of cigarettes to the researchers. These subjects are followed over time; their cigarette consumption, as reported by the subject, is tabulated, and the incidence of diseases such as lung cancer is also noted. This gives a risk of lung cancer based on quantities of cigarettes smoked. These estimates are then extrapolated down to estimate the risk from one cigarette. This is how the risk of 1.4 cigarettes was calculated in the risk table shown earlier. Note that these extrapolated risk numbers have extremely wide confidence bands, but these bands are neither reported in the press nor are they understood by the general population. Nor do these numbers reflect causality issues such as who smokes in the first place and why.

The final methodology available to researchers in the dose–response analysis is still in its infancy. Computer simulations of the effects of a chemical on specific tissues have been used in biology and chemistry for some time. Computer simulations of the entire human system are just starting to be developed. These will allow testing of substances/behaviors on computers rather than humans or animals. This will require immense amounts of data concerning the whole system's response to an individual stimulus.

Every step along the risk assessment path has data gathering, data analysis, data aggregation, and extrapolation problems leading to difficulties in drawing conclusions. Students are often surprised at how tricky the process can be and how these estimates can vary from study to study. This does not negate the entire process, it simply means that informed consumers need to be aware of the methodology used in determining these numbers. Including discussions of how race, gender, and age may affect these risk assessments is appropriate but touchy. The methods by which risk is defined, measured, aggregated, and estimated have major consequences for individuals as well as social groups. This leads into discussions of governmental policy and benefit-cost regulations.

The National Academy of Science notes risk assessment can be defined as the use of scientific methods, models, and data to develop information about risks, while risk management is much broader and includes the balancing of risks against other possible societal criteria. Conceptions of risk management will be socially designed and may include analysis of the possible risk and benefit tradeoffs in decision making. Many would agree that risk management is much more of a political or social decision than risk assessment since it incorporates the goals of a society and which risk and benefit tradeoffs are considered to be socially acceptable. As such, risk management is as controversial as any other political matter. The role of risk assessment is to help the public debate over risk management.

Once the risk has been identified and quantified, the process of risk management begins. Risk management can be used to prevent the risk producing process, to reduce exposures, to educate, to compensate for damages, and to ameliorate effects. There may be no easy or correct choice among the tradeoffs faced by society. These tradeoffs, and the public's willingness to accept them, are part of the risk management and risk communication process.

Over the past few decades, society has tended to switch the focus in risk management from the work or home environment to a focus on individual susceptibility to risk sources. It has become fashionable to look for genetic explanations for health and response to risk. The argument runs like this: environmental factors may govern many aspects of health, but some smokers get lung cancer while others do not. So something other than smoking distinguishes those who get lung cancer from those who do not. Indeed, inherited factors may have an impact on health, but inherited effects are embedded in a network of environmental factors. We literally eat, sleep, sweat, breath and move through our environments. Isolating environmental factors from genetic factors is difficult at best.

While everyone may agree that some biological variation may exist in response to exposures to risky substances, the current trend is to identify high-risk individuals based on statistical associations between particular genetic findings/abnormalities and specific traits or diseases. Proponents of this approach view this as a value-neutral way to reduce overall health risks to society. The danger lies in that categorizing people as "high-risk" can be translated into determining a "genetic susceptibility" with racial or sexual overtones. Given the pervasive influence of the environment, such risk measures as calculated in the aggregate and then applied to any one individual are not purely scientific or technical. Institutional arrangements, power structures, social forces, employment patterns, and cultural views can be used to determine which individuals are viewed as at risk from a substance. For example, women are now counseled away from certain jobs based on suspected fetal hazards. The push to research and find the genes that control "this" or "that" condition could lead to tests for these conditions based on genetic markers. Ultimately this could be used to exclude workers from jobs based on their genetic tests, whether or not a worker actually showed the disease in question.

Our ideas of race and gender are influenced by the way we look at one another. We tend to notice differences among ourselves rather than similarities. In describing other humans, we concentrate on our differences since we know the similarities of two eyes, two ears, two arms and so on. And so, we describe each other by differences such as skin color, eye color, etc. Therefore, our age, gender, and race may be seen as the cornerstones of our identity as an individual. And indeed, age and gender are concrete and measurable. On the other hand, race is a classification that suffers from sociological, biological, cultural, and semantic interpretations. Asking how different groups of individuals may be affected by some risk factor is potentially opening a can of worms, particularly if a group's predisposition toward susceptibility for a risk factor is used to exclude that group from an activity.

Genetics, as a science, focuses on the differences between organisms, not the similarities. Modern technologies such as DNA testing have vastly improved genetic analysis. Humans are remarkably different on a genetic level around the world. Yet these genetic differences pale beside the genetic differences between humans and other similar species such as monkeys. It is all a matter of perspective. On the surface level (our eyes, our skin, etc.) we may look very different, but at the deeper anatomical/physiological level, there is a great deal of similarity among all of us.

Our personal DNA code may differ only slightly from a random stranger. Current genetic research has pointed out that despite obvious physical differences among individuals, the vast majority of human variations on the genetic level occur within a population group not between population groups. On a personal level, differences among individuals of Irish descent are greater than the differences between an individual of Irish descent and one of West African decent. Richard Lewontin, a geneticist from Harvard, showed in his classic study in 1972 that only about 6 percent of differences between individuals can be accounted for by race (Shreeve 1994). Patterns of variation in genetic material cut across many obvious and visible selection criteria, such as race or national origin. Our genetic knowledge is increasing, but our social understanding of how these genetic techniques are applied is still lacking. In fact, anthropologists cannot agree on what constitutes a definition of race and whether or not biological races even exist.

Despite the controversy over exactly what constitutes race, medical researchers seem to have little question about the validity of racial categories. Each year, dozens of reports in respected medical journals use race as an explanatory variable in showing susceptibility to disease, infant mortality rates, life expectancy, IQ, and other markers of public health and well-being. The true question underlying all of these statistics is that of correlation versus causality. Are these studies pointing to actual genetic differences among these groups of people, or are they using race as a convenient scapegoat to cover differences in social, cultural, medical, and economic environments for the different groups? Trying to track down a single genetic cause for a condition is difficult since health problems can be the result of many factors. For example, high blood pressure can be the result of smoking, dietary sodium levels, exposure to environmental hazards, and workplace stress, as well as other factors. Until genetic sequences of a large number of people have been examined, real and significant correlations between genes and health will be impossible to distinguish from accidental correlations. Scientific papers that give rise to positive correlations receive a large amount of press, while later retractions do not even rate a mention in the press.

Managing the environmental, technological, and other public health risks has become an arena for disagreements in our society. Controversies have not been limited to any one type of technology or behavior. How we choose to define and calculate risk; how high risk individuals or groups are identified; the proper use of technology; all have major implications for individual workers, the health care system, governmental policy, and society. In general, scientists attempt to assess the risk, governmental agencies must choose whether or not to regulate the risk, and the public will actually experience the risk. Therefore, increasing the public's awareness of how risk is measured and managed is important. Economics has a large role to play in discussing the tradeoffs inherent in any choice and noting that every choice carries some degree of risk. We end the discussion with the fact that there must always be a tradeoff between conflicting uses of society's resources. Resources devoted to eliminating pollution can't be used for worker training and so on. Students should come away with a different perspective on risk. They should realize that risk cannot be completely eliminated, and that many risk values carry additional uncertainty due to measurement errors, differences in people, genetics, body weight, and overall health. Evaluating the risk in any proposed product, governmental plan, or program will become increasingly important. I close with reminding students that despite any obvious differences, what unites all of us as members of the human species is much more than the petty differences that separate us.

Additional suggested readings

1 Glickman, T. S. and Gough, M. (1990) *Readings in Risk*, Baltimore, MD: Resources for the Future.

2 Dawes, Robyn M. (1988) *Rational Choice in an Uncertain World*, New York: Harcourt Brace.
3 *Risk Analysis*, quarterly journal, New York: Plenum Publishing.

BIBLIOGRAPHY

Baum, A. and Fleming, I. (1993) "Implications of Psychological Research on Stress and Technological Accidents," *American Psychologist* 48: 665–72.
Beach, L. R. (1990) *Image Theory: Decision Making in Personal and Organizational Contexts*, New York: Wiley Publishing.
Covello, V. and Hadlock, C. (eds) (1985) "Probabilistic Risk Assessment: Status Report and Review of the Probabilistic Risk Assessment Model," *Document NUREG-1050*, Washington, DC: National Science Foundation.
Draper, E. (1991) *Risky Business: Genetic Testing and Exclusionary Practices in the Hazardous Workplace*, Cambridge, UK: Cambridge University Press.
Fiksel, J. and Covello, V. (1986) *Biotechnology Risk Assessments: Issues and Methods for Environmental Introductions*, New York: Pergamon Press.
Fischhoff, B. (1983) "Predicting Frames," *Journal of Experimental Psychology: Learning, Memory and Cognition* 9: 103–16.
Hubbard, R. and Wald, E. (1993) *Exploding the Gene Myth*, Boston, MA: Beacon Press.
Levin, M. and Strauss, H. (1991) *Risk Assessment in Genetic Engineering: Environmental Release of Organisms*, New York: McGraw-Hill.
Martin, B. (1989) "The Sociology of the Fluoridation Controversy: A Reexamination," *Sociological Quarterly* 30: 59–76.
Miller, A. (1983) "The Influence of Personal Biases on Environmental Problem Solving," *Journal of Environmental Management* 17: 133–42.
Miller, H. and Gunary, D. (1993) "Serious Flaws in the Horizontal Approach to Biotechnology Risk," *Science* 262: 1500–1.
Morgan, M. G. (1993) "Risk Analysis and Management," *Scientific American* 32–41.
National Academy of Science (1983) *Risk Assessment in Federal Government: Managing the Process*, Washington, DC: National Academy Press.
Nelkin, D. (1989) "Communicating Technological Risk: The Social Construction of Risk Perception," *Annual Review of Public Health* 10: 95–113.
Plough, A. and Krimsky, S. (1987) "The Emergence of Risk Communication Studies: Social and Political Context," *Science, Technology, and Human Values* 12: 4–10.
Redenbaugh, K., Hiatt, W., Martineau, B., Kramer, M., Sheehy, R., Sanders, R., Houck, C., and Emlay, D. (1992) *Safety Assessment of Genetically Engineered Fruits and Vegetables; A Case Study of the Flavr Savr Tomato*, Boca Raton, FL: CRC Press.
Russell, C. (1990) "What, Me Worry?" *American Health* 12: 45–50.
Sharlin, H. I. (1986) "EDB: A Case in Communication," *Risk Analysis* 6: 61–8.
Shreeve, J. (1994) "Terms of Estrangement," *Discover*, November: 57–63.
Slovic, D., Fischoff, B., Lichtenstein, S., Read, S., and Combs, B. (1978) "How Safe is Safe Enough? A Psychometric Study of Attitudes Towards Technological Risk and Benefits," *Policy Sciences* 15: 127–52.
Slovic, P., Flynn, J., and Layman, M. (1991) "Perceived Risk, Trust, and the Politics of Nuclear Waste," *Science* 254: 1603–7.
Stern, P., Dietz, T., and Black, S. J., (1986) "Support for Environmental Protection: The Role of Moral Norms," *Population and the Environment* 8: 204–22.
Tversky, A. and Kahneman, D. (1981) "The Framing of Decisions and the Psychology of Choice," *Science* 211: 453–8.

Vaughan, E. (1993) "Individual and Cultural Differences in Adaptation to Environmental Risk," *American Psychologist* 48: 673–80.

Vaughan, E. and Seifert, M. (1992) "Variability in the Framing of Risk Issues," *Journal of Social Issues* 48: 119–35.

Vlek, C. and Keren, G. (1991) "Behavioral Decision Theory and Environmental Risk Management: What We Have Learned and What Has Been Neglected?" paper presented at conference on Probability, Utility, and Decision Making, Fribourg, Sweden.

Vlek, C. and Stallen, P. (1981) "Judging Risks and Benefits in the Small and in the Large," *Organizational Behavior and Human Performances* 28: 235–71.

Viscusi, K. (1993) "The Value of Risks to Life and Health," *Journal of Economic Literature* 31: 1912–46.

Wandersman, A. and Hallman, W. (1993) "Are People Acting Irrationally? Understanding Public Concerns about Environmental Threats," *American Psychologist* 48: 681–6.

Wilson, R. (1979) "Analyzing the Daily Risks for Life," *Technology Review* 81: 40–6.

Part III

Integrating race and gender topics into introductory macroeconomics

This part of the book is devoted to macroeconomic examples for balancing the introductory economics course. There are five examples that show how to take a traditional economic concept and examine it from race and gender perspectives. The authors provide background information, pedagogical guidance, and examples of how to integrate information on race and gender. The introductory economics course syllabus in Chapter 1 uses four of the examples provided in this section.

Rachel Nugent's "A Critique of National Accounting" is a good complement to most textbook treatments of national income accounting. She looks at the distinctions made between market and non-market activities, the definition of progress, choice of measurement technique, and the non-objectivity of the numbers. The pedagogy is one of active learning where students collect and manipulate data.

In the second part of her chapter, Nugent discusses the importance of the errors of omission with respect to GDP and how these errors are not inconsequential. The discussion is enriched with historical quotes from the National Income Accounting Debates. The third part of her chapter talks about new approaches to national income accounting. She discusses whether modifying the current way is helpful or whether there should be wholesale substitution. Here Nugent provides a wealth of activities for students to do.

William Kempey, in "General vs. Selective Credit Controls: The Asset Required Reserve Proposal, specific tools by the Federal Reserve". His example should be used after the definition of money is defined and the structure and purpose of the Federal Reserve system are examined. Next the purpose of general and selective controls need to be discussed in order to provide the context within which to discuss the Asset Required Reserve Proposal. Students can discuss how different areas of a community can be encouraged to develop and grow by using different selective reserve requirements for different types of loans.

Margaret Ray's "Race and Gender in a Basic Labor Force Model" should be introduced when talking about the overall aggregate labor market, particularly when discussing the definition of the labor force and components of the population. The material is first presented in a traditional approach, and then Ray redoes the analysis from a race and then gender perspective. The analysis is accentuated by first focusing on the size of various groups or blocs in the labor force picture. Then she suggests how the flows between and among the various blocs can be discussed. Ray also adds some suggestions for discussing race and gender labor force differences over time and over the business cycle.

Finally, Irene Powell and Jane Rosetti, in "A Disaggregated CPI: The Differential Effects of Inflation," provide data that enables students to compute the Consumer Price Index (CPI) for various demographic groups: white and non-white, low-income groups and high-income groups, young and old, low-income versus high-income. Students who work through these examples will not only have a good idea not only of how the CPI is calculated, but also of how the overall CPI may give a very limited picture of the importance of price increases.

Each of these examples provides students of Economics 190 R&G additional opportunities to make economics more meaningful by exploring "real-world" applications of the concepts to race and gender data. While the concepts could easily be applied to real world data that does not specifically focus on race and gender issues, a direct application helps meet the goals of the course.

8 Race and gender in a basic labor force model

Margaret A. Ray

The field of macroeconomics necessarily focuses on economic aggregates. The study of macroeconomic principles is, by definition, the study of the "big picture." This approach often leaves students with the impression that individuals' experiences in the aggregate economy are homogeneous. By overlooking (aggregate) differences between demographic groups, important systematic differences between cohort groups become imbedded in the "total" figures presented. Often these differences are ignored. For example, a book titled *Unemployment: Macroeconomic Performance and the Labour Market* (Layard *et al.* 1991) states "As everybody knows, unemployment rates differ widely...across age, race and (sometimes) sex groups." This book's treatment of these differences can be quoted here in its entirety. "We shall also say little about race differences, which are acute and reflect mainly differences in inflow rates into unemployment, or about sex differences, which in most but not all countries are fairly small." But issues of differences between race and gender in the labor force should not and need not be left for microeconomic issues classes. These issues can be treated within the structure of a traditional macroeconomic principles course.

It is important, if students are to get a true picture of the macro economy, to bring out differences between demographic groups. The question is then, how to do this within the curricular confines and resource limitations of an existing macroeconomic principles course. How can the issues be integrated into a course, without becoming a footnote or appendix, and still leave time to cover important foundations? The example that follows expands an existing teaching technique, in a foundation area, to both highlight race and gender differences and reinforce basic content. The traditional unemployment definitions and material are covered and enriched using the data and experiences of demographic groups in the economy.

A LABOR MARKET EXAMPLE

The model adapted here is a standard approach frequently used to illustrate the concepts and definitions of the labor force and unemployment, and the flows between the categories "not in the labor force," "in the labor force,"

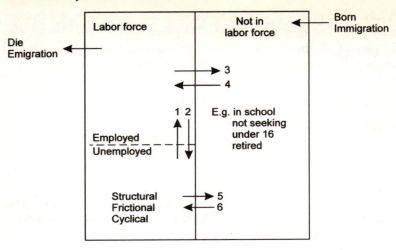

Figure 8.1 Population

"employed," and "unemployed." This model is often used to depict the (US) population as a whole. Stopping with the treatment of the aggregate economy, however, covers up the differing experiences of women and non-whites in the economy. A simple way to bring in these differences while teaching traditional material is to use the model first with the entire population and then go through it again (either in class or as an assignment) using female and non-white populations.

The model, illustrated in Figure 8.1, is a pictorial representation of the population, divided into labor force and non-labor force components. The whole box represents the population (approximately 250 million in the United States). Births and immigrants flow into the box (population) and deaths and emigration flow out of the box (population). The population is then divided, roughly in half, to show the two parts; "in the labor force" and "not in the labor force." The labor force half of the box is divided into two parts; "employed" and "unemployed."

The instructor can use this model to talk about the definitions of each box, who falls into each category, and how individuals flow from one category to the other. For example, those under sixteen, retired, disabled, institutionalized, in school and who do not actively seek employment are "not in the labor force." Individuals with jobs and those seeking jobs are considered "in the labor force." Individuals can move into the labor force by graduating and getting/seeking a job, returning to work, etc. Individuals can move out of the labor force if they stop actively seeking, go back to school full-time, retire, etc.

The unemployed box can be further divided into the "types" of unemployment (structural, cyclical, etc.). Individuals can move from the unemployed box by getting a job or when they stop seeking employment. Those with jobs are employed. They may become unemployed by losing their job or may move out of the labor force by going back to school, retiring, etc. This "picture" of the economy is a commonly used model that helps students visualize and understand the divisions and flows in the labor market.

INTEGRATING RACE AND GENDER INTO THE MODEL

It is fairly easy to see how this model can be used, reinforced, and expanded to include the experiences of women and non-whites. Discussion and/or assignments can focus on differences in the size of the boxes, the flows between boxes, changes in the boxes over time, changes in the box sizes over business cycles, and other differences unique to the region, school, etc. (e.g. differences for Asian or Hispanic subgroup populations). Actual figures can be used for illustration or as part of student homework assignments.

Differences in the size of boxes

Each sub-population has unique and important differences in the distribution of the population between the categories. Table 8.1 shows population, birth rate, and death rate differences. These differences, and factors that might contribute to these differences, are a good area for discussion questions. Labor force participation and unemployment rate differences are systematically different for sub-populations (see Table 8.2). Women experience lower labor force participation rates, while non-whites experience

Table 8.1 Population, birth and death rates by race, 1991

Race	Population (1,000)	Birth rate	Death rate
Black (non-Hispanic)	29,667	24.0	8.5
White (non-Hispanic)	189,116	13.7	9.3
Hispanic	22,950	24.6	4.7

Source: Statistical Abstracts of the United States, 1993, p. 20.

Table 8.2 Unemployment and labor force participation rates by race and gender, 1992

Race/gender	Unemployment rate	LFPR
Total	7.4	66.3
Male	7.8	75.6
Female	6.9	57.8
White	6.5	66.7
Black	14.1	63.3
Hispanic	11.4	66.5

Source: Statistical Abstracts of the United States, 1993, p. 395. (Data in this table also include these figures back to 1960.)

significantly higher unemployment rates. Reasons for these differences are also good points for discussion. *Gender and Race Inequality at Work* (Tomaskovic-Devey 1993) is an excellent source here. Finally, there are differences when unemployment is broken down into sub-categories. The distribution of the types of unemployment experienced (i.e. why people are unemployed) will differ for the demographic groups.

Differences in flows between boxes

There are also important differences in the reason for and size of the flows between the categories for the different groups. For example, women leave and enter the work force for various reasons and at various stages (see, for example, Tomaskovic-Devey 1993). Also, differences in educational attainment affect the size of the flows of the subgroups (see Table 8.3). Further, the groups experience different rates of discouragement that can influence the statistics (for a discussion see Stevans *et al.* 1985). Finally, the groups have different experiences in the work force that affect their abilities to increase schooling and other human capital, retire or maintain employment (last hired—first fired, poverty rates, discrimination, etc.). Sources that discuss these issues include *Economics of Poverty and Discrimination* (Schiller 1989) and *Economics of Women, Men, and Work* (Blau and Ferber 1986).

Table 8.3 Labor force statistics and educational attainment by race and gender, 1991

	Less than High school	High school graduate	Less than college grad	College graduate
Total				
LFPR	40.7	66.2	75.1	81.2
U rate	11.4	6.8	5.6	3.2
Male				
LFPR	53.8	78.0	83.6	86.8
U rate	11.4	7.3	5.9	3.3
Female				
LFPR	29.4	56.7	67.7	74.7
U rate	11.4	6.2	5.3	3.0
White				
LFPR	40.8	65.4	74.5	80.9
U rate	10.7	6.0	5.0	3.0
Black				
LFPR	39.7	72.3	80.5	85.6
U rate	15.1	12.3	9.8	4.4
Hispanic				
LFPR	55.9	75.2	62.1	83.0
U rate	12.8	9.0	7.7	5.0

Source: Statistical Abstracts of the United States, 1993, p. 398.

Changes over time

In addition to cross-sectional differences, there are differences in female and non-white experiences over time. Tomaskovic-Devey (1993) is an excellent source looking at the experience of women and minorities in the workplace throughout history in the United States. Social, cultural and political reasons for participation differences are discussed, as is discrimination. This is an excellent way to integrate history and outside readings into a class or assignment.

Changes over the business cycle

Students in a macroeconomics course are also introduced to the business cycle. The importance of graphical techniques makes this a good area to combine these topics. Looking at or drawing graphs illustrating the differences that groups experience over the business cycle (see Figures 8.2 and 8.3) will help students strengthen graphing skills, empirically investigate the business cycle, as well as address race and gender issues.

Other Differences

Clearly, there are other differences and other demographic groups that can be considered using this model. For example, the population and labor force growth rates of Hispanic and Asian groups (see *Statistical Abstracts*

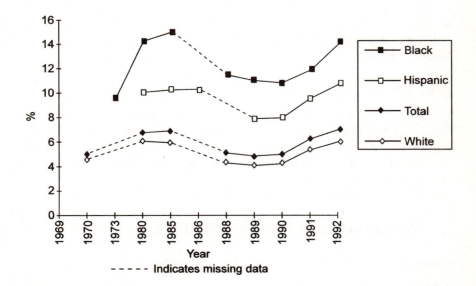

Figure 8.2 Unemployment rate

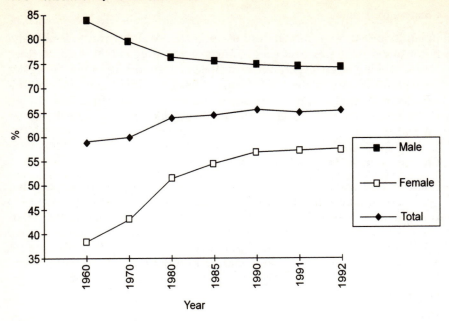

Figure 8.3   Labor force participation rate.
Source: Statistical Abstract of the United States (1993), p. 395

of the United States, 1993, p. 20). It is not possible thoroughly to investigate all the possible important groups and differences. It is, however, possible to adapt this approach to the specific needs, interests and populations of a class or institution.

CONCLUDING REMARKS

Taking the time, in class or using enrichment assignments, to follow up the basic model in this way has dual benefits. First, the traditional material is reinforced. And more importantly, the aggregate approach is not used to mask the different experiences of economic minorities. Students will consider race and gender issues more closely when they are viewed in the context of the main body of material than when it is presented as an afterthought.

STUDENT EXERCISES

Problems

1 Use the data provided in Table 8.4 to calculate population of each of the following demographic groups as a percentage of the total population: whites, blacks, Hispanics, women, men.

2 Use the data provided in Table 8.4 to calculate the labor force of each of the following demographic groups as a percentage of the total labor force: whites, blacks, women, men.

3 Use the data provided in Table 8.4 to calculate the labor force participation rate for each of the following groups: blacks, whites, Hispanics, women, men.

4 Use the data provided in Tables 8.4 and 8.5 to calculate the unemployment rate for the entire population, men, women, whites, and non-whites.

5 Use the data provided in Table 8.6 to graph the labor force participation over time for women, men, and the entire population.

6 Use the data provided in Table 8.6 to graph the unemployment rate over time for whites, blacks, and the entire population. (Why do you think the data for blacks begins in 1973 rather than 1960?)

7 Label the phases of the business cycle on your graph.

Table 8.4   Population by race and gender, 1991

Race/gender	Population (1,000)	Labor force
Total	252,177	101,171
Male	122,979	55,554
Female	129,198	45,617
Black	29,667	10,863
White	189,116	86,776
Hispanic	22,950	

Source: Statistical Abstracts of the United States, 1993, pp. 20–1 and 394.

Table 8.5   Labor force statistics by race and gender, 1992

Race/gender	Unemployed (1,000)
Total	9,384
Female	4,005
Male	5,380
White	7,047
Black	1,958

Source: Statistical Abstracts of the United States, 1993, p. 395.

Discussion Questions

1 What factors might explain the lower labor force participation rate of women?

2 What has been happening to the labor force participation rate of women over time? What factors might explain this change? Do you expect this trend to continue? If so, until when? If not, why not?

3 What factors might help to explain the difference in unemployment rates by race?

4 Comment on sensitivity differences of the race categories to fluctuations in the business cycle.
5 What is "discouragement"? How might you expect rates of discouragement for demographic groups to differ from overall rates of discouragement? Why? Use the data presented in Table 8.7.

Table 8.6   Labor force participation and unemployment by race and gender, 1960–92

Year	LFPR	U rate
Total		
1960	59.4	5.5
1970	60.4	4.9
1980	63.8	7.1
1985	64.8	7.2
1990	66.4	5.5
1991	66.0	6.7
1992	66.3	7.4
Male		
1960	83.3	5.4
1970	79.9	4.4
1980	77.4	6.9
1985	76.3	7.0
1990	76.1	5.6
1991	75.5	7.0
1992	75.6	7.8
Female		
1960	37.7	5.9
1970	43.3	5.9
1980	51.5	7.4
1985	54.5	7.4
1990	57.5	5.4
1991	57.3	6.3
1992	57.8	6.9
White		
1960	58.8	5.0
1970	60.2	4.5
1980	64.1	6.3
1985	65.0	6.2
1990	66.8	4.7
1991	66.6	6.0
1992	66.7	6.5
Black		
1973	60.2	9.4
1980	61.0	14.3
1985	62.9	15.1
1990	63.3	11.3
1991	62.6	12.4
1992	63.3	14.1

Source: Statistical Abstracts of the United States, 1993, p. 395.

Table 8.7 Labor force and educational attainment by race and gender, 1970–1991

Year	Less than high School	High school graduate	1-3 years college	College graduate
Total				
1970	36.1	38.1	11.8	14.1
1980	20.6	39.8	17.6	22.0
1985	15.9	40.2	19.0	24.9
1990	13.3	39.4	20.8	26.5
1991	12.8	39.2	21.3	26.7
Male				
1970	37.5	34.5	12.2	15.7
1980	22.2	35.7	17.7	24.3
1985	17.7	36.9	18.3	27.1
1990	14.9	37.3	19.8	28.0
1991	14.5	37.1	20.3	28.2
Female				
1970	33.5	44.3	10.9	11.2
1980	18.4	45.4	17.4	18.7
1985	13.7	44.4	19.9	22.0
1990	11.2	42.1	22.1	24.6
1991	10.7	41.8	22.5	25.0
White				
1970	33.7	39.3	12.2	14.8
1980	19.1	40.2	17.7	22.9
1985	14.7	40.7	19.1	25.6
1990	12.5	39.4	20.8	27.3
1991	12.1	39.1	21.3	27.5
Black				
1970	55.5	28.2	8.0	8.3
1980	34.7	38.1	16.3	11.0
1985	26.2	39.5	19.2	15.0
1990	19.4	43.0	21.8	15.8
1991	18.4	43.0	22.5	16.0

Source: Statistical Abstracts of the United States, 1993, p. 394.

6 Represent this data on a graph to illustrate how educational attainment of the labor force differs for the demographic groups. (Show what percentage of the labor force is in each educational category.)

7 What factors might explain these differences in educational attainment?

8 What do you think happens to unemployment rates for groups as educational attainment increases?

9 Relate the data on educational attainment to the data on unemployment rates (Table 8.6).

10 How do you think educational attainment might be related to labor force participation and discouragement rates?

11 What has been happening to educational attainment in the groups over time?
12 What other demographic groups are you familiar with that may have labor force market experiences different from the total (e.g. other race groups or age groups)?
13 Collect and present data for some other group that illustrate the different labor market experience of some demographic group.
14 Find data that tells you what happened to LFPRs for the entire population and for women during World War II. What factors help explain the changes in LFPRs (especially for women) during this time?

BIBLIOGRAPHY

Blau, F. and Ferber, M. (1986) *Economics of Women, Men, and Work*, Englewood Cliffs, NJ: Prentice Hall.
Goldin, C. (1990) *Understanding the Gender Gap*, New York: Oxford University Press.
Layard, R., Nickell, S., and Jackman, R. (1991) *Unemployment: Macroeconomic Performance and the Labour Market*, Oxford: Oxford University Press.
Schiller, B. R. (1989) *Economics of Poverty and Discrimination*, Englewood Cliffs, NJ: Prentice Hall.
Stevans, L., Register, C., and Grimes, P. (1985) "Race and the Discouraged Female Worker: A Question of Labor Force Attachment." *Review of Black Political Economy* 14, 1 (summer): 49–59.
Tomaskovic-Devey, D. (1993) *Gender and Racial Inequality at Work*, Ithaca, NY: ILR Press.

9 General vs. selective credit controls: the Asset Required Reserve Proposal

William M. Kempey

The proposal developed below is for inclusion in a typical introductory Economics I (Macro) course. It is assumed that the instructor has already discussed the several definitions of money and spent a little time developing the purpose and organization of the Federal Reserve System. With that much background, most introductory texts then turn to a discussion of the tools or methods which the Fed possesses and uses to change the money supply (McConnell and Brue 1993: 283–90; Samuelson and Nordhaus 1993: 257–65; Waud 1989: 301–44).

The first step of such a discussion is the development of the conflicting arguments surrounding the use of selective vs. general credit controls. The Fed has consistently argued in favor of using mechanisms like the discount rate, required reserve changes, and especially open market operations (general credit controls) instead of such devices as setting down-payment requirements and interest rate maximums on mortgage loans (selective credit controls used during World War II and the Korean War). The preference for general credit controls flows from the Fed's conservative and long-held view that it should, in creating monetary policy, interfere as little as possible with the market system. Using selective credit controls would force the Fed to use monetary policy in a discriminatory way by forcing the Fed to allocate credit within the system. In the case of required reserves, the Fed argues that it is preferable for the monetary authority to set the total amount of reserves (changing the percentages up or down as needed) and let the market system then allocate the amount of funds to different uses and users. Table 9.1 shows the typical textbook balance sheet for a commercial bank assuming a 10 percent required reserve.

Most introductory courses then go on to show (using a typical "T" account as in Table 9.1) how a change in required reserves produces a multiple change in the supply of money as primary deposits are created and moved from bank 1 through bank 2, etc. A simple money supply multiplier can then be constructed (McConnell and Brue 1993: 283–90; Samuels and Nordhaus 1993: 257–65; Waud 1989: 301–447).

Table 9.1   Bank 1's balance sheet

Bank 1			
Assets		*Liabilities*	
Required reserves	$1,000	Demand deposits	$10,000
Loan and investments		Other liabilities and net worth	
(a) local real estate	$0		
(b) non-local loans	$9,000		
Other loans	$0		
	$10,000		$10,000

THE ASSET REQUIRED RESERVE PROPOSAL

The approach and philosophy outlined as the Fed's position differs significantly from that envisioned by the Asset Required Reserve Proposal.[1] In the first place, supporters of such an approach argue that the Fed's view, that general credit controls are preferable because they do not discriminate, is in reality not completely accurate. What, in fact, happens (as other chapters of this book point out) is that significant discrimination in the market economy already exists and what the Fed is doing by choosing general credit controls is simply agreeing with and supporting the existing uses and users of credit. Thus, the non-discrimination argument is a codification of existing practices and is, in fact, discriminatory. For example, it has been noted that some urban banks, despite the Community Reinvestment Act, export funds from the communities in which they are deposited for use in other, more affluent suburban areas (Cushman 1993: D2). The net result of such lending is to direct funds away from monetary borrowers. Existing state and federal laws appear to be unable to produce the desired change in bank lending behavior. A different approach (one using a carrot and not the stick of legal sanction) would be for the Fed to change its position on the use of selective credit controls to manage the required reserve mechanism.

Specifically, the Asset Required Reserve Proposal would work in the following way. At present, required reserves are assets held against the liability (deposits) side of the "T" account of a bank's balance sheet. The Asset Required Reserve Proposal would shift required reserves to the asset side of the balance sheet, i.e. it would tie the amount of required reserves to the amount of assets a bank holds. Required reserves, for example, could be held against different loans and investments of the bank (see Table 9.2).

By shifting the amount of required reserves a bank must hold from different types of liabilities to different types of assets, the Fed would be able to impact various credit flows while also changing the nation's supply of money. In the example in Table 9.2 bank 1 would be encouraged to lend within its community to improve housing (or for some other project) by the Fed creating a negative required reserve on such loans (i.e. for every dollar lent for those purposes deemed desirable, the Fed would pay the bank ten cents while a +10 percent required reserve would be charged on similar loans outside of the designated local area).[2] The use of differential required reserves on the loan and investment portfolios of banks could be used to redirect credit from areas deemed undesirable to areas which society believes to be more deserving or productive. Thus, if one accepts the view that the market system does not produce the desired results sought, then a serious review of selective credit controls in general, and the Asset Required Reserve Proposal in particular, would seem to be in order.

Table 9.2   Bank 1's balance sheet

		Bank 1	
Assets		*Liabilities*	
Loans and investments	$10,000	Demand deposits	$10,000
Required reserves −10%			
(a) local real estate lending			
Required reserves + 5%			
(b) non-local lending		Other liabilities and net worth	
Other loans			
	$10,000		$10,000

CONCLUSIONS AND PROBLEMS

The presentation of the Asset Required Reserve Proposal can be completed in one ($1\frac{1}{4}$ hour) lecture. One should attempt to avoid technical discussions (e.g. the accounting theory behind the "T" account) and focus more on the overall differences in philosophies envisioned by supporters of general vs. selective controls and to focus on how an amended required reserve mechanism might be used in other areas. Issues of race and gender are likely to arise when discussing the allocation of credit. It is important in talking about these issues within the context of the Required Reserve Proposal to create a "safe" environment, one open to free discussion, with arguments judged on their merit. A technique to help develop such an environment would be to create a debate on the topic of Asset Required Reserves, with students being assigned to pro or con positions. Other methods discussed in other chapters may also be applied. Finally, the issue of who sets the priorities and thus differentiated reserves should lead to a discussion of the independence of the Federal Reserve System. Such a discussion, while important by itself and more so in connection with the Asset Required Reserve Proposal, may be time-consuming and may not be amenable to full debate in the time constraints of Economics I.

NOTES

1 Commission on Money and Credit (1961). This report contains an analysis of the Asset Required Proposal.
2 Differential rates, in reality, would probably not have to be large and required reserves may not have to be negative, but "just enough" below those on other loans.

BIBLIOGRAPHY

Commission on Money and Credit (1961) *Money and Credit: Their Influence on Jobs, Prices, and Growth*, Englewood Cliffs, NJ: Prentice Hall.
Cushman, J. H. (1993) "Plan to set Banks' Role in Community Lending," *New York Times*, June 23: D2.
McConnell, C. R. and Brue, S. L. (1993) *Economics*, twelfth edition, New York: McGraw-Hill.
Samuelson, P. and Nordhaus, W. D. (1993) *Economics*, thirteenth edition, New York: McGraw-Hill.
Waud, R. N. (1989) *Economics*, fourth edition, New York: Harper and Row.

ACKNOWLEDGEMENTS

The author wishes to thank Robin Bartlett for her comments and Susan Feiner and those colleagues who attended the Workshop on Integrating the Latest Scholarship on Race and Gender into the Economics Curriculum held at the College of William and Mary for their knowledge and support.

10 A critique of national accounting

Rachel A. Nugent

One of the least-liked sections of a principles course is when the instructor turns to discussion of national income accounting. Students unsuspectingly approach this chapter when, after being introduced to "the economic question" and the tools of supply and demand, they are developing some confidence in their ability to handle economics and its relevance to their lives. The instructor generally starts by saying, "This is boring, but necessary," and plunges into the morass of definitions, acronyms, and exceptions that constitute a system of national income accounts. Students quickly decide economics isn't relevant after all.

The purpose of this chapter is to present a brief critique of the textbook approach to GDP accounting from the point of view of missing social, cultural, and environmental measures, to suggest approaches to remedy these omissions, and provide examples of classroom techniques for enhanced critical thinking about national income accounting.

The usual goal of introducing principles students to national income accounts is to provide a common framework and vocabulary for assessing economic conditions and progress. With a more inclusive approach, this section of the course can also help students consider:

1 Relationships between market and non-market activities.
2 The philosophical basis for defining progress.
3 Difficulties arising from choice of measurement techniques.
4 The non-objectivity of numbers.
5 The difference between a narrow economic approach and one that blends multiple perspectives.

The pedagogical goals of looking at national income accounts in this way are to engage students in some data collection and analysis, to encourage collaboration, and to help them fit economic measurement into a broader social and scientific framework. It is a particularly useful approach for principles classes that are oriented toward development or environmental issues, and for "non-traditional economics" students from the humanities or interdisciplinary programs.

The teaching and learning techniques that can be employed in this section are varied. National income accounting is not particularly well suited to a standard lecture format because the high level of aggregation prevents students from perceiving the relevance to their own lives, and the abstract detail easily leads to snoozing. Thus, an active learning technique is more appropriate. The recommended approach is to combine a teacher-led discussion of issues with small group development of solutions. Students can then share their results from groups with the larger class to engender a discussion of whether a measure can be found that adequately meets the informational needs and value sets of all the groups. The data-oriented nature of the subject suggests exercises in which students collect and manipulate some data on their own, and since income accounting is used as a yardstick, many comparative exercises can be developed.

The national income accounting section of the course generally comes early in the semester, as the definitions are used throughout the course. Presenting the idea of inclusive income accounting early in the course also offers the opportunity to discuss very broad issues such as the uses of economics, the blurring between normative and positive analysis, and the inherent biases of counting all people as identical. The material could also be presented in conjunction with the standard textbook chapter on national income accounts, or as part of a discussion of market failure or non-market issues at a later stage in the course.

This chapter proceeds with a discussion of the problems of standard GDP accounting and suggestions for classroom use of this material. A good way to motivate the whole topic is by having students debate the purpose of income accounting, and establish some of their own ideas of what such a measure should accomplish. This section should include some account of the history and purpose of income accounting among economists. These are discussed in the second main section. The third proposes a classroom treatment of a new income accounting approach by describing ways in which students may develop more inclusive measures. This material can be considered using the current income accounts as a basis and developing modifications to it, or it can be considered through a search for a substitute measure of welfare. Both possibilities will be treated briefly in the chapter. Finally, potential problems are mentioned in the fourth section.

Instructors know that national income accounting is central to every other lesson the students face in economics and so feel compelled to include it in their classes, despite negative associations they may hold from their early introduction to the subject. In the effort to end the ordeal as soon as possible, they often fail to consider the implications of relaxing the assumptions of the standard method, or broadening the definition of "income." An important first step in teaching a new approach to income accounting is for the instructor to shed these attitudes and begin at the beginning. If you consider the reason for having an economic measuring system and the uses to which it will be put, the subject becomes very interesting. One goal of this chapter is to present ideas for making income accounting more exciting both to students and the instructor.

PROBLEMS WITH GDP ACCOUNTING

The standard textbook treatment of national income accounting develops the dual approach of adding up expenditures by category and summing income by source with appropriate adjustments so the results are equivalent to output. Output (GDP or GNP) is then used as a measure of national welfare and the figures are used to compare changes in national welfare across time and to compare across countries. The textbooks will mention the weaknesses of using these monetary measures as indicators of welfare, and list several of the important omissions or distortions that arise. The student is left believing that these problems are relatively minor and irresolvable.

To the contrary, the problems with the standard approach to national income accounts are neither minor nor necessary. GDP is not a "good" measure of national welfare. At best it is misleading, at worst it can lead to absolutely false conclusions. These distortions have serious gender, class and ethnic implications.

For instance, Waring (1988: 2) describes how

as a politician, I found it virtually impossible to prove—given the production framework with which we were faced—that child care facilities were needed. "Nonproducers" (housewives, mothers) who are "inactive" and "unoccupied" cannot, apparently, be in need. They are not even in the economic cycle in the first place.

Economic growth is defined by economists as an increase in GDP, with no regard for the composition of that output, the non-market effects of producing it, the possibility of depleting natural resources, and the quality of lives achieved for the people in the economy. Growth in GDP is generally seen, if not by economists, then by the press and politicians, as a measure of improvements in societal welfare. As such, it has been established as an official and unofficial goal. However, it excludes the value and values of those individuals and objects unrepresented by the monetary counting-up system. Even the *New York Times* indicates problems with conventional GDP measures, calling GDP comparisons "a faulty way of calculating the economic scorecard" (Nasar 1992).

Anderson (1991) presents several categories of problems with conventional national income accounts. They include mismeasurement of income, welfare, and stocks and omitted or inefficient measures of welfare. As most of these issues are familiar to instructors, I will briefly list those omissions or distortions relating to gender, class, race, and the environment. Refer to Anderson (1991) or most texts for elaboration and examples.

1 Income and output are distorted when unpaid labor and non-money transactions are ignored. This often involves gender-based differences in work conditions and roles, especially in developing countries, and devalues volunteerism and other unpaid labor. It leads to incorrect comparisons across time and across countries.

   One recent example is the redefinition of US unemployment rates to take account of respondents (mostly women) who say their primary occupation is work in the household because of the time they put into housework, but who nevertheless also work outside the home. They have not heretofore been considered among the unemployed when they lost their paid work. A revision to include these workers "in the labor force" raised the official unemployment rate in early 1994 by 0.3 percent.

2 Average per capita output is used as a measure of welfare for comparisons. This ignores distributional issues, differing needs of people, and sometimes even exchange rate fluctuations that should affect cross-country comparisons. These distinctions are important for understanding class, gender and cultural differences.

   For instance, cross-country comparisons of GDP are often made by converting GDP using official exchange rates. A more careful comparison will use a measure of purchasing power parity to account for glaring differences in cost of living across countries. But nowhere do the comparisons account for differences in social and cultural choices and behaviors that affect measured GDP. For instance, foreign aid programs usually define women as "non-producers." According to Waring (1988: 12), women are then either denied aid on the grounds they are "less productive" or they are not recognized as a development problem because it is assumed that males bear the economic burden of caring for women and children.

3 Stocks and depreciation are either ignored or poorly measured. These issues affect gender, class, and the environment when human capital is devalued, wealth changes are ignored until realized, and environmental stocks are ignored until harvested.

   A gender-based example is that education of women is not seen as valuable if the returns from it cannot be measured in the paid labor market. Another important example is the situation that national income accounts ignore the value of environmental stocks (forest habitat or food sources of indigenous peoples) until they are harvested and marketed.

4 Non-income sources of welfare such as leisure and quality of work are ignored. This clearly exposes social and cultural value systems that need examination. A specific example is the implication that the aesthetic enjoyment of the environment has no worth in economic measurement.

5 Distortions of welfare are implied by the bias toward more expensive provision of goods and services, new rather than used or old, and use of society's resources dictated by the wealthier regardless of differences in marginal utility of income. These issues contain class-based and cultural

biases and environmental implications. Waring (1988: 42) quotes a Norwegian member of parliament,

> Women researchers are concerned about the fact that growth in many sectors of the economy takes place by adding more work to the existing unpaid work performed by women. For instance, all over the Western world, supermarkets replace small retailers. This requires housewives to increase the time needed for shopping.

A good start for classroom discussion is to ask students the meaning of GDP (they may respond more quickly to GNP, as that term is still in common use). This can be simply a brief classroom discussion to stimulate their thinking about national income accounting, or they could be requested to bring in a newspaper or magazine article that uses the term and discuss its use and interpretation. The discussion will raise a number of different uses and suggested meanings of the term, but will likely converge towards "the money value of total production or purchases in the economy in a given year," or something appropriate.

In order to prompt thinking about the fallacies and weaknesses of the above definition, several types of questions can be posed for classroom discussion, small-group consideration, or even short writing assignments. These include:

1 What activities have you (your family members, friends) done that are not included in GDP?
2 What makes GDP grow faster, slower? (This may be a good time to clarify the difference between nominal and real if that issue hasn't arisen yet.) Are these "good" events? You should get or encourage answers about types of production, prices of goods and services, converting non-marketed into marketable goods, perhaps population growth or women entering the labor force. Students may wish to consider the difference between producing guns or weapons and education. Waring (1988: 72) provides the example that $600 million in transfer payments for AFDC will not show up in the GDP statistics (and is therefore easy to eliminate), while $600 million will pay for the surge in GDP from producing 688 nuclear submarines.
3 Which people or activities have the most weight in measured GDP? (Encourage examples such as Michael Jordan or David Letterman, Donald Trump, expensive cars, etc.)[1]
4 How does GDP in the US compare with that of other countries? If the students have spent time abroad, they can look up these numbers (there will be some comparisons in the text) and discuss whether they noticed the difference in GDP where they have been. Why is GDP so different across countries, especially the developing compared to developed countries? This should lead to discussion about non-market activities, perhaps even gender-based roles in different countries and female labor force

participation. The cultural and social differences implied by various means of agriculture, food processing, handicrafts, and other cooperative activities in some countries could be explored with photos, stories (even literature), and other examples.

After these questions have been considered and digested, it's a good time to ask students what the GDP should measure. They can begin considering the purpose of an income accounting system, and an historical lesson about the development of GDP as a measure can be introduced here. Little attention was paid to keeping national accounts until the 1930s' depression brought high and enduring unemployment to the United States. Keynesian solutions were based on principles of tracking and manipulating government and private aggregate spending, and eventually the NBER took on some of this work, and its staff grew accordingly.

Much debate ensued during the next twenty years over the purpose and uses of a national income accounting system. Simon Kuznets was a primary developer of early methods, but later critiqued the adopted UN System of National Accounts for being too narrow. He wrote (1954: 177–8):,

> The refusal to extend discussion ... to a fuller coverage of consumption levels, of levels of living, and of experimentally established functional equivalents—is not due to the possibly low yield of such explorations. On the contrary, they promise results of great value. They might explain more satisfactorily ... the basic differences between industrial and pre-industrial economies, and the conditions on which the latter might be industrialized ... they might provide a more effective basis for comparison and help overcome the difficulties imposed by differences in the goods composition of national product.

The eventual system owes much to the usefulness of aggregate economic statistics in tracking the expenses and expenditures of World War II in Britain and the United States. Keynes co-authored a paper entitled "How to Pay for the War" (Keynes and Stone 1939) which provided the analytical framework for present-day national accounts. Thus, what we have today derives in large part from Keynesian economics and Hitlerian politics.

Tracing the other use of GDP and GNP measures back to the eighteenth and nineteenth centuries, one finds much debate over the meaning of "value." Economists find the simple use of price as a measure of value to be relatively compelling as a measure of utility. However, the simultaneous attributes often given those measures by politicians as measures of overall progress and success in an economy have little validity. At this point, in small groups or as a class, students can be asked to consider what they would like an income accounting system to include, and perhaps wrestle briefly with some of the measurement difficulties. Discussion of the alternative meanings of "value" in an historical and philosophical context may be interesting and useful.

This discussion may revolve around the meaning of the term "welfare." To economists, it is the sum of consumer and producer surplus. When these areas increase, other things held equal, welfare has improved. While students have probably not at this stage been introduced to this definition of welfare, they will understand some of the examples that show its internal inconsistencies. For instance, GDP increases when subsistence farmers join the labor force, when domestic help is substituted for in-home labor, when war or natural disaster destroys infrastructure and it is rebuilt, and when money is spent to correct environmental degradation. It is now time to address the development of a modified or new system of national accounts with the aim of better representing welfare.

NEW APPROACHES TO NATIONAL INCOME ACCOUNTING

There are two main approaches that can be used in considering appropriate changes in GDP accounting: modifications to the current method, or wholesale substitution of alternative measures. While the latter is more difficult to explore in a standard principles course because the text discussion is confined to standard measures, a more complete exploration of non-economic issues can be conducted when considering substitute measures. This section presents classroom techniques for exploring the two approaches.

Adjustments and additions to GDP

Textbooks will typically include a section at the end of the chapter on national income accounting that recites the weaknesses of standard GDP. This is a place for instructors to begin as their classes consider adjustments and additions to GDP. The section generally mentions unpaid household labor, other non-market transactions such as the underground economy, volunteer or self-help work, leisure and other amenities and environmental externalities.

A classroom exercise (again, probably in small groups) can be organized in which the students attempt to fill in the gaps by calculating the value of some of these items. They will soon find that valuation is difficult, and discussion can ensue of the implications of excluding household or other "women's" work from consideration. This can be particularly enlightening when applied to developing countries, as there is good documentation of the role of women's labor in indigenous and other societies. A study from the International Labor Organization estimated domestic activities in developing countries account for 40–5 percent of total labor time of all household members, with similar results indicated for the United Kingdom (Dixon-Mueller and Anker 1988: 65; Carr-Hill and Lintott 1986: 152).

Students are often amazed to consider the value of non-market transactions, whether the instructor provides data or they attempt to calculate it themselves. These topics provide a good opportunity not only for consideration of measurement problems, but the moral implications of devaluing or ignoring such efforts. Of course, not only gender, but race and class issues arise.

This section also provides the opportunity to consider the environmental issues that are ignored in GDP accounts: both externalities and valuation of environmental stocks can be considered, although externalities are often handled by textbooks in a chapter devoted to market failure. The instructor can point out several dramatic examples if students are having trouble, such as the increase in current GDP from harvesting Indonesian rainforest timber while depleting ecosystem resources, and the health, congestion and other costs of auto travel. (See Repetto 1988.)[2]

A few other potential adjustments to GDP are fun for students to consider. Should GDP increase after a natural disaster or should there be some alternative accounting? Can accumulation of human capital such as their education be considered explicitly in national accounts? What should be done to show species extinction? Some of these issues have clear gender, ethnic and cultural implications, while others are simply ways for students to consider what information GDP is intended to convey.

In general, it is relatively easy to stick close to the standard textbook treatment of income accounting by simply allowing the class to elaborate on and try to correct the list of omissions and distortions the book provides. This exercise can be accomplished as quickly as class time allows, either by adding some discussion time, or by sending students to collect information to adjust the official numbers. These adjustments can be simple adjustments to the students' own household income calculations, or can be based on national figures and aggregate estimates of necessary changes.

As an example, Anderson's (1991: 39) adjusted national product would be calculated as:

Gross national product – Capital depreciation + Money value of unpaid domestic labor + Money value of non-money transactions outside the household – Environmental depreciation

This approach has the advantage of being quick, low-cost and in close conformance with the text, but also allows students to develop insights into the changes in standard measures that would take place under different systems of accounting, and the values that underlie the current system. The disadvantages are that it would still not be a good measure of welfare as it would ignore issues of distribution, inefficiencies, and non-monetary issues such as discrimination in labor markets, quality of life issues, and social/cultural differences.

Alternative welfare measures

A more radical departure from standard treatments of national income accounting is to explore alternative measures of national welfare, either through inspection of existing alternatives, or in-class development of alternatives. The advantages of this approach are that it allows for consideration of a broader range of indicators, avoids reliance on monetary measures that may be distorted, and can use readily available data for a wide variety of social, economic, and environmental indicators.

There are several ways of approaching this material. A good start may be to motivate the discussion by looking at some of the alternative measures that have been developed. The well-known and readily available GDP substitutes are the United Nations' Human Development Index, the Index of Sustainable Economic Welfare created by Herman Daly and John Cobb, natural resource accounts developed by World Resources Institute, and Nordhaus's efforts. Other indicators have been compiled to emphasize specific types of issues, such as "The Index of Social Health," distributed by Fordham University that monitors Census Bureau statistics on social and family issues.

These alternatives will show a wide variance in the conditions of countries compared to a simple GDP measure. In general, they will emphasize one or another aspect of society, but are intended as a broader measure of overall conditions than GDP. A review of these indexes can prompt a class discussion of the meaning of progress, whether economic growth is a "good" or adequate goal, and what the difference is between growth and development. This is particularly useful in a class in which you may wish to explore development or environmental issues, as it raises the central issue of what rate of economic growth is desirable for developing countries, and the inherent inequities of differential rates of growth between the developed and developing world. Of course, this leads into discussion of culture, race, and class differences.

Even if the focus is not on development, a class discussion of the conflicting outcomes of economic growth as conventionally measured is fruitful. The published indexes generally provide information for a variety of countries and it is instructive for students to examine what factors are responsible for changing the rankings of countries from the conventional economic measure. For instance, Scandinavian countries typically top the United States and other western European nations because of more equal distributions of income, better health measures and higher literacy rates. Even some developing countries with relatively low per capita incomes exceed the US position with respect to health and equality measures.[3]

At this point students have probably developed their own preferences for what to include in a measure of welfare, and you may ask them to begin assembling actual data for the United States, or if they are in small groups, for a variety of countries. The instructor can provide assistance by listing reference materials available in the library, bringing in the reference librarian, or providing the data directly if time is short. The data collection aspect of this exercise proves to be very valuable practice for students, as well as imparting to them a clear understanding of the difficulties of empirical work.

The fruits of this data collection work can be used in a variety of ways, from simple classroom discussion and comparison to the creation of multimedia presentations by small groups of their alternative measures. If they have studied a variety of countries, the cultural exploration can extend as far as videos that you may show in class, poster presentations, an international potluck day, and many other diversions.

The next step is to have the class develop its own alternative measure of national welfare, as a whole or in small groups. Typically this will mean choosing a variety of indicators, and either combining them statistically to arrive at a composite, or listing them to provide the broad detail. The students' analysis should include some system for comparing a common set of indicators they have chosen and drawing conclusions about country rankings. They should also compare their results in some time series analysis with the GDP change over the same period, considering whether the welfare changes are in the same direction.

It is useful to provide some framework for this effort. Anderson (1991) lists the characteristics of good indicators:

1 Easily and cheaply available.
2 Easy to understand.
3 Measurable.
4 Representative of something important.
5 Available with little delay.
6 Comparable at different levels.

A brief list is provided here of the readily available indicators in the five categories that Anderson (1991) recommends. They are not all equally available on a comparable basis across countries, but students can be asked to consider the reliability and credibility of some data sources as part of their exercise.

Social

Educational attainment or literacy rates, especially disaggregated by race and gender.

Work and unemployment

Unemployment rates disaggregated by race and gender are the easiest measure, but a measure of time spent at all types of work by gender would be more revealing. This, of course, is almost impossible to get, even for developed countries.

Consumption

Simple measures of satisfaction of basic needs are not difficult to get. These would include calories as a percentage of minimum requirements, percent of people with access to clean drinking water, and sanitation. Others included as proxies of level of development include telephones per capita, square feet of living space per capita, etc.

Distribution of income/wealth

The standard measure is percent of income earned by the top 20 percent of the population divided by the percent of income earned by the bottom 20 percent of the population. When possible this can be supplemented with some measure of wealth distribution.

Health

The most revealing single measure is the infant mortality rate. This can be supplemented by the under-five mortality rate and the life expectancy at birth. Any of these disaggregated by race or income group would be particularly revealing.

Environmental

There are many choices here, and the biggest problem presented with this category is the difficulty in comparing countries because of vastly different resource bases. However, students can select those most pertinent to individual countries. They could select the deforestation rate, rate of species extinction, carbon dioxide emissions, population growth rate, energy intensity, and others.

PROBLEMS WITH CLASS APPLICATION

The primary difficulty is the balance which an instructor must achieve in teaching a heterodox approach to an important subject. Can the students appreciate the uses and abuses of the conventional system and explore alternatives without becoming cynical about the entire subject? Students at the principles level take economics extremely literally.

Many of the above measures present problems in interpretation themselves. These should be carefully considered by students and choices made about which best meet the criteria outlined above. If students have elected (or the instructor has required) to create a composite index, they will need to establish some common indexation for the different indicators to make the data comparable and a method of weighting them. Successful creation of a composite measure would make comparisons to GDP much easier, but is fraught with interpretive and statistical difficulties that will create frustrations for a principles class.

Of course, there are many problems getting data for students to use, or sending them out to find data—especially about developing countries and environmental values.

NOTES

1 Incidentally, some economists responsible for developing national income accounts were quite concerned about the lack of regard for distribution and other qualitative effects implied by the developing system of national accounts. Jacob Viner (1953: 99–100) wrote, "The numbers of those living at the margin of subsistence may have grown consistent with a rise in the average income of the population as a whole."
2 Repetto's adjustments for depletion of environmental resources shows substantially altered growth rates from the standard GDP growth rate. For instance, Indonesia's fifteen-year growth record during the 1971–84 period would have been cut almost in half by including depletion.
3 For examples based on UN Human Development Index, see *New York Times*, March 8, 1992, p. 5.

BIBLIOGRAPHY

Anderson, V. (1991) *Alternative Economic Indicators*, London: Routledge.
Carr-Hill, R. and Lintott, J. (1986) "Social Indicators for Popular Planning," in P. Ekins (ed.) *The Living Economy*, London: Routledge.
Dixon-Mueller, R. and Anker, R. (1988) *Assessing Women's Economic Contributions to Development*, Geneva: ILO.
Keynes, J. M. and Stone, R. (1939) "The National Income and Expenditure of the United Kingdom, and How to Pay for the War," *Times* (London), July 26: 15 b.
Kuznets, S. (1954) *National Income and Industrial Structure*, London: Economic Change.
Lewenhak, S. (1992) *The Revaluation of Women's Work*, London: Earthscan Publications.
Nasar, Sylvia (1992) *New York Times*, March 8: 5.
Nordhaus, W. and Tobin, J. (1972) *Is Growth Obsolete?* Cambridge, MA: National Bureau of Economic Research.
Repetto, Robert (1988) "Tropical Forests: The Sale that Sells the Future," *Christian Science Monitor*, June 15: 13, col. 1.
World Resources Institute, *Resources*, various issues.
Viner, J. (1953) *International Trade and Economic Development*, Oxford: Clarendon Press.
Waring, M. (1988) *If Women Counted*, New York: Harper and Row.

11 A disaggregated CPI: the differential effects of inflation

Irene Powell and Jane Rossetti

Most introductory economics texts discuss the CPI, the PPI, and the GNP deflator early on in the macro section. They explain how the CPI is used to calculate inflation rates. They also provide, either in the text or in the accompanying student workbooks, or both, examples of CPIs to calculate. These calculations may be made for imaginary economies or using actual US data for periods of particular historical interest. What the exercises have in common is that they calculate "the" CPI or deflator. However, since different groups (by age, race, income, household composition) spend different percentages of income on different categories of consumption or saving, (on average) the inflation rate a group experiences is not the same as "the" CPI. Having students calculate CPIs for different groups not only gives them practice in weighting and summing, but also reinforces the idea that the macro economy is made up of different groups of people, who are differentially affected by particular fiscal or monetary policy. In this particular case, the numbers also illustrate that different groups have different marginal propensities to consume/save, a point which can be elaborated later in the course.

In a course designed to ensure economic literacy, a solid understanding of the construction, interpretation, and use of the CPI is crucial. It is one of the most widely cited statistics in the newspapers, on the television and the radio. Students, no matter their backgrounds, will hear or read reports of the current CPI on a regular basis. An exercise exploring the CPI helps to fulfill this primary goal. This particular exercise also helps satisfy the complementary goal of introducing and investigating differences in race, class, and gender in the economy. This example serves the goal of practise in calculating the CPI at the same time it illustrates the differential impact of inflation on different groups. It encourages students to remember that aggregation has its limits, particularly in evaluating government policy.

We see this example as fitting early in the introductory macroeconomics class during the section on macro measurement and its limitations, and discussion of macro goals. It could be presented in class as a lecture, but is probably more effective as an exercise for the student or a group of students to perform on their own, which could then form the basis for either class discussion or a short essay. The amount of information the instructor provides the students can be adjusted to reflect actual or desired student research skills and the time the instructor would like the student to spend on this one example. There are no institutional or departmental constraints, as long as the library carries the periodicals in which current data appear.

The examples below use data from 1988–89. The data on inflation rates for particular categories of goods are not difficult to find. They appear in the *Monthly Labor Review*, a periodical put out by the Bureau of Labor Statistics, and in *Economic Indicators*, a periodical put out by the Council of Economic Advisors, and in other places including the *Survey of Current Business* (US Department of Commerce), *Business Statistics* (US Department of Commerce), and *Economic Indicators* (Joint Economic Committee, Council of Economic Advisors). Data on average expenditure by different category is found in the *Consumer Expenditure Survey*, US Department of Labor, Bureau of Labor Statistics. The data below are presented for race. Many other subsets of population (e.g. by age, income) are possible.[1]

Tables 11.1 and 11.2 show the inflation rates for the categories above (from Table 26, "Historical CPI-U: US City Average, by Commodity and Service Group and Detailed Expenditure Categories," pp. 86–90, *CPI Detailed Report*, US Department of Labor, Bureau of Labor Statistics) and the percentage expenditures on each category for the two groups: black and white/other (*Consumer Expenditure Survey*).

Table 11.1   Percentage change in CPI from previous December (December 1987–December 1988)

All	4.4
Food	5.1
Housing	4.0
Apparel	4.7
Other	7.0

Table 11.2   Percentage expenditure on given category out of total expenditure 1988

Category	Black	White/other
Food	16.38	14.34
Housing	33.51	31.03
Apparel	7.20	5.64
Other[a]	17.16	18.89

a "Other" includes alcoholic beverages, personal care products and services, reading, education, tobacco, miscellaneous, contributions, insurance and pension, health care, transportation and entertainment.

If December 1987 is the base year, the "price" in December 1987 is taken to equal 1.0 for each category. Thus, the price in December 1988 for each category of expenditure can be calculated based on the inflation rates between December 1987 and December 1988, as given above. For example, the inflation rate for food in 1988 was 5.1 percent; the new price of food in December 1988 is 1.051. To calculate the CPI for each group, multiply the new price times the quantity (in percent expenditures on each category). So, for example, p*q of food in December 1988 for African Americans is 16.38 * 1.051 = 17.22; for white/others it is 14.34 * 1.051 = 15.07. (See Table 11.3.)

Table 11.3 Solution worked out

Category	p*q black	p*q white/other
Food	17.22	15.07
Housing	34.85	32.27
Apparel	7.54	5.90
Other	45.91	52.42
Sum = CPI	105.52	105.66
% Δ CPI	5.52	5.66

Whites/others experience a higher inflation rate, implying that, if equity/distribution is a concern, the government might logically tolerate a higher inflation rate than it has in the past. Also note that the CPI figures, when released, are themselves usually partially disaggregated (e.g. food prices this month are responsible for holding down/propelling inflation) and that these statistics might themselves be of importance in decision-making.

The exercise above can be replicated for age (this might be of interest to our students) or income category. These data are presented in Appendix 11.1. The replication might serve as a good method of evaluating student understanding, either in simplified form on in-class work, or as a short paper. An interesting example to have them research would be to construct the CPI for their own expenditures, or for a group of current policy concern in your area or nationally, for instance single mothers with children. These require the students to learn how to search for and find the appropriate data, which may be one of your course goals.

In addition, Alan Blinder, in *Hard Heads, Soft Hearts (Reading, MA: Addison-Wesley)*, in chapter 2, titled "Striking a Balance Between Unemployment and Inflation," discusses the differential impact of inflation on the sources of income side for the most recent big episode of inflation in the 1970s. He concludes that on the income side only higher-income groups suffered much from that inflation. Again, the implication is that if equity/distribution is a policy goal, the government might tolerate a higher inflation rate than it has in the past (especially, given Blinder's evidence in the same chapter on the differential impacts of unemployment).

APPENDIX 11.1

In these examples as well, richer people experience a higher rate of inflation.

Table 11.4   Expenditure disaggregated by income quintile

Category	Lowest 20%	Highest 20%
(Average income	4,942	67,199)
(Gender	60% female	86% male)
Expenditure	10,893	48,718
% expenditure		
Food	17.90	12.46
Housing	36.33	29.63
Apparel	5.27	6.21
Other	32.67	41.85
Sum (p*q)	104.96	105.13
% Δ CPI	4.96	5.13

Source; Consumer Expenditure Survey, table 10.

APPENDIX 11.2

Table 11.5   Expenditure disaggregated by household type, age, gender, and income: females in one-adult households, of at least fifty-five years of age, by income (%)

Category	Low income	High income
Food	18.9	8.6
Housing	39.4	20.1
Apparel	3.6	4.5
Other	38.1	66.8
Sum (p*q)	105.38	106.13
% change CPI	5.38	6.13

Source: Statistical Abstract of the United States.

NOTES

1 The data for highest/lowest income quintile are presented in Appendix 11.1. Data for one comparison between older adults by income (here women over fifty-five in single-adult households) are presented in Appendix 11.2.

ACKNOWLEDGMENTS

With thanks to Bob Cherry of Brooklyn College for the original idea, and for suggestions of which differences to investigate.

12 An active learning exercise for studying the differential effects of inflation

Sherryl Davis Kasper

The exercise developed below is proposed for use during the macroeconomics section of a typical introductory economics course. It presupposes that the instructor has defined inflation, has identified key price indexes and demonstrated how they are used to measure inflation, and has presented a historical survey of movements in rates of inflation. Typically most introductory texts proceed to discuss who gains and who loses from inflation, focusing on anonymous groups such as creditors vs. debtors or savers vs. people on fixed incomes (Case and Fair 1994; Colander 1994; Rohlf 1993). This exercise aims to bring to life the differential effects of inflation on various groups in society using active learning techniques.

CLASS FORMAT

The instructor begins the discussion by informing the students that they are going to analyze the effects of inflation on various groups in society by studying the impact of changes in the Consumer Price Index (CPI). He or she should remind the students that the CPI measures changes in the prices of a market basket of goods and services such as food, housing, and medical care. Likewise, the CPI serves as an important indicator of social well-being to members of Congress and officials in the executive branch and the Federal Reserve as they determine the course of monetary and fiscal policy.

The instructor next presents statistics that chronicle recent changes in components of the CPI as reported in the most recent edition of the *Economic Report of the President* (See Table 12.1). As the students examine these statistics, the instructor should insure that they recognize that price changes in the components of the CPI occurred at different rates, some greater and some less, than the average for all goods and services. As a result, consumption patterns determine the real effect of inflation on the household's ability to purchase goods and services and, as a consequence, its level of social well-being. For example, from 1982–84 to 1993 consumer prices rose at an average rate of 44.5 percent, while the costs of medical care increased 101.4 percent. For a household that received medical benefits, the CPI overstated the effect of inflation, and for a household that did not, it understated inflation's impact on real consumption. Thus, the aggregate CPI does not necessarily provide an accurate measure of social well-being, and, as a result, its use as an indicator for policy decisions can be misleading.

Table 12.1   Consumer price indexes, December 1993 (1982–84 = 100)

All items	144.5		
Food and beverages	141.6	Apparel and upkeep	133.7
Housing	141.2	Transportation	130.4
Shelter	155.7	Medical care	201.4
Fuel and other utilities	121.3	Entertainment	145.8
Furnishings and operating	119.3	Other goods and services	192.9

Source: Economic Report of the President, 1994.

To study the differential impact of inflation in more detail, the instructor should divide the class into small groups of three to five students. The instructor then provides each group with a short description of a household that includes information such as source of income, geographical location, gender, race, age, and educational level. Examples include the following:

1 An Appalachian household headed by a single woman with two children. This woman works as a sewing machine operator in a garment factory earning just above the minimum wage.
2 A retired steel worker and his wife living in Ohio. Their main sources of income consist of a pension that contains a COLA and Social Security.
3 A dual career couple consisting of an orthopedic surgeon and a dentist living in Florida.
4 A middle-aged, middle-income household consisting of a husband, wife, and two children living in the suburbs of Washington, DC. The husband works for the federal government and has received annual raises of approximately 3 percent since 1984. The wife re-entered the labor force as a nurse when her oldest child enrolled in college in 1988.
5 An aerospace engineer and a computer programmer who were laid off by their employers in southern California in the early 1990s owing to cuts in defense expenditures by the US government. The engineer remains unemployed; the computer programmer participated in a government-funded retraining program and now works in a welfare office earning a 25 percent smaller income.

If the class is large, the instructor may assign several groups the same household description. The instructor is also encouraged to develop other examples that will have particular meaning for his or her students. The goal in devising the examples is to develop scenarios that illustrate the differential effects of inflation on individuals according to race, gender, or class characteristics. The instructor should be careful not to devise hypothetical households that will perpetuate stereotypical views held by students of particular groups across the nation or in a particular region. For example, in the scenarios listed previously, the household representing the poor and disenfranchised is a rural, female-headed family in Appalachia rather than the typical media presentation of an unwed, teenage, African-American welfare mother living in an inner city housing project. The Appalachian household reminds students that poverty also exists in rural areas and also addresses stereotypical views of the white underclass held by some students from the southeastern section of the United States.

The instructor should ask each group to use the data presented in Table 12.1 to evaluate how the household changed its income level and consumption patterns to cope with the effects of inflation over the same time period. The students should then prepare a three to five minute oral presentation of their findings. This group work can take place either during the class period or as a homework assignment, depending on the preferences of the instructor.[1]

The instructor should encourage the students to fill in detail about the households as they complete their analysis. For example, low-skilled workers in Appalachia frequently compete with foreign workers in northern Mexico and Asia; as a consequence, they are often subject to threats of plant closings. Fear of job loss leads to a lack of bargaining power that limits their ability to raise their incomes in step with changes in the costs of living. Like many of their contemporaries, the retired couple could have an adult child who has been recently laid off from the steel mill owing to automation; as a result they are trying to help him meet the quickly escalating costs of obtaining a college education necessary to compete in the new global economy. One of the households could have a member with a pre-existing medical condition that prevents that person from obtaining health insurance. The amount of detail the instructor can expect will depend on both the background knowledge of and the time available to the students to complete the assignment.

Each group is asked to present its findings to the class. These presentations serve as the basis for a discussion of the differential effects of inflation on various groups in society. Themes that can be drawn out and emphasized include: (1) the effect of sex, gender, age, and geographical location on consumption expenditures; (2) the role of bargaining power in maintaining purchasing power; (3) factors that determine a household's ability to obtain bargaining power; (4) the problems associated with using a simple average rate of inflation both as a measure of social well-being and as a basis for policy deliberations. The instructor should allocate one class period for the group presentations and subsequent discussion.

CONCLUSION

The exercise using a disaggregated CPI to study the differential effects of inflation on various groups in society presents the instructor with several opportunities. First, it helps students to see that the average CPI does not equally reflect the problems faced by a household as it tries to cope with effects of inflation. As a result, students are encouraged to become more critical consumers of common economic statistics both as measures of social well-being and as policy guides. Likewise, they learn the role of bargaining power in coping with inflation and how race, gender, and class characteristics influence the level of bargaining power held by each household. Second, this exercise offers the instructor an opportunity to use active learning techniques that develop both oral communication and critical thinking skills. Both the small group discussion and the report to the class require students to practice their ability to communicate orally. In the small group discussions, students are required to think creatively about the situation of a particular household as it copes with effects of inflation over the past decade. In the class discussion, the students are encouraged to draw general conclusions from the particular examples of the households about the differential effects of inflation. Both activities require them to develop their critical thinking skills.

NOTE

1 If the instructor opts to use this exercise as a homework assignment, he or she can also request the students to find the statistical information themselves in the *Economic Report of the President* or similar source. The collection of these statistics can acquaint the students with sources of economic data and provide them with practice in gathering this information.

BIBLIOGRAPHY

Case, K. E. and Fair, R. C. (1994) *Principles of Macroeconomics*, third edition, Englewood Cliffs, NJ: Prentice Hall.
Colander, D. (1994) *Macroeconomics*, Burr Ridge, IL: Richard D. Irwin.
Economic Report of the President (1994) Washington: Government Printing Office.
Rohlf, Jr., W. D. (1993) *Introduction to Economic Reasoning*, Reading, MA: Addison4-Wesley.

ACKNOWLEDGMENTS

The author wishes to thank her colleagues who attended the Workshop on Integrating the Latest Scholarship on Race and Gender in the Economics Curriculum held at Denison University, for their knowledge and inspiration.

Part IV

Additional considerations in integrating race and gender into Economics 190 R&G

These chapters cover a variety of issues that surface when race and gender issues are integrated into introductory economics: Why do it, how to do it, how instructor and student prejudices can affect students, how different students may use affective versus cognitive learning realms, and finally, how data should be used with caution.

Marianne Ferber, in "Gender and the Study of Economics: A Feminist Critique," discusses the elements of economics and, in particular, introductory economics, that might put off female students. She pushes aside the notion that overt sexism is the main culprit and focuses on three more subtle reasons. First, she examines the lack of women in the field of economics and the message sent to female students. With few role models to emulate, other fields of study may seem more appropriate. Second, there seems to be a gender bias in the presentation of material. To illustrate her point, Ferber looks at nine leading introductory economics textbooks and finds errors of omission with regard to women's economic contributions. Finally, Ferber hypothesizes that economics may not be attractive to women students because of its narrow neoclassical approach. A broader methodological approach may be of interest to more students.

Robert Cherry, in "Integrating Race and Gender Topics into Introductory Microeconomics," examines seven topics found in an introductory microeconomics class and demonstrates how race- and gender-related topics can be analyzed within a neoclassical framework. Cherry acknowledges that most introductory microeconomics classes are geared to develop technical frameworks for analyzing economic phenomena in the output market and chooses his examples accordingly. For example, he uses the production possibilities curve to examine the trade-offs between equity and efficiency rather than guns and butter. In this section he also develops a wage offer curve which uses wage and safety data for immigration workers. Demand and supply curves are used to illustrate the crowding hypothesis with regard to the labor supply of women. Elasticity is used to explain why stores in low-income neighborhoods may be able to charge higher prices. Marginal benefit and marginal cost analysis is applied to crime and the optimal job search for women with employed husbands. The theory of competition is illustrated with the cotton market in the antebellum South. He uses an interesting example of the beauty-care industry to demonstrate the notion of optimization. Finally, Cherry has a great example of the integration of professional baseball teams for labor markets. Cherry uses seven graphs to look at race and gender issues within a neoclassical framework. His examples are insightful and provide interesting data for students to examine.

Akira Motomura, in "Thoughts on Teaching Asian-American Undergraduates," provides insights into how to deal with the issue of stereotyping. He cautions instructors from thinking that "all aspirin is alike." Not all Asian-American students are newly immigrated and not all Asian Americans are the "model minority." Motomura attempts to show instructors of economics that there is greater diversity within groups than there probably is between groups. Moreover, Asian Americans are often ignored or wrongly categorized as white or people of color. Despite the diversity, Asian Americans share some common experiences. In the eyes of non-Asians, Asian students look very similar. Motomura discusses the harmful effects the model minority syndrome can have on student performance. Despite the damaging effects of the model minority stereotype, there are some valuable lessons that can be learned from Asian-American students. Motomura offers advice on how to deal with stereotypes in the classroom.

Vernon Dixon, in "Some Thoughts on Teaching Predominantly Affective-oriented Groups," moves instructors out of the familiar cognitive realm of abstract ways of knowing into the affective realm of connected ways of knowing. He begins by discussing the traits of affective-oriented learners. There is a certain wholeness to what is to be learned, not compartmentalized, as is typically done in economics. In terms of values, affective-oriented learners find meaning in nature and interpersonal relationships or affiliations. Affiliations can be more important than individual preferences. The production of knowledge by affective-oriented people comes from the emotions, from feeling connected. Dixon gives several examples of these ways of knowing drawn from African and Hawaiian cultures.

Finally, Carolyn Shaw Bell, in "Race, Gender, and Economic Data," explores the relationships between race and economic data and gender and economic data. She writes a fascinating history of the census data and how various races have been categorized over the years. She also discusses the history of the poverty measures and their shortcomings. Even the definition of elderly is questioned. This chapter is an excellent illustration of the importance of the definitions when measuring economic concepts, and the importance of having the data fit the questions being asked.

13 Gender and the study of economics: a feminist critique

Marianne A. Ferber

For some time now there has been concern about the small representation of women and minorities among students of economics, and about their slow rate of increase. This paper focuses very largely on women because far more work has been done on that subject. But many of the problems are likely to be similar for both groups, and certainly both deserve attention.

There is also evidence that women do not perform as well as men in introductory economics courses[1] (Siegfried 1979). This may, however, at least in part be an artifact of the type of tests used (Ferber *et al.* 1983; Lumsden and Scott 1987; Morawetz 1976). Further, women appear to be more disadvantaged than men by large class sizes, and hence to benefit more from different approaches to teaching (Allison 1977).

For all these reasons, there has been considerable interest in the "chilly classroom climate" for women students in economics courses as they are presently taught (Feiner and Morgan 1987; Ferber 1984). In this chapter, the focus will be on the small representation of women among economics faculties, the biased subject matter, and the narrow approach of traditional economics.

WOMEN'S REPRESENTATION IN ECONOMICS

As seen in Table 13.1, women's representation in higher education has been increasing rapidly, but the rise in economics has lagged considerably. The disparity between economics and the other social sciences at all degree levels, except for M.A.s in political science, is particularly striking. It is frequently suggested that mathematics requirements inhibit women's entry, and that women are not interested in business-related fields. However, the fact that women earn a substantially larger share of degrees in mathematics than in economics at the B.A. and M.A. level, and a larger share of business degrees at all levels, suggests that the explanations must lie elsewhere.

Similarly this evidence of unusually low representation of women in economics rules out general sexism in the classroom, from the greater attention of teachers to boys, the tendency to encourage boys to be more aggressive in class participation, and the use of sexist language, to disparaging illustrations

Table 13.1 Proportion of degrees awarded to women in economics and other selected fields (%)

Field	1949–50	1975–76	1988–89
		B.A.s	
Total, all fields	23.9	45.5	52.5
Econ.	7.6	19.6	32.5
Math.	22.6	40.7	46.0
Bus.	–	19.7	48.3
Pol. Sc.	15.5	25.3	40.9
Psych.	36.7	54.3	70.8
Soc.	50.6	59.3	68.8
		M.A.s	
Total, all fields	29.1	46.4	51.9
Econ.	12.4	15.9	28.4
Math.	19.5	34.0	39.9
Bus.	–	11.6	33.6
Pol. Sc.	15.9	21.6	32.6
Psych.	28.0	46.6	67.4
Soc.	32.4	42.0	56.8
		Ph.D.s	
Total, all fields	9.6	22.9	36.5
Econ.	4.5	10.6	19.0
Math.	5.6	11.0	19.4
Bus.	–	3.4	26.6
Pol. Sc.	7.9	16.3	25.7
Psych.	14.8	30.9	56.2
Soc.	18.4	30.2	50.9

Source: National Center for Education Statistics, *Digest of Education*, 1977–78, 1991.

of incompetent women as the main culprit, for they have been found to be pervasive regardless of subject-matter (Sadker and Sadker 1979; Sandler 1987). Instead, we must look to factors that are not general to all fields.

REPRESENTATION OF WOMEN ON FACULTIES

The persistently small proportion of women among economics faculties, especially at senior levels, shown in Table 13.2, is likely to be a contributing factor.[2] The dearth of female role models and mentors in departments with few women faculty was found to be a decisive obstacle for women graduate students (Berg and Ferber 1983). Other problems, specific to economics, need to be considered as well.

SUBJECT-MATTER BIAS

The best available indicator of the content of introductory economics courses is the content of widely used texts. A review of nine recent editions

Table 13.2 Faculty, by type of institution

Faculty	1984–85			1988–89		
	Men	Women	Percent women	Men	Women	Percent women
Undergraduate institution						
Full prof.	105	15	12.5	130	16	11.0
Assoc. prof.	107	12	10.1	129	17	11.6
Asst. prof.	152	24	13.6	143	29	16.9
Instructors	47	8	14.5	24	8	25.0
Total	411	59	12.6	426	70	14.1
Graduate institution						
Full prof.	567	20	3.4	588	20	3.3
Assoc. prof.	270	15	5.3	230	21	8.4
Asst. prof.	320	48	13.0	313	64	17.0
Instructors	28	3	9.7	18	2	10.0
Total	1,185	86	6.8	1,149	107	8.5
All institutions						
Full prof.	672	35	5.0	718	36	4.8
Assoc. prof.	377	27	6.7	359	38	9.6
Asst. prof.	472	72	13.2	456	93	16.9
Instructors	75	11	12.8	42	10	19.2
Total	1,596	145	8.3	1,575	177	10.1

Sources: 1984–85, 1988–89 Report of the Committee on the Status of Women in the Economics Profession, *American Economic Review* 80, 2 (May 1990): 488.

of best-selling books shows, on the one hand, that there has been progress over time, but, on the other hand, that there is room for substantially more improvement.[3] One interesting fact is that texts have come full circle regarding references to "women" in their subject index. They multiplied initially as attention to women's issues increased, but have now once again virtually disappeared (except for Samuelson and Nordhaus 1992). This may be for the same sound reason that there are no references to men: they are now likely to be taken for granted. On the other hand, the fact that among references to individuals (including non-economists) the proportion of women is, on average, only 5 percent, ranging from zero (Parkin 1990) to 15 percent (Dolan and Lindsay 1991) suggests there has not been much change in this respect. Further, topics of special importance to women, and discussions of significant differences between men and women, are still all too frequently ignored.[4] A few examples will suffice to illustrate this point.

More than half of the texts make no mention of the rise in women's labor force participation, arguably one of the most important economic developments of the last fifty years; two of them mention it only as a purported reason for lower productivity. Several of the books discuss GNP without noting that non-market work is excluded; one briefly mentions household production under the heading of "leisure;" none discusses possible ways of calculating its value, or the need for such information in order to get more reasonable estimates of the poverty level of today's diverse households. About half of the books discuss income distribution without remarking on the "feminization of poverty," or the disproportionate representation of children among the poor. Households and families as institutions receive virtually no attention, in spite of the proliferation of research on the "new home economics."

CRITIQUES OF "THE ECONOMIC APPROACH"

Sins of omission, such as the ones cited above, have long received attention. More recently, feminist economists have also challenged the mainstream view represented by Blaug's (1962) statement that the story of economics is "yesterday's blunders now corrected." In other words, they do not agree that it is a story of unidirectional progress toward objective truth.[5] Like other feminists they emphasize "holism, harmony and complexity rather than reductionism, domination, and linearity" (Rose 1986: 72).

Even some prominent mainstream economists have been casting a jaundiced eye on the narrow neoclassical approach. Thus, for instance, Blank (1993) questions strict adherence to the concept of rationality.[6] She says she was startled to realize that many economists "really believe all this stuff about individuals constantly making fully informed rational choices accounting for all expected lifetime costs and benefits,"[7] and believes that this goes a long way toward explaining why ninety-nine out of a hundred students in introductory courses are likely to find the economic approach sort of crazy, even though they may also find it interesting. Only the one student in a hundred who thinks this way is likely to become an economist.

Leibenstein (1969, 1976) proposed the novel concept of "X-efficiency," which posits that the behavior of interacting individuals is determined by differences in personality and varying conditions, as opposed to the usual model of autonomous, optimizing agents. Equally unorthodox is Solow's (1990) suggestion that wages may be the result of commonly accepted rules of equity and of institutional controls, both of which constitute substantial hurdles to the operation of equilibrating forces. He then goes further and argues that wages have to be regarded as an independent variable, likely to be important in determining the productivity of labor.

These challenges to established dogma are not unlike those posed by feminists. Yet Blank fails to note that the model of the detached, rational maximizer is particularly inappropriate for a young woman making a traditional career choice because she has been socialized to believe that, whatever else she plans to do with her life, she will have to assume primary responsibility for family members (parents, children, or spouse) who need care. The same is true for young people, and especially members of minorities who do not believe they have little or no choice because they have grown up in the inner city or a rural slum, where unemployment is rampant, and good jobs are virtually nonexistent. Nor does Blank suggest that the one student who will find this model congenial is not likely to be a woman or a member of a minority group.

Similarly, Leibenstein discusses his innovative concept of X-efficiency in the context of the firm, but does not appear to be aware that it is particularly applicable to the family. And Solow does not point out the obvious relevance of his analysis to the notion of comparable worth, a concept well-nigh universally condemned by neoclassical economists as unwarranted interference with the market, where wages of workers are presumably determined by their productivity.

These omissions help to explain why even such critics, who have most likely increased the appeal of economics to students who would not tend to be attracted to the orthodox model, are not likely to have made many converts among women and minorities. This is more likely to be accomplished by feminists, and "Africanists," as Williams (forthcoming) calls them. They explicitly begin from the premise that ideology is, at the very least, bound to make a difference in what problems are selected for research, how research is operationalized, and how findings are interpreted (Blau 1981). They not only question the established dogma, but also apply their analysis to issues previously either entirely neglected, or forced into especially inappropriate molds. Again, a few illustrations will suffice.

Madden (1975) offered a theory of discrimination consistent with profit maximization, and therefore not subject to the usual charge that it cannot continue in the long run. Bergmann (1974) developed an explanation of lower pay for women not in conflict with workers being paid according to their marginal contribution. Ferber and Birnbaum (1977) and Sawhill (1977) were among the early critics who challenged the "new home economics" (Becker 1965, 1973, 1981) as a blatant justification and reinforcement of the *status quo*.[8] England (1982, 1984) forcefully contested Polachek's (1976, 1981) view of occupational segregation as the result of voluntary, rational choices of women. Reskin and Roos (1990), Strober (1984), and Strober and Arnold (1987) instead offered an alternative explanation, which essentially relegates women to jobs men do not want.

CONCLUSIONS

Numerous articles have been written for some time, suggesting how to improve the climate for women students in general, and in economics in particular.[9] Many of the suggestions made in this literature are, regrettably, still timely. This chapter has, once again, noted topics that would be likely not only to be of greater interest to women, but to offer a fuller picture of the real world as it is, and to contribute to a more informed discussion of current policy issues. It has, however, taken the additional step of pointing out that a fundamental review of the traditional economic approach is needed if the field is to appeal to more than the one in a hundred students, and particularly to women and members of minorities.

NOTES

1 A recent paper (Waldauer, Duggal and Williams, 1992) reports that no such differences were found among women and men in an intermediate economics course. This could, however, be the result of selection bias, to the extent that only women who did relatively well in their introductory course go on to become economics majors, or even just to take some additional economics courses.

2 The low proportion of women among economics students in turn contributes to the low proportion of women faculty, but does not explain the continued sub-stantially lower representation of women at higher ranks. This circular problem of very low representation among both students and faculty appears to be even more serious for minorities.

3 The texts reviewed are Baumol and Blinder (1990); Dolan and Lindsay (1991); Fischer *et al.* (1988); Gwartney and Stroup (1991); Leftwich (1984); McConnell (1987); Parkin (1990); Samuelson and Nordhaus (1992); and Schiller (1991). These are compared with similar sets of textbooks reviewed in Ferber and Teiman (1981) and Ferber (1990).

4 It is also worth noting that such neglect is not confined to textbooks. In a two-page summary of "Working and Earning under Different Rules: What the United States can learn from Labor Market Institutions in other Countries" (*NBER Reporter*, summer 1991) Richard Freeman has nothing to say about differences in women's labor force participation, in the male–female earnings gap, or in policies that would influence both.

5 As suggested in Ferber and Nelson (1993), feminist critics may be divided into three groups. All go beyond what is often disparagingly termed "Add women and stir." The first is "postmodernism," concerned with "deconstruction" of intellectual concepts, and mainly associated with such literary critics as Foucault and Derrida. The second consists of proponents of "feminist difference," who tend to espouse women's superiority in creating knowledge, based on "women's ways of knowing." The third, termed "feminist empiricists" by Harding (1986), up to a point accept existing methodological norms of scientific inquiry, but argue that they must be more strictly adhered to if prevailing biases are to be corrected. An interesting and more extensive discussion of these issues can be found in Seiz (1992).

6 Strober (1987) reports on the result of an experiment by two psychologists. Two groups of students were asked to choose between two ways of responding to an outbreak of disease. One was told that program A would save 200 people, while program B would result in a one-in-three probability that nobody would die and a two-out-of-three probability that 600 people would die. The second group was given precisely the same choice, but told that 400 people would die, and there was a one-in-three probability that nobody will die and a two out of three probability that 600 people would die. In the first group, 72 percent chose the first approach, but in the second group 78 percent chose the second approach. So much for rationality.

7 Just how far this can be carried is seen when Gregory Mankiw is quoted in "Macroeconomics in disarray" (*NBER Reporter*, summer 1991): "Let me start with the widespread acceptance of rational expectations. Economists routinely assume that firms rationally maximize profits, and that consumers rationally maximize productivity. It would be an act of schizophrenia not to assume that economic agents act rationally when they form their expectations of the future."

8 Bergmann (1987b: 132–3) suggests that "To say that the "new home economists" are not feminist in their orientation would be as much of an understatement as to say that Bengal tigers are not vegetarians."
9 In addition to the ones already mentioned are, among others, American Sociological Association Committee on the Status of Women in Sociology (1979); Bergmann (1987a); Jackstadt and Grotaert (1980); Roby (1973); and Solmon (1976).

BIBLIOGRAPHY

Allison, E. K. (1977) "Three Years of Self-paced Teaching in Introductory Economics at Harvard," *American Economic Review* 66, 2 (May): 222–8.

American Sociological Association Committee on the Status of Women in Sociology (1979) "How to Recognize and Avoid Sexist Bias in Sociological Research: Some Problems and Issues," Washington, DC: American Sociological Association.

Baumol, W. J. and Blinder, A. S. (1990) *Economics*, Reading, MA: Addison-Wesley.

Becker, G. S. (1965) "A Theory of the Allocation of Time," *Economic Journal* 75 (September): 493–517.

—— (1973) "A Theory of Marriage" I, *Journal of Political Economy* 81 (July/August): 813–46.

—— (1974) "A Theory of Marriage" II, *Journal of Political Economy* 82 (March/April): 1063–93.

—— (1981) *A Treatise on the Family*, Cambridge, MA: Harvard University Press.

Berg, H. M. and Ferber, M. A. (1983) "Men and Women Graduate Students: Who Succeeds and Why?" *Journal of Higher Education* 54 (November–December): 629–41.

Bergmann, B. R. (1974) "Occupational Segregation, Wages and Profits when Employers discriminate by Race or Sex," *Eastern Economic Journal* 1, 2–3 (April–July): 103–10.

—— (1987a) "Women's Roles in the Economy: Teaching the Issues," *Journal of Economic Education* 18, 4 (fall): 393–407.

—— (1987b) "The Task of Feminist Economics: A More Equitable Future," in Christie Farnham (ed.) *The Impact of Feminist Research in the Academy*, Bloomington, IN: University of Indiana Press.

Blank, R. M. (1993) "What Should Mainstream Economists learn from Feminist Theory?" in M. A. Ferber and J. A. Nelson (eds) *Beyond Economic Man: Feminist Theory and Economics*, Chicago: University of Chicago Press.

Blau, F. D. (1981) "On the Role of Values in Feminist Scholarship," *Signs: Journal of Women in Culture and Society* 86 (spring): 538–40.

Blaug, M. (1962) *Economic Theory in Retrospect*, London: Heinemann.

Dolan, E. G. and Lindsay, D. E. (1991) *Macroeconomics*, Chicago: Dryden Press.

England, P. (1982) "The Failure of Human Capital Theory to explain Occupational Sex Segregation," *Journal of Human Resources* 17 (summer): 358–70.

—— (1984) "Wage Appreciation and Depreciation: A Test of Neoclassical Economic Explanations of Occupational Sex Segregation," *Social Forces* 62 (March): 726–49.

Feiner, S. F. and Morgan, B. A. (1987) "Women and Minorities in Introductory Economics Textbooks," *Journal of Economic Education* 18 (fall): 376–92.

Ferber, M. A. (1984) "Suggestions for Improving the Classroom Climate for Women in the Introductory Economics Course," *Journal of Economic Education* 15, 2 (spring): 160–8.

—— (1990) "Gender and the Study of Economics," in P. Saunders and W. B. Walstad (eds) *The Principles of Economics Course*, New York: McGraw-Hill.

Ferber, M. A. and Birnbaum, B. G. (1977) "The New Home Economics: Retrospects and Prospects," *Journal of Consumer Research* 4 (June): 19–28.

Ferber, M. A., Birnbaum, B. G., and Green, C. A. (1983) "Gender Differences in Economic Knowledge: A Reevaluation of the Evidence," *Journal of Economic Education* 14, 2 (spring): 24–37.

Ferber, M. A. and Nelson, J. A. (forthcoming) "The Social Construction of Economics and the Social Construction of Gender," in M. A. Ferber and J. A. Nelson (eds) *Beyond Economic Man: Feminist Theory and Economics*, Chicago: University of Chicago Press.

Ferber, M. A. and Teiman, M. (1981) "The Impact of Feminism on Economics," in D. Spender (ed.) *Men's Studies Modified*, Oxford: Pergamon Press.

Fischer, S., Dornbusch, R., and Schmalensee, R. L. (1988) *Economics*, New York: McGraw-Hill.

Freeman, R. (1991) cited in *NBER Reporter* (summer).

Gwartney, J. D. and Stroup, R. L. (1991) *Macroeconomics*, San Diego, CA: Harcourt Brace.

Harding, S. (1986) *The Science Question in Feminism*, Ithaca, NY: Cornell University Press.

Jackstadt, S. L. and Grotaert, C. (1980) "Gender, Gender Stereotyping, and Socioeconomic Background as Determinants of Economic Knowledge and Learning," *Journal of Economic Education* 12, 1 (winter): 34–40.

Leftwich, R. (1984) *A Basic Framework for Economics*, Dallas, TX: Business Publications.

Leibenstein, H. (1969) "Organizational or Frictional Equilibria: X-efficiency and the Role of Innovations," *Quarterly Journal of Economics* 84 (November): 600–23.

——(1976) *Beyond Economic Man: A New Foundation for Microeconomics*, Cambridge, MA: Harvard University Press.

Lumsden, K. G. and Scott, A. (1987) "The Economics Student Reexamined: Male–Female Differences in Comprehension," *Journal of Economic Education* 18, 4 (fall): 365–75.

McConnell, C. R. (1987) *Economics*, New York: McGraw-Hill.

Madden, J. F. (1975) *The Economics of Discrimination*, Lexington, MA: D. C. Heath.

Mankiw, G. (1991) cited in *NBER Reporter* (summer).

Morawetz, D. (1976) "Correlations between Student Performance on Multiple Choice and Essay Type Examinations at the Hebrew University, 1966–1974," Research Report 93, Jerusalem: The Hebrew University of Jerusalem.

Parkin, M. (1990) *Economics*, Reading, MA: Addison-Wesley.

Polacheck, S. W. (1976) "Occupational Segregation: An Alternative Hypothesis," *Journal of Contemporary Business* 5, 1 (winter): 1–12.

——(1981) "Occupational Self-selection: A Human Capital Approach to Sex Differences in Occupational Structure," *Review of Economics and Statistics* 63, 1 (February): 60–9.

Reskin, B. F. and Roos, P. A. (1990) *Job Queues, Gender Queues*, Philadelphia: Temple University Press.

Roby, P. (1973) "Structural and Internalized Barriers to Women in Higher Education," in A. S. Rossi and A. Calderwood (eds) *Academic Women on the Move*, New York: Russell Sage Foundation.

Rose, H. (1986) "Beyond the Masculinist Realities: A Feminist Epistemology for the Sciences," in R. Bleier (ed.) *Feminist Approaches to Science*, New York: Pergamon Press.

Sadker, M. and Sadker, D. (1979) "Between Teacher and Student: Overcoming Sex Bias in the Classroom," unpublished report to the Non-sexist Teacher Project of the Women's Educational Equity Program, US DHEW, Office of Education.

Samuelson, P. and Nordhaus, W. D. (1992) *Economics*, New York: McGraw-Hill.
Sandler, B. R. (1987) "The Classroom Climate: Still a Chilly One for Women," in C. Lasser, *Educating Men and Women Together: Coeducation in a Changing World*, Urbana, IL: University of Illinois Press.
Sawhill, I. V. (1977) "Economic Perspectives on the Family," *Daedalus* 106 (spring): 115–25.
Schiller, B. R. (1991) *The Economy Today: Micro*, New York: McGraw-Hill.
Seiz, J. A. (1992) "Gender and Economic Research," in N. de Marchi (ed.), *The Methodology of Economics*, Boston, MA: Kluwer Nijhoff.
Siegfried, J. J. (1979) "Male–Female Differences in Economic Education: A Survey," *Journal of Economic Education* 10, 2 (spring): 1–11.
Solmon, L. C. (1976) *Male and Female Graduate Students: The Question of Equal Opportunity*, Special Studies in US Economic, Social and Political Issues, New York: Praeger.
Solow, R. M. (1990) *The Labor Market as a Social Institution*, Cambridge, MA: Blackwell.
Strober, M. H. (1984) "Toward a General Theory of Occupational Sex Segregation," in B. F. Reskin (ed.) *Sex Segregation in the Workplace: Trends, Explanations, Remedies*, Washington, DC: National Academy Press.
—— (1987) "The Scope of Microeconomics: Implications for Economic Education," *Journal of Economic Education* 18 (spring): 135–49.
Strober, M. H. and Arnold, C. L. (1987) "The Dynamics of Occupational Segregation among Bank Tellers," in C. Brown and J. Pechman (eds) *Gender in the Workplace*, Washington, DC: Brookings Institution.
Waldauer, C. (1992); Duggal, V. and Williams, M.L. "Gender Differences in Economic Knowledge: A Further Extension of the Analysis," *Quarterly Review of Economics and Finances* 32 (winter): 138–43.
Williams, R. M. (forthcoming) "Race, Deconstruction, and the Emergent Agenda of Feminist Economic Theory," in M. Ferber and J. A. Nelson (eds) *Economic Man: Feminist Theory and Economics*, Chicago: University of Chicago Press.

14 Integrating race and gender topics into introductory microeconomics courses

Robert Cherry

For many instructors wishing to teach microeconomics in a multicultural manner, the options appear limited. The main objective of introductory microeconomics courses is to develop some basic technical frameworks. These frameworks are often developed generically with limited references to social applications, particularly ones which may be controversial. Since race and gender topics are often controversial, they are generally ignored in the core development of economic tools. In addition, most presentations emphasize output markets so that the labor process, which clearly has race and gender components, becomes an optional topic, not covered in a substantial way in introductory microeconomics courses. This chapter will indicate that, even within the confines of a traditionally structured micro-economics course, there is a great deal of room to present topics which touch on race and gender. Let us look at some of the ways economic tools can be presented.

Production possibility curves are developed so that students begin to understand the concepts of feasibility and constrained optimization. Often specialization and comparative advantage are introduced by developing a simple international trade model. Instead, these concepts can be developed by focusing on the so-called equity versus efficiency trade-off as illustrated through the input–output Table 14.1. Here women have an absolute

Table 14.1 Output per unit labor

	Female	*Male*
MFG	10	5
AGA	15	9

advantage in both manufacturing and agriculture but a comparative advantage only in manufacturing.

Many instructors shy away from this presentation because it has a very conservative thrust. While we should indicate that this model is an alternative to one which would emphasize labor market discrimination, it allows an entry point quite early in the course for discussions of labor market segmentation and alternative explanations for inequality presented by different economists.

More broadly, courses can present feasibility-set examples which have a multicultural aspect. It is quite simple to develop a wage-offer curve to describe the situation faced by immigrant workers. This wage-offer curve represents all the combinations of safety and wages which would yield zero economic profits. The curve can be derived from information on the MC of each unit of safety yearly, together with the number of full-time equivalent workers. For example,

Units of safety	1	2	3	4	5
MC ($000)	40	40	60	80	120

If there are 100 full-time equivalent workers (employed 2,000 hours/year) then the first unit of safety would require the hourly wage rate to decline by $0.20. If we assume that the firm is willing to pay $7 per hour with no safety requirements, we could then construct the wage-offer curve (Figure 14.1).

As long as output markets are competitive, so that firms do not obtain excess profits in the long run, labor market outcomes must be on the wage-offer curve. In this context, workers must "pay" for the safety they receive, and some workers—those who place a low value on safety—are harmed by safety regulations. In particular, suppose some workers value the third unit

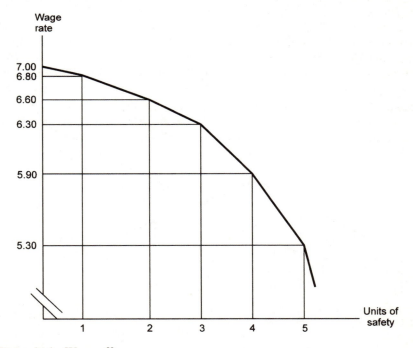

Figure 14.1 Wage offer curve

of safety at less than $0.30 per hour. If government regulations required firms to supply at least three units of safety, these workers would be harmed.

This model has been applied by Thomas Sowell and others to argue that turn-of-the-century sweatshops were in the best interest of immigrant workers. This analysis will force students to see the critical role the competitive assumption plays in economic analysis and how explanations for unsafe working conditions other than discrimination are possible.

Supply and demand frameworks are generally used to describe the movement of prices in the marketplace. When both supply and demand curves shift, the direction of change of only one of the variables—either equilibrium price or equilibrium quantity—can be predicted with certainty. Gender issues can be introduced to demonstrate this result. In particular, students can be asked to use supply and demand to determine the effect on the market for restaurant meals if more women entered the labor market.

Students immediately note that there would be an increased demand either because of an income effect—households have more income—or a substitution effect—the opportunity cost of home-cooked meals has risen. Some also realize that the supply curve may also shift if the entry of women increases the supply of restaurant workers, thereby lowering wages. While both shifts increase equilibrium quantity, they have contrasting impacts on equilibrium price. In Figure 14.2 the net effect is to leave the equilibrium price for restaurant meals unchanged.

In addition, the growth of female labor supplies provides an entry point to discuss the crowding hypothesis, which can be illustrated using supply and demand curves for two labor markets. This model illustrates one

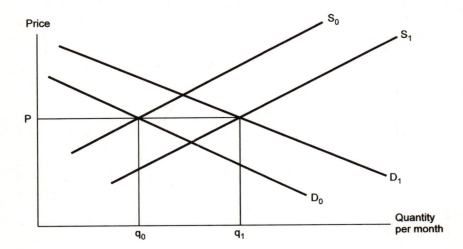

Figure 14.2 Market for restaurant meals

explanation for the lower earnings in female-dominated than in male-dominated occupations even after adjusting for skill differences. Note that while for Barbara Bergmann this crowding results from discrimination against women in male-dominated occupations, for Becker it results from differential preferences.

The supply and demand framework can also be utilized to describe the movement of prices for social goods, such as children. In particular, we might use it to assess why the quantity of children yearly has declined. On the demand side we could discuss how economic growth and social security have eliminated some of the economic benefits derived from children; on the supply side we could discuss the opportunity cost changes when shifting from rural to urban locations and the increased access of women to higher-paying jobs.

Elasticity can be applied to multicultural topics. For example, one way to demonstrate that the ability to raise prices is a function of price elasticity of demand rather than the size of the market is to discuss pricing at stores in low-income neighborhoods. There are variety of reasons why these stores have higher prices. There are technological reasons; since the stores have a lower sales volume they are unable to use cost-saving technology, such as price scanning at checkout counters. In addition, these stores may have higher security costs. However, it is also possible that since low-income households have more limited mobility they have an inelastic demand for goods and services purchased at local stores. Facing inelastic demands, these stores have a financial incentive to raise prices independent of costs.

Multicultural dimensions can also be included when presenting the topic of income elasticity. First, elasticity allows for another entry point to discuss family size. On the one hand, it might appear that children are an inferior good: as incomes have increased, family size has decreased. On the other hand, there continue to be political demands that the generosity of welfare encourages women to have additional children. As discussed above, family size has decreased for reasons other than income changes. In particular, the cost of children has risen so that "price" changes rather than income changes may have dominated. Thus, even though children are a "normal" good, demand declined.

Second, the use of excise taxes to raise revenues can be related to income distribution through income elasticity information. That is, placing excise taxes on goods which are inferior is the equivalent of a strongly regressive tax. Excise taxes on goods which are normal but income inelastic would also be regressive. This could then be related to alcohol and cigarette consumption in low-income (black and Latino) neighborhoods.

Marginal benefit, marginal cost analysis is generally associated with the theory of the firm, with marginal revenue reflecting marginal benefit. Courses could also use this method of analysis in multicultural settings. The economics of crime provides a number of areas. Youth crime can be discussed in terms of the benefits and costs associated with illegal activities. Not only does this focus on criminal behavior as rational but it provides a framework to demonstrate the relationship between unemployment and crime rates. In particular, deterrents to crime like longer sentences only change behavior if there is a significant opportunity cost on lost time in jail. For unemployed workers living in slum conditions, opportunity cost may be negligible. Thus, decent jobs may be a stronger deterrent to crime than harsher sentencing.

In addition, the economics of crime quickly derives the concept of an optimal crime rate: as long as criminal resources have some economic cost, crime should be undertaken only up to the point where it is cost-effective so that it is irrational for society to try and minimize the crime rate. This is understandable but becomes more complex when the crime is violent, as for example with rape. How do we view the concept of an "optimal rape rate?" Are rapists rational? Do they respond to changes in costs?

The natural rate of unemployment can also be discussed in the context of benefits and costs, using the arguments presented by Martin Feldstein in the 1970s—the exact same arguments that justified taxing unemployment insurance in 1979. Feldstein focused on the benefits and costs of job search to married women with working husbands. He argued that for a large portion of these women, especially those who held low-wage jobs, there was little cost to remaining unemployed, so that, for them, the optimal job search time was much longer than for men or single women. This highlights the continued assumption in economics that women place more value on non-market time than men and how this assumption impacts on economic analysis and public policy.

The *competitive theory of the firm* can be applied to the cotton market in the antebellum South. Cotton was produced in a highly competitive market so that in the long run there should have been zero economic profits as a result of the production process. At the simplest level, this would indicate that the lower (in-kind) payment to slave labor than to free labor enabled consumers to obtain goods at lower prices than they would have otherwise. Thus, consumers, not plantation owners, were the financial beneficiaries from slavery.

At a deeper level, however, plantation owners were beneficiaries. When presenting the competitive model, textbooks generally identify the case of increasing-cost industries: industries in which changes in output demand impact on wages. In the plantation model, there was a relative fixed supply of slaves (4 million in Figure 14.3) so that the price of slaves must rise to accommodate the increased demand for plantation workers. The rise in price of slaves shifted 600,000 slaves from other activities, such as domestic work, to work on cotton plantations. This is reflected in the upward-sloping long-run industry supply curve, SS_0. Thus, plantation owners benefited from growing demand for cotton, not necessarily as producers, but as owners of slaves.

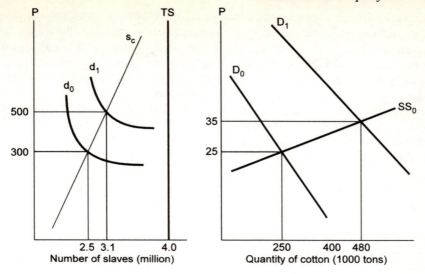

Figure 14.3 The impact of increased demand for cotton on cotton prices and the price of slaves

Optimization in unregulated markets requires that income distribution and preferences are exogenously given and that there are no externalities. In each of these areas, there are entry points to introduce race and gender issues. With respect to preferences, we could discuss the beauty-care industry. To what extent are conceptions of female beauty determined by women or imposed on women by social pressures? With respect to dollar votes, issues of homelessness and world famine can be presented.

With respect to externalities, the issue of pollution in black communities in the South—often by the sole industry in the town—could be presented. Here the focus can be on the inability of an individual town or individual state to place pollution restrictions greater than the national norm on firms which operate in competitive markets. It may be that these regulations harm workers who lose employment. This points out that pollution standards may be beneficial to all workers only when imposed at a national level.

One interesting example of the impact of positive externalities is the decision on building maintenance in low-income areas. The traditional neoclassical explanation for the blighting of buildings in these areas is that low-income households are willing to trade off housing "amenities" for lower rents. It follows that housing regulations cause homelessness since they take a choice away from tenants. One can certainly question the competitive assumption—owners make zero economic profits—which underpins this viewpoint.

Alternatively, blighting may result because positive externalities create a free-rider problem among owners of rental units. Positive externalities exist because of neighborhood effects—the value of each owner's building is influenced by the maintenance decision of other owners. Even though it is in the economic interest of all owners to maintain, each may choose not to maintain. As a result of these neighborhood effects, blighting may occur even when tenants are willing to pay higher rents for maintenance.

Suppose the neighborhood is comprised of identical rental buildings owned by Sam and Freda. If both do not maintain, tenants are willing to pay only $510 monthly to live in this blighted neighborhood. However, if both maintain, they are willing to pay $600 monthly. The higher rent reflects both an improved apartment and the ability to live in a well-kept neighborhood. If only one owner maintains—say Freda—her tenants would be willing to pay only $65 more, since the neighborhood is only half improved. However, Sam's tenants will increase the rent they are willing to pay to $535, reflecting the neighborhood effect of Freda's decision to maintain her buildings. Now suppose the cost of maintaining each apartment is between $65 and $90 monthly. Since each owner can raise rentals in their units by only $65, each will choose not to maintain even though the total benefits are $90. This demonstrates that even when the benefit of maintenance to tenants is sufficient, positive externalities may create under-investment in maintenance and a blighting of the neighborhood.

Labor market topics should be brought into the early part of the course. As already mentioned, the crowding model does not require anything other than the manipulation of supply and demand curves. The Becker model of discrimination is also a straightforward application of the self-regulating mechanism often described early in courses. According to the *laissez-faire* thesis, whenever problems appear there will be self-regulating mechanisms which will overcome them without the need for government intervention. According to Becker, the profit motive would discipline owners in competitive markets to hire the most productive workers.

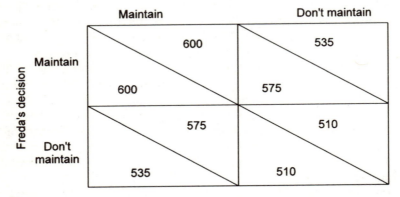

Figure 14.4 Rent tenants in each building are willing to pay, depending upon the level of maintenance in each building in the neighborhood

Table 14.2 Integration of baseball (number)

Team	First year	Black starters 1947–59	46–50	Average wins 51–59	Diff.
Milw	1950	18	83.2	85.7	2.5
LA	1947	27	92.0	91.6	−0.4
SF	1950	22	75.8	81.8	6.0
Chi WS	1950	24	64.4	87.4	23.0
Clev	1948	25	85.2	90.2	5.0
Average					7.2
StL	1958	2	88.8	77.7	−11.1
Phila	1957	1	73.8	75.1	1.3
Wash	–	0	62.6	63.7	1.1
Detr	–	0	87.4	71.4	−16.0
Bos	–	0	94.6	80.0	−14.6
NY	1959	2	94.6	94.1	−0.5
Average					−6.6
Pitts	1955	6	67.2	63.2	−4.0
Cinc	1956	7	66.4	75.0	8.6
Chic Cub	1954	12	68.0	67.6	−0.4
Balt	1955	5	59.2	63.8	4.6
KC	1954	8	68.8	63.6	−5.2
Average					0.9

The clearest example of this process was the integration of baseball teams between 1947 and 1960 before anti-discrimination laws were adopted. Taking the average wins per team during the period 1946–49 as a benchmark, Table 14.2 indicates the changes in number of wins per year during the 1950s. Teams are grouped according to how quickly they integrated. Two measures of integration can be used: the year each team employed its first starting black player or, alternatively, the number of starting positions 1947–60 filled by black players. Using either method, each team falls into one of three categories: those which integrated quickly and strongly; those which integrated slowly and modestly; and those which had not integrated by 1960.

Those teams that delayed integration became less competitive, winning 6.6 fewer games annually during the 1950s. Teams which integrated rapidly averaged 7.2 more wins annually, while those which had not integrated by 1960 averaged 6.6 fewer wins. Particularly, after television revenues changed baseball from a hobby to a business, owners were disciplined to employ ballplayers in a non-discriminatory manner.

Does the baseball example illustrate a general principle of how markets self-regulate or are there special attributes which make the baseball industry a special case which should not be generalized from? In baseball there are wide productivity differentials among players which are not typically found in other occupations. Wide productivity differentials generate large benefits from hiring in a non-discriminatory manner; without these differentials there may be little cost to those who hire in a discriminatory manner. Indeed, since there is little productivity differential among applicants for executive positions in baseball, it is not surprising that in this area of hiring the percentage of black and Latino employees is dramatically lower than their percentage of players.

Government programs to raise the incomes of low-wage workers can also be presented early in the course. In many books this is limited to a discussion of the minimum wage. Certainly this topic should be covered with race and gender dimensions discussed. With respect to race, the lack of evidence in support of the often-voiced contention that the minimum wage disproportionately harms black youth should be presented. Indeed, there is much current research which brings into question the claim that there is a significant disemployment effect. With respect to gender, discussion of the minimum wage can be linked to the low wages adult women without a college degree continue to earn. Thus, a rise in the minimum wage may be one method of bringing gender equity to the nonprofessional labor market.

Rather than waiting until the optional section on poverty, I believe that courses should bring the earned income credit (EIC) program into the discussion when the minimum wage is presented. The EIC program has consistently been promoted as an alternative to the minimum wage and with the 1993 tax bill will have shifted up to $3,560 to qualifying households by 1996. It allows a focus on female-headed households, since they make up a large portion of qualifying households. In addition, it presents an oppor-

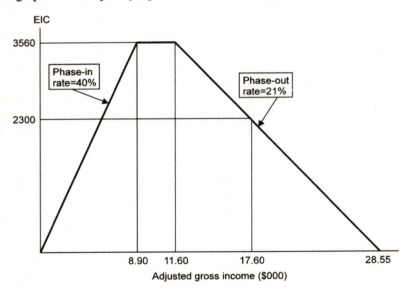

Figure 14.5 Earned Income Credit (EIC) for household with two dependent children

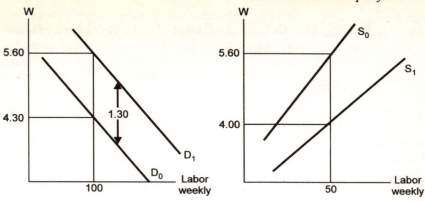

Figure 14.6 Labor vourcher (*left*) and Earned Income Credit program (*right*)

tunity to demonstrate the importance of income and substitution effects. In particular, in the *phase-out* region of the EIC program, there will be a *decline* in labor supply as a result of both the income and substitution effects. This occurs because for each $1 of additional wage income, the EIC to qualifying households declines by $0.21. Finally, the EIC program has an impact on marriage rates, since a qualifying female head of household would generally lose the EIC by marrying a man who is employed.

Finally, traditional courses usually demonstrate how vouchers and subsidies shift supply and demand curves respectively. Rather than using vouchers in output markets— coupons to consumers—labor market examples can be utilized. In particular, pilot programs have tested the impact of providing employment vouchers to black youth as a means of lowering their high unemployment rates. The left-hand panel in Figure 14.6 indicates the impact if an employment voucher equal to $1.30 for each hour the worker is employed was given to workers.

Subsidies to suppliers can also be illustrated with examples from the labor market. In particular, the EIC program in its *phase-in* region is essentially a subsidy program. In that region, households with two dependent children qualify for $0.40 for each $1 of wage income. As a result, a worker in a qualified household would obtain $1.60 in credits for each $4 of wage income. As the right panel indicates, the worker would supply the same fifty hours weekly at $4 per hour after the institution of the EIC program, as she would have at $5.60 per hour without the program. Since these workers are a portion of the total supply in the low-wage labor market, the total labor supply curve is shifted downward, lowering the price paid by labor demanders. Indeed, this vision is undoubtedly one of the reasons why the business community has been a strong proponent of the EIC program. Note that this analysis ignores the impact of the EIC program on the labor supply of households in the phase-out region.

15 Thoughts on teaching Asian-American undergraduates

Akira Motomura

This chapter is part of a volume whose intended audience is economics professors who wish to put more race- and gender-related material into their introductory economics courses or do a better job of handling more diverse classes. This chapter is aimed at the second purpose.

A recent applicant for a responsible position at my institution introduced himself to me by saying, *"Ohaiyo gozaimasu"* (Good morning), a common and appropriate greeting in Japanese. While I'm sure the person meant well, the incident contained a disturbing parallel to the racial insults and hostile comments that Asian Americans endure throughout the United States. He assumed that I was a "foreigner," though he placed less of a negative connotation on that label than would the insult hurlers. At least he knew enough to determine my ancestral country from my name. Nevertheless, he made an incorrect assumption about my personal background, ignoring a history of ethnic Asians in America that dates back to the nineteenth century.

The ignorance of those individuals reflects a broad lack of understanding about Asian Americans. Even as "multiculturalism" has become a buzzword (and lightning rod) on college and university campuses, all too often Asian Americans are assumed to have assimilated with the majority white population or to be "people of color" who can be lumped with African Americans, and, if one is being multicultural rather than bicultural, Latinos and Native Americans. American society often fails to allow for the existence of Asian Americans. A young Asian-American woman I know recently learned this when stopped by the police. In reporting the incident on the radio, the officers involved classified her as "white." The only other possible racial categories were "black" and "unknown."

The assumptions cited above are dubious. While many Asian Americans achieve educational and financial success, and may live in predominantly white neighborhoods, they often do not feel fully accepted on their own terms by whites. Ethnic Asians are distinguishable from whites to the most casual observer, making complete assimilation impossible in a country whose history is full of racial categorization. While people of color face some common struggles in the United States, each racial group has unique elements in its history. Some issues today, like Asian-American–African-American tensions in many cities, highlight rather than suppress the differences among these groups.

In this chapter, I raise issues about Asian-American students for teachers of undergraduate economics and college professors in general to consider. A fundamental point is that ethnic Asian undergraduates in the United States are a very diverse population about whom it is difficult to generalize accurately. I cannot offer readers simple answers or formulas for "how to deal with" Asian-American students. That said, I think my observations will help professors better understand and serve Asian-American students in their classes and on their campuses.

I write from my personal experience as an Asian American who grew up in a West Coast city, was active in an undergraduate Asian-American student group at an Ivy League university in the late 1970s, and has been a faculty advisor to an ethnic Asian student group at a small predominantly white liberal arts college far from any major Asian-American population center. I am not a professional expert on Asians or Asian Americans.

In the next section, I offer some statistical data about Asian Americans as useful background. The following section contains observations and some specific pieces of advice about Asian-American students. The concluding section offers general suggestions about teaching Asian-American students and about dealing with anti-Asian prejudice against those students or your colleagues.

SOME DATA

Asian Americans are a rapidly growing racial group. The 1990 United States Census reported 6.9 million persons whose race was classified as Asian, about 2.8 percent of the total US population. Those numbers indicated rapid growth since 1980. Like other racial groups of color, ethnic Asians are unevenly distributed geographically. The largest numbers live in urban areas like Los Angeles, San Francisco, Honolulu, Seattle, and New York, with smaller communities in Washington, Boston, Philadelphia, and Chicago.

Asian Americans are ethnically diverse. The largest ethnic groups are the Chinese (1.65 million), Filipinos (1.41 million), Japanese (848,000), Asian Indian (814,000), Korean (799,000), and Vietnamese (615,000). The first groups of immigrants, spanning from about 1850 to the 1924 Immigration Act, came mostly from China, Japan, and the Philippines. From 1924 to 1952, Asians could not enter as immigrants. Since the Immigration Act of 1965, they have come from a wider variety of countries. Over 60 percent of ethnic Asians in the 1980 census are foreign-born, but that percentage varies across ethnic groups, from more than 80 percent among Vietnamese and Koreans to less than 30 percent among Japanese. I suspect those percentages are lower among ethnic Asian undergraduates.

Asian Americans attend college in high proportions and are relatively likely to graduate. This academic success goes back to greater success in high school and is correlated with more hours spent studying.

Being an Asian American continues to be an economic disadvantage. Although the mean nominal Asian-American family income exceeds the national average, several factors more than adequately explain that statistic, leaving a negative residual to being Asian American. Those factors are more workers per household, higher educational achievement, and concentration in high cost of living areas like Hawaii, California, and New York (Takaki 1979, pp. 475–6). Within most educational and occupational groups, Asian Americans have lower average incomes than their white counterparts. In every one of the thirteen states with the largest aggregate Asian-American income, the per capita income of Asian Americans is below that of whites. The poverty rate among Asian Americans exceeds that of the general population. Disparities occur throughout the income distribution, suggesting that no explanation specific to one occupational or educational group can fully account for the difference.

There is some evidence of a "glass ceiling" that may particularly concern Asian-American students. Studies of engineers and journalists find that Asian Americans face greater difficulty than white Americans in gaining promotions and managerial positions (Kerwin 1990; Tano 1993).

SOME OBSERVATIONS

As the above data suggest, Asian Americans are a diverse and complex racial group about which it is dangerous to generalize. Nevertheless, some common aspects of culture and experience ease bonding among Asian Americans and distinguish them from persons of other races.

Background and identity

Ethnic Asian students come from a wide variety of backgrounds. There are the US-born, immigrants who came as small children, recent immigrants for whom English is a second or third language, and Asians born and raised in Asia. Some, mainly of Chinese ancestry, have roots in more than one Asian country. Most US-raised ethnic Asians, whom we can define as Asian American, seem to come from neighborhoods in which there are either many ethnic Asians or very few. Those from the suburbs of cities with large Asian-American populations may have either extensive or minimal contact with ethnic Asian communities. Among the Asian-raised, many students are uncertain about whether to settle in the United States after graduation. In deciding, they usually weigh how comfortable they feel in each society and how well they can do professionally. The issue is especially complex for women, who face more traditional social and professional expectations in Asia compared to the United States.

The reader may have noticed that I use the term "Asian American" and not "Oriental." The former has been preferred among younger and now middle-aged Americans of Asian ancestry for more than twenty years, especially on the West Coast. "Oriental" is about as current as "Negro." It carries many negative connotations and defines "Oriental" people with reference to those of European ancestry.

Asian-American students identify themselves in different ways. I mean here what one feels inside, not which box one marks on registration forms asking for race. These differences are not necessarily determined by how long one has lived in the United States. While some see themselves, perhaps wishfully, as true-blue Yankees who just happen to look (and perhaps eat) a little differently from Euro-Americans, others view themselves as more (fill in an Asian country) than American.

These perspectives are stereotypically familiar, but many young Asian Americans do not identify with either one. They see themselves as a mix of American and Asian cultural influences, different from either Americans of other racial groups and from Asians. Students vary in how much they like that self-image. Some embrace an Asian-American identity, while others dislike it even as they accept its accuracy.

For example, as a Japanese American born and raised in the United States, I cannot ever hope to live in Japan as a full member of Japanese society. Unspoken expectations and modes of thinking in Japan are so different from those common in the United States that I could never fully adopt them even if I dedicated myself to doing so. It is appropriately symbolic that, if I filled out an official form in Japan, I would have to write my name in Latin, not Japanese, characters. To "go back where you (or your ancestors) came from" would be similarly impossible for other Asian Americans, including many immigrants.

At the same time, I cannot become a full member of white America. Strangers and acquaintances often think I am foreign because of my facial appearance (it can't be the clothes). Comments about "our" Western or Judeo-Christian heritage exclude my ancestors. From the Naturalization Act of 1790 which reserved naturalized citizenship for whites to the internment of ethnic Japanese during World War II, ethnic Asians have been discriminated against by federal and state governments (Takaki 1979, p14).

Many young Asian Americans view themselves as persons of color, but may not identify completely with other non-whites. Persons of color face some common experiences, especially facing isolation and perhaps discrimination because of skin color or culture. Also widespread is the feeling of uncertainty over whether a slight one has suffered was racially motivated. Even if no racial motive is explicit, race has been so important in American history that many people of color cannot avoid spending mental energy wondering about others' motives. There are wide differences in culture, experiences, identity, and reactions to white society within and across racial groups of color.

Many Asian-American students feel some degree of Asian-American identity that bridges ethnic groups. Some may identify more strongly with their specific ethnic group. Among undergraduates, one's self-identification seems to depend at least three factors. One is that ethnic Asians look alike to many non-Asians and thus endure many of the same misunderstandings, slurs, and innocent but troubling remarks. The most infamous example of anti-Asian-American violence in the early 1980s was the beating to death of Vincent Chin, a Chinese American who was mistaken for Japanese by his assailants, laid-off auto workers.

Second, Asian cultures share common elements relative to other cultures in America, even if Asian cultures differ from each other in absolute terms. Asian Americans find they do not have to explain some experiences and assumptions to each other, reducing the work in socializing. Anyone who has been visibly different in some environment can probably identify with the relief that comes from talking with another from the same culture who already understands aspects of one's background life ranging from eating utensils to family customs. Common experiences provide an opportunity to bond in a more relaxing way for Asian Americans.

A third important factor in self-identification can be the size of the Asian-American student population at a school. Students naturally want to be part of a group. Forging bonds as Asian Americans across ethnicities can expand the group to a better size. The Asian-American Student Association was the dominant formal group among the roughly 300 Asian-American students at my undergraduate institution in the late 1970s. Now, it is an umbrella organization uniting groups dedicated to single ethnicities or to multiracial students among the 800 or so Asian-American undergraduates at the same school.

Campus environments

Asian-American students coming from a wide range of ethnicities and environments must often adapt to a new racial environment in college. Ironically, this is most true at institutions with "multicultural" or "diverse" student bodies in which Asian Americans compose from 3 percent to 10 percent of the population. Being a student of color in such an environment can be a powerful learning experience. One is part of a racial grouping which is small enough to be a minority, yet usually large enough to provide the basis for a group that can generate support and activities.

Students from heavily Asian-American backgrounds must adapt to being part of a numerical minority in an environment where their presence is not as routinely accepted as at home. These adjustments take time. Growing up in San Francisco, I never heard anyone seriously question whether I "belonged" in America. Since leaving California, many have done so, either directly or implicitly. Students find their identity questioned when there are few people around who have shared the experience and can offer advice on how to cope.

Asian-American students from backgrounds with few other Asian Americans often wonder if they are supposed to feel a bond to other Asian Americans on campus. This issue is especially difficult if the students have ancestral homelands which are traditional enemies or if they have opposing political ideologies which may be closely related to family histories. Many have never encountered an Asian-American organization before and must decide whether to join, an act which broadcasts an unsubtle message about one's self-perception to Asians and non-Asians. Students from predominantly white backgrounds often already feel like outsiders at home, belonging to but not feeling fully part of the crowd. As a sample of one, a student cannot know: Is it me? The way I look? My parents' quirks? Their Asian culture? Some students from predominantly white environments embrace the chance to learn more about their cultural roots through other Asian Americans, while others reject any contact with groups of Asian Americans, either informal or formal.

While each student has a right to make an individual choice about his/her associations, it seems important for non-Asians to recognize that Asian-American students can learn a lot from spending time with each other, within and across ethnic lines. They can learn about what elements of their background, culture, and history are common and different; I certainly did. The experience is all the richer if Asian students are around to relate what it's like in the ancestral homeland. Students can more easily discern what's Korean, Japanese, Asian, or Asian American. There is no substitute for this experience, especially at schools lacking courses that examine Asian-American history and culture. Once these students leave the academy, the diverse "multicultural" community will never exist for them again.

Campus environments facing Asian Americans vary widely. A large number of Asian Americans makes any single Asian face unremarkable and usually means that more non-Asian students will have Asian-American friends. On the other hand, Asian Americans may be viewed as a threatening group, giving rise to resentments like those which have led some to call UCLA the University of Caucasians Living among Asians. Institutions with few Asian-American students may think they do not have an "Asian problem." Instead, they may have students who feel isolated or conspicuous, or who are the objects of racial attacks. Those students are often viewed as foreigners by non-Asians who have had little exposure to Asian Americans. Overall, there may be no correlation between the size or share of the Asian-American student population and the net balance of attitudes toward Asian Americans.

The "model minority" myth and Asian culture

Economic and educational success for some and low levels of political activity have fed a myth of Asian Americans as a "model minority" that is in many ways harmful. While the stereotype is based on real accomplishments by some, it masks real difficulties faced by Asian Americans and sometimes imposes trying stresses. Instructors might examine whether they have any preconceptions of their Asian-American students or assistants based on race rather than on individual behavior.

Asian culture can exert a strong influence even on US-born Asian Americans. Parental authority tends to be great in ethnic Asian families. The primacy of age discourages speaking up to elders, a tendency that can inhibit students from "bothering" their professors by asking questions or seeking help. These tendencies to be quiet may be reinforced by the relative lack of emphasis on verbal expression in Asian culture and by a desire to avoid calling attention to oneself, because of racial difference or language difficulty for some. Professors might take more initiative to encourage Asian-American students to see them or speak up in class.

Asian-American students who succeed tend to do so for the usual reasons, but success is often twisted into a negative stereotype. Uri Treisman (1992) found that Chinese-American students at the University of California did well in calculus largely because they learned from older students that long hours (often more than the professor stated) were necessary to succeed and they discussed their homework in groups. Treisman's incorporation of the "secrets" of success into explicit course expectations and structure has been very successful with other students of color at Berkeley and the University of Texas. I cite this study not to suggest that Asian Americans are a "model minority" for other persons of color. Instead, I maintain that behavior we admire in students like hard work and application of effective study methods are often twisted into negative stereotypes ("work all the time," "clannish") when talking about ethnic Asians. Are members of the swim team criticized for their disciplined lives when successful? Is a racial inference drawn? Also, Treisman's work suggests ways in which economics professors can help students who come to college lacking inside knowledge of the secrets to success in problem-solving fields like economics.

Asian Americans' visibility and success in mathematics and the natural sciences can combine with strong parental influence to exert unreasonable pressures on Asian-American students whose interests lie elsewhere or who struggle in science courses. Even A-students may be affected. Young Asian Americans talk knowingly about their parents' high expectations and efforts to steer their offspring toward math and science majors and beyond into the medical or engineering professions. That parental pressure often comes from good intentions. Many parents believe their children are less likely to encounter discrimination in forms like the glass ceiling or political tests in fields that have more "objective" standards. Immigrant parents fear their children will be disadvantaged in fields where mastery of English is important.

A possible implication for economics professors is that talented Asian-American students may not pursue economics or some supposedly more "subjective" fields related to it like business or public policy out of unspoken fear rather than lack of interest. Professors might try to get a more complete picture of a student's true interests, and encourage those who seem to be fearful of pursuing their real interests to do so. If racism persists in economics or business, it presumably also does in the sciences. Also, entering non-stereotypical professions is an important part of breaking down stereotypes. Don't ask students to be pioneers, but do encourage them to do what will give them greatest enjoyment and satisfaction.

While I have written mostly about how Asian Americans differ from the white majority, they also differ from other persons of color. For example, Asian Americans seem less likely to be politically active. I suspect this is true within socio-economic strata. Many Asian Americans prefer to deal with the specter of discrimination by avoiding politics or open confrontation. This strategy may comfort many whites, but it is not necessarily the most effective way to deal with the problem. Undergraduate political activity can profoundly change the lives of those students who become active.

Gender, interracial relations, and identities

Interracial sexual relations are an explosive topic among Asian Americans, as they are among other Americans of color. Because they are often on students' minds, I mention them here. Relationships involving Asian-American women with men of other races, like those in the novel and movie *Joy Luck Club* are more common and even trendy on the West Coast, while Asian-American man–white woman relationships are less common. The gender differential creates tensions among Asian Americans. Interracial marriage is common, with rates of 50 percent or higher sometimes quoted for Japanese Americans. Interracial marriage is very controversial, as some consider it to be something predictable in a multiracial society, while others see it as promoting the extinction of Asian-American culture.

Gender roles can play out in unexpected ways among Asian Americans. Some Asian-American women rationalize a preference for non-Asian men on a stereotype of Asian men as being too quiet or too authoritarian in their relationships. While many Asian-American men may be less vocal or more authoritarian than American men in general (if such traits can be measured), that characterization is certainly not universally true. The popularity of Asian-American women in interracial relationships is often based on a stereotype that they are more submissive than American women in general. In terms of educational expectations, there are cases of daughters in Asian immigrant families being discouraged from pursuing professions (more than college) while their brothers are encouraged. On the other hand, Asian-American women seem more likely to attend college and to major in scientific fields than are American women in general.

The offspring of interracial marriages face complex issues of identity. Some large universities have groups of partly Asian multiracial students.

While as recently as ten years ago many such students came from American GI–Asian woman marriages, multiracial undergraduates are increasingly likely to be the offspring of two Americans, with some having Asian-American fathers. They vary widely in how they view themselves. Racially unmixed Asian Americans tend to accept multiracial persons as fellow Asian Americans, but acceptance is not universal. This pattern resembles that among other racial groups of color. Whether one's last name is Asian or European can be important among those who do not know each other well.

Some students are biologically Asian but adopted by non-Asian families. A large percentage of these are Korean women. The students I have known have experienced a wide range of support from their adoptive parents in learning about their country of birth. College offers some of these students their first opportunity to know others who are viewed similarly because of facial appearance and to learn about growing up Asian-American. These interracial adoptees face great complications in shaping their identity while undergraduates.

SOME CONCLUDING ADVICE

Given these observations, how can professors deal with Asian-American students in a more sensitive way? How can they deal with the display or possibility of racism against Asian Americans? Just as one cannot make strong generalizations about Asian Americans, it is impossible to offer a simple formula for how to act. I offer some general advice to supplement the more specific pointers scattered throughout the last section. Some ideas are general but more applicable to Asian Americans and perhaps students of color more broadly. Its usefulness depends on the situation at your institution.

First, remember that young Asian Americans are often forced to confront their identity and their relation to society. Students of color often try different images on for size. Asian-American students face additional pressures from negotiating a new racial environment that is often politicized. They may change views even within a semester; don't assume the radical firebrand of the first week won't sound like a mainstream conservative by the end of the semester, or vice versa.

Clear course expectations may eliminate unnecessary anxiety or failure for those students who do not have inside information on how to succeed in college courses. If you assign "killer" problems that are meant to stretch the best students rather than serve as simple exercises, say so. If you expect creative or synthetic thinking in an assignment, it will help willing but unknowing students if you make that clear.

In terms of course content, readers of this volume can include data on Asian Americans where possible; some of the references in this chapter may help as a start. The growing Asian-American population is making it easier for researchers to get large enough samples for good econometric studies.

Be alert for signs of racism or unfriendly ignorance which may be directed at students, teaching assistants, or colleagues. Sometimes prejudice is coded, as in complaints made at one university (with hundreds of Asian-American undergraduates) about the "accent" of an Asian-American TA who was born and raised in California. How you deal with a situation depends on the particulars and your personality. Sometimes you can put the issue in non-racial terms, perhaps by telling students to pay attention to fellow students who speak in class; or commenting that hard work is necessary for any student to do well in a course. At other times it may be best to confront the racial issue directly. Personally, I like seeing racists made to look absurd with a biting question or comment. This strategy may be most effective in situations like the one above in which the complaint is coded, groundless, and based on a false assumption. ('So, what is it about his California accent that makes him so difficult to understand?') Some complaints must be taken more seriously but can be turned into educational experiences. You might ask yourself how Europeans who have spent a comparable amount of time living in the United States would be treated in a parallel situation. Be careful not to indulge prejudices. Use your judgment about whether to make some preemptive mention about anti-Asian prejudice if it has been a problem on your campus; I face an inherently different situation than do most readers of this chapter. Asian-American TAs and junior faculty will generally, I think, appreciate a clear private indication that you, as a head instructor or senior colleague, will be supportive if they experience any race-related problems; don't signal this support unless you mean it.

Last but not least, learn more about the Asian and Asian-American students at your school. Go beyond the aggregated numbers or percentages in official sources and get a sense of the individuals and distribution, even if you are a macroeconomist. Encouraging students to speak to you and listening to them will help you to avoid the stereotyping against which I've cautioned in this chapter. Where do the students come from? What are their families like? What kind of reaction do they get from other students on campus? Is there an active organization of Asian-American students? What are they up to? Don't assume an Asian-American student in your class will know these things or trust you enough to discuss their feelings about race right away. You might begin by asking students less threatening questions about their academic lives or about their future plans. Listening to and knowing about one's students is useful for effective teaching; one often has to work more to learn about minority populations. Asian Americans are a diverse group, just as other groups of students are, be they Euro-Americans, African Americans, Latinos, athletes, musicians, suburbanites, or economics majors. Don't assume a representative student.

BIBLIOGRAPHY

Bunzel, J. and Au, J. (1987) "Diversity or Discrimination: Asian-Americans in College," *The Public Interest* 87 (spring): 55.

Commission on Wartime Relocation and Internment of Civilians (1982) *Personal Justice Denied*, Washington, DC: Government Printing Office.

Gall, S. B. and Gall, T. L. (1993) *Statistical Record of Asian Americans*, Detroit: Gale Research, 479–515.

Kerwin, A. M. (1990) "Asian Americans and Journalism," *Editor and Publisher* 123, 36 (September 8): 18.

Portes, A. and Rumbaut R. G. (1990) *Immigrant America: A Portrait*, Berkeley: University of California, 192–5.

Takaki, R.T. *Iron Cases*. New York, NY: Alfred A. Knopf, 1979.

Tano, J. (1993) "The Career Attainment of Caucasian and Asian Engineers," *Sociological Quarterly* 34, 3 (fall): 467– 96.

Treisman, U. (1992) "Studying Students Studying Calculus: A Look at the Lives of Minority Mathematics Students in College," *College Mathematics Journal* 23, 5 (November): 362–72.

United States Bureau of the Census (1990) *Census of Population and Housing Summary*, Tape File 1C.

16   Some thoughts on teaching predominantly affective-oriented groups

Vernon J. Dixon

This chapter evolves in the following way. First, there is a brief presentation of the traits that characterize the term "predominantly affective-oriented groups." Second, there ensue some suggestions, when teaching such groups, about adjustments in some of the introductory course content. Third, and finally, a very brief section will be offered on some pedagogical styles that may facilitate the educational interaction between professors and affective-oriented groups. Since space constraints will not permit a thorough and rigorous development of these ideas, an apology is offered. Hopefully, the thoughts set forth below will excite you to ruminate about your own experiences, to critique your categories of analyses and to apply any results in your own way.

PREDOMINANTLY AFFECTIVE-ORIENTED GROUPS

The non-exhaustive set of traits discussed below does not imply that only these traits characterize people in affective-oriented groups; rather, it implies that this set of traits is dominant, relative to their embodiment of alternative sets, i.e. their dominant profile or their first-order preference. No attempt can be undertaken here to evaluate the degree of pervasiveness of these set of traits, i.e. their variation in differing situations or among differing classes. Several traits which may assist in understanding an affective framework are: (a) language, (b) values concerning nature, human relations and time, and (c) knowledge production.

Language

In an affective-oriented view of the world, there is no gap or separation among people, nature and the supernatural. One is simply an extension of the other. Their unity creates a conception of wholeness. There is no separation of the self; rather the self must feel, must experience, must internalize, must personalize the phenomenal world. There is no distance, no discontinuity, no gap, no empty perceptual space between the self and the phenomenal world. The self is one with it. One affective group reflects this personification of the inanimate in their use of language: "That record is saying something," "That sound is bad," "The eagles fly on Friday," or "You put the hurt on me." (In effect, the phenomenal world becomes personalized, a "person," a "thou.")

This usage involves words whose meanings are embedded in a specific phenomenal context. Words are concrete, with much use of visual and tactile symbols, for example, money eagles, bread, bundle, a little bit of dust (primarily welfare payments). Meaning depends upon the unique context of the event, its time and place, the characteristics of the interacting communicants' age, sex, authority, social relationships to each other—and other non-verbal clues such as inflection, body movements, etc. When spoken, the language is characterized by fluency, by the use of strong and colorful expressions which are intended to communicate and to evoke emotion, and by a wide range of vocal intonation and inflection. All this is consistent with the orientation of non-separation of self from the phenomenal world. Accordingly, the use of non-affective English becomes very difficult for affective-oriented groups because it obscures, by either the speaker or the writer, non-verbal clues in its expression of meaning.

Values

Nature

Arising from an affective view of themselves and the phenomenal world as mutually interdependent, they experience themselves in harmony with nature. Their aim is to maintain balance or harmony among the various aspects of the universe. Disequilibrium may result in troubles such as human illness, drought, or social disruption. Illness, for example, may take the form of the "miseries" where no empirical measures of sickness (temperature, congestion, etc.) are present, yet they are physically incapacitated as if they had the flu. They personalize nature and work with its elements; magic, voodoo, herbs, mysticism are the use of forces in nature to restore a more harmonious relationship between man and the universe. Technology also has this characteristic of working with nature. According to my grandfather, Trinidadians undertook voyages spanning many hundreds of miles of open ocean with techniques that did not include even a compass, chronometer, sextant, or star tables. Instead of technology which masters nature, they relied on the direction of the wind and waves, the sound of the waves hitting the hull, the feel of the boat traveling through water, and, on a clear night, the rising and setting of the stars. Reports exist of similar phenomenona for Truskee sailors.

Human relations

Affective-oriented groups view the individual's position in social space this way—"I am, because we are; and since we are, therefore I am." Whatever happens to the individual happens to the whole group, and whatever happens to the whole group happens to the individual. The individual becomes conscious only in terms of other people of his/her own being, duties, privileges, and responsibilities towards himself/herself and others. Thus, the individual suffers and rejoices not alone but with kinsmen, relatives, and neighbors, i.e. the corporate group. During the 1970s, the Trinidadian government paid all its employees a bonus of a half-year's salary. Rather than save and invest this windfall gain, virtually all Trinidadians ceased working and had a two-week fete. Similar communal rejoicing occurs when an affective person hits the numbers. Alternatively, in a housing complex in Watts, California, set up along the lines of a *ujamaa* village, people who had moved away returned in order to regain their individual identity created or produced by that community. Critical functions such as leadership, child care and discretionary use of funds were widely and periodically shared by all members of the group. These functions were not formally defined and attached to statuses. Furthermore, in a communal orientation, an individual cannot refuse to act in any critical capacity when called upon to do so. For example, affective-oriented persons unquestioningly going against their own personal welfare for other group members, even though the former know that the latter are wrong. They will cosign loans for friends, while aware that their friends will default and that their own finances will suffer. An orientation towards interpersonal relationships has predominance over a purely personal one.

Effectively, value is embodied in the affiliated relationship among individuals. Sensitivities become predominantly affiliation-oriented and affective persons, with this view, attain their highest self-value through the maximization of interpersonal harmony and satisfaction of their group. This affiliative orientation has relevance in the problem of adoption and pregnant, unmarried, affective mothers. Children obtain the benefits of the strengths inherent in an extended family rather than "get ahead" through adoption by a nuclear family. Old people are considered part of extended families; they have affiliation roles in the household as models for children and as purveyors of oral history and culture, rather than being sent to nursing homes or old people's towns. In this context, children become a form of saving and investment for old age. Finally, this maximization of interpersonal affiliation means in economics that the marginal conditions (based on assumptions of independent utility and production functions) for optimal resource allocation no longer hold.

Time

For predominantly affective groups, time has to be experienced in order to make sense or become real. The future constitutes part of time, only as part of the rhythm of natural events, such as sunrise, sunsets, etc. The drive for future-oriented investment becomes substantially less important. The unison of affective people with their phenomenal world also means that time becomes felt and continuous. It is not numerical or linear. Rather there are *phenomenon calendars*. Time is a composition of events that are experienced or felt. For example, among some affective-oriented groups, August may be called "The Sun," because the sun is very hot at that time. Yet this may be for twenty, thirty, or forty numeral days. The actual number of days is irrelevant, since a month is in terms of felt phenomena rather than reckoned in mathematical terms. Without the assumption of the linearity of time, such notions as upward social mobility or the calculation of future benefits from saving money or the present value of future net benefits are qualitatively less significant.

This felt time orientation, for example, appears in some African Americans in their operation according to "CP time" or in "Hawaiian time" for some Hawaiians or in "Indian time" for some Native Americans. Time-scheduled, planned activities simply do not take precedence over a person continuing to respond to other events in which he/she is immediately experiencing. For example, a mental health clinic in Watts, California, was facing 80 percent no-show rates for prearranged, psychological counseling appointments, thereby losing state reimbursement funds. Our research revealed that clients would appear on other days as "walk-ins," for which there were no state reimbursements. They came to the clinic only when they felt they needed help, which only accidentally corresponded to their prearranged appointments. To them, it made no sense to "bottle up" feelings until some set future date arrived; or to come at that date, if there were no felt need. A simple switch to a procedure of phoning for an appointment on the day a felt need arose resulted thereafter in a 78 percent show rate.

Knowledge production

The concern here is not intelligence. Rather, the focus is on how, or the way in which one knows reality or phenomena; i.e. the grounds or method of knowledge. The affective-oriented mode of knowing reality I call Affect-Symbolic Imagery Cognition. Affective-oriented persons know reality predominantly through the interaction of Affect and Symbolic Imagery, i.e. the synthesis of these two factors, like the Marshallian cutting action of two blades of a scissors, produces knowledge. Affect refers to the feeling self, the emotive self engaged in experiencing phenomena holistically. For example, affective plumbers who fix sinks may also include as part of the experience the enjoyment of a "rap" or conversation and, perhaps, even a "taste" or drink. Similarly, affective-oriented football players have to experience their scoring touchdowns not only by crossing the goal line, but also by "doing their thing" in the end-zone. Affect personalizes the phenomenal world. It is one factor in the affective mode of knowing. Affect, however, is not intuition, for the latter term means direct or immediate knowledge (instinctive knowledge) without resource to inference from or reasoning about evidence.

Affect does interact with evidence, evidence in the form of Symbolic Imagery.

For example, consider the way in which Trinidadian and Hawaiian sailors came to know the proper ocean course to travel between islands without the use of mechanical aids. Although aware of their destinations, they could not plot beforehand or *a priori* their courses on a chart. The courses could only be formulated *ad hoc*, i.e. as they usually sailed towards their destinations. Their Affects had to experience and integrate with the combinations of motion, sounds, wave patterns, wind directions and force all unknown until actually encountered. These latter factors were symbolic images necessary for cognition. In effect, the input (these images and the feeling self) and its synthesis were a continuous process involving multiple simultaneous operations to produce output (the knowledge of the actual course). It is undeniable that this process of navigating between islands reflects a high order of intellectual functioning.

Since symbolic images convey multiple meanings, are there discernible principles or generalizations by which these many meanings are weighted and combined in order to obtain the meaning that is reality, for example, the proper course? Verbal, discernible principles or generalizations exist. One form of these generalizations is the proverbs of affective groups. Proverbs represent the collective experience of the community as a whole. They arise from the analyses of various generations of peoples, each generation testing the veracity of its proverbs and, if valid, passing them on to the succeeding generations. Areaw and Dundes (1964: no. 6) point out that:

> The impersonal power of proverbs is perhaps most apparent in the well-known African judicial processes in which the participants argue with proverbs intended to serve as past precedents for action. In European courtrooms of course, lawyers cite previous cases to support the validity of their arguments. In African legal ritual, an advocate of a cause uses proverbs for the same purpose. Here, clearly it is not enough to know the proverbs; it is also necessary to be expert in applying them to new situations. The case usually will be won, not by the man who knows the most proverbs, but by the man who knows best how to apply the proverbs he knows to the problem at hand.

As a consequence, it is not surprising that proverbs provide principles of analysis for major events. Consider the analysis of the boycott of the 1979 Olympics. Congolese Jean-Claude Ganga, general secretary of the Supreme Council for Sports in Africa and a director of that boycott, offered the following analysis on how it could have been averted by certain actions of New Zealand:

> Just deploring apartheid isn't enough. When the crocodile is hitting you, it's crying at the same time. You need acts and action, not only declarations.

> (*New York Times*, July 21, 1996: 21)

In this context, Malcolm X used a principle or proverb to analyze the particular details of the assassination of President Kennedy—"a case of chickens coming home to roost." He was harshly condemned by the press. In effect, Malcolm had used a proverb as a criterion for synthesizing the input of his Affect and the Symbolic imagery of government actions. The US government could not hatch assassination plots of foreign leaders (Castro, for example) without giving birth to similar plots of its own leaders. Alternatively, others stated: what goes around, comes around. In sum, Affect–Symbolic Imagery Cognition means this: "I feel phenomena; therefore I think; I know."

INTRODUCTORY ECONOMIC CONTENT

The purpose of this section is to offer some suggestions for recasting the usual introductory economic content to introduce the traits of pre-dominantly affective-oriented groups. More specifically, we will focus on (a) economic goals, (b) human activity, and (c) hypothesis testing.

Economic goals

Consider a definition of economics in which rational action implies seeking to minimize the effect of the use of available means or outlays, i.e. a logic of rational choice which aims at the maximization of preferences—utility for the household and profits for the business firm. On the basis of the assumptions of absolute consumer sovereignty, independent utility and production functions, static time, a uniform motivation for all economic action of the maximization of private gain (expressed in monetary terms), and on the basis of other simplifying assumptions summarized in the notion of perfect competition, economists can state the optimum use of scarce resources in very simple terms: an equilibrium between demand and supply within a pattern of relative prices which corresponds to marginal costs and marginal utilities, and a remuneration of the factors of production which corresponds to their marginal productivities.

As a consequence, the institutional conditions of the optimal allocation of resources are those of the free play of the classical market mechanisms, in both national and international economics. For the latter, the principle of comparative advantage provides the foundation for the international division of labor and trade. Additionally, the "economic laws" of this static analysis (the law of diminishing returns, etc.) are stated un-equivocally and are considered to be universally valid, i.e. independent of specific social, historical, and cultural contexts. The definition or assump-tion of economic rationality means the conquering of spontaneous, erratic, transitory impulses and temptations in the use of scarce resources, or else the lack of impulse control must, in a contradictory fashion, be systematic.

The rigorous application of the rules of economic calculation to the comparability of diverse ends and means requires their expression in a *numeraire* such as money. Thus, the maximization of preferences, utility, and profits involves the acquisition of money and ultimately goods and services (Objects). In this context, there follow naturally such notions as "consumerism"—the unrestricted pursuit of utility or pleasure through the acquisition and use of an ever-increasing volume and variety of goods and services; and "growth-fetishism"—the attachment of exaggerated importance to growth indices as decisive criteria of the efficiency of an economic system or policies that exclude non-economic factors such as the quality of life, etc. Increasing technological innovations in the form of mastery-over-nature, then, become important as a way of reducing any bending constraints of scarce means in order to increase output.

For an affective-oriented group that unites the emotive self and the phenomenal world, a single aspect of behavior can be understood only in its context of interconnection and interaction with other aspects. The optimum use of scarce means or the principle of economic rationality, therefore, has meaning only in relation with other phenomena to which the feeling self relates. That is to say, the repairing of sinks by affective-oriented plumbers (production of useful goods and services) has meaning only in relation to their production of utility for themselves and their customers, through their mutual engagement in the enjoyment of a "rap" and "taste." Alternatively, a chief in Africa had been entrusted with a friend's sheep which died. He gave his friend a sheep in compensation, then another, finally a third, and for good measure 100 francs as well. Only then could his friend forget the sorrow of having lost his sheep. In this interactive process, each element impinges upon others and is, in turn, acted upon by them. Optimization or the search for principles that fulfill the principle of economic rationality is relative to its phenomenal context and is sociohistorically conditioned. With this affective orientation of universal oneness, we may, for example, still speak heuristically of economics, sociology, history, etc., but these categories merge into one discipline. As a consequence, the content of assumptions and models includes factors which traditional economics considers given from other disciplines and/or subjective.

Human relations

The assumption of consumer sovereignty places the individual in the center of social space in economics in the form of the assumption of independent utility functions, i.e. one argument is not simultaneously in two or more utility functions, as an individual pursues his/her self-interest. Such preference functions effectively rule out any interpersonal comparisons of utility, given the present immeasurability of cardinal utility. Welfare economics erected an entire prescriptive system on the assumption of the existence of such functions, subject to maximization. Accordingly, the Pareto formulation of optimality means that social welfare is increased only if the satisfaction of an individual can be increased without decreasing another person's satisfaction in his/her own estimation. More sophisticatedly, social welfare increases where the gainers can compensate the losers and the former still be better off. In any event, the definition of what increases *social* welfare depends on what increases *individual* welfare. Theoretically there is no recognition of the common welfare as such. In an orientation of individualism there is no conception of the group as a whole, except as a summation of individuals. In addition, this welfare formulation assumes the structure of income distribution, is given from outside. Thus, the redistribution of income or the enjoyment of individuals through systematically sharing their goods with others is not considered in that view of economic welfare. Some recent theoretical work on income redistribution also indicates similar individualistic orientations, treating income redistribution as one good in the utility function of an individual or using interdependent utilities, but requiring that transfers be Pareto optimal. Finally, the concept of externality together with the compensation principle also implicitly reflects, for analogous reasons, the orientation of individualism.

The affective orientation means the assumption of the maximization of affiliative or interpersonal and group preferences. According to affective orientation, they pursue both self-interest and non-self-interest, i.e. their own welfare, the welfare of others, and the welfare of the group. In turn, these latter two welfares are at the same time their own welfare. In economic parlance, individual utility is also collective utility and conversely. Consider, for example, the problem of the allocation of a given sum (means) to one of two firms to erect housing in an Afro-American community (end). One is a low-cost firm located outside the community, which can supply 23,000 housing units; the other is a high-cost company located within the community which can supply 19,000 units. Traditionally oriented economics would theoretically dictate allocation to the firm which optimizes the use of scarce resources based on the principle of comparative advantage. Thus, the external firm, supplying the maximum real product, receives the contract, unless the community firm can advance successfully an infant industry argument.

A more sophisticated theoretical formulation for allocating funds to the community firm could be a variant of Johnson's (1992) theory of protectionism. First, the assumption is made that there exists a collective preference for the development of housing production in the community which yields a flow of satisfaction independent of the utility derived directly from the consumption of housing. This assumption of a "preference for industrial housing development" as a collective consumption leads to a maximization of real income consisting of the individual utilities from the consumption of housing and the collective utility from the joint consumption by community members from having their own housing firm. In this context, the real product, forgone 4,000 housing units, becomes a cost of the development of the community's housing firm that may be offset by the utility of joint consumption. The allocation to the community firm that formerly may have been a suboptimal use of resources may now become optimal.

These analyses, however, are not consistent with an affective orientation. The first analysis does not consider collective utility, while the second separates individual and collective utilities. The utility derived from the consumption of the 19,000 units produced by the community firm is also the collective utility of the community. In this view, the forgone 4,000 units are neither costs nor losses of any type of utility. Similar paradoxical identity of seemingly contradictory utilities occurs in affective behavior set forth earlier. Consider the previously cited situation of an affective individual cosigning a note for a friend whom he/she knows will default. The former has, at the same time, positive utility from helping his/her friend and negative utility from the effects of his/her defaulting. Alternatively, consider an affective individual who shares his/her income with members of his/her extended family. The marginal conditions for optimal resource allocation no longer hold. For example, the affective individual's wages, the social marginal cost, do not adequately reflect his/her private marginal cost, since part of his/her earnings is analogous to rent paid to non-productive factors, i.e. members of his/her extended family. Similarly, price, the social marginal utility of the goods purchased by the individual, no longer indicates his/her own private marginal utility, since the latter includes the private marginal utilities of a number of other consumers. In sum, affective-oriented evaluations allow for the simultaneity of individual and collective utility as well as positive and negative ones.

The marginal productivity theory which measures accomplishment in a form external to the individual has limited validity for understanding affective behavior. More relevant is the degree of the union between one's individual utility and that of others and the group. For example, my research on manpower training programs in the Bedford–Stuyvesant area revealed a successful completion rate (job placements) of 21 percent of the enrollees over a seventeen-month period (Dixon 1973: 13–28). Many of the dropouts had finished the program, but did not obtain employment. They simply refused to go for a job interview without the accompaniment of each other. In part, this reflected their need to express intertwined utilities.

Hypothesis testing

The mode that characterizes the method of verification in economics is the use of quantifiable measures as a basis for knowing economic behavior. For example, ends and means expressed in money terms become fully comparable and allow for the strict application of the rules of economic calculation to determine net advantages or disadvantages. This empirical orientation toward measurement appears in the remarkable expansion of quantitative methods of economic analysis. Some have evolved into several new disciplines such as econometrics, programming theory, operations research, etc. Theoretical hypotheses are formulated in such a manner that they can be tested by statistical methods. There are very few aspects of economic behavior in which some attempt is not made to approach the phenomena quantitatively.

Specifically, econometric methods are widely used in impartial analysis to statistically verify the interdependence of two or more variables. These variables usually result from the narrow formulation of working hypotheses, whose validity the econometric testing serves to confirm or reject. In this way, concrete, quantitative regularities in economic behavior become knowable. These hypotheses or models are stated in terms of cause (independent variables) and effect (dependent variables). This construct establishes an exclusive relationship between two events or two sets of events. In effect, the separation of these variables from the rest of the phenomenal world through the use of *ceteris paribus* attributes to them more power and significance for explaining reality than they really possess. If all events are part of a total, continuous interacting network of reality, then the *ceteris paribus* approach becomes an interruption in this unity. In turn, the introduction of differential, difference and probability calculus, game theory, decision theory, etc., reinforce the notion of precision in economics even though the difficulties of measuring (utility, wealth, etc.) and of aggregating economic magnitudes are still present. Effectively, then, economists have a predisposition towards measurement and precision, whether in the form of mathematics, statistics, money prices, shadow prices, or quantitative probabilities, etc.

The affective-oriented method of verification of models and hypotheses follows naturally from the affective nature of knowledge production. This mode of verification involves the synthesis of the feeling self with evidence in the form of words, gestures, things, forces, numbers, etc. Researchers are participant observers, involved observers. They are part of what is being observed through their affective selves. They become part of the lives of the people, while at the same time seeking to understand the forces which mold them and to which they respond. This permits researchers to unite their affects with symbolic imageries of the evidence obtained.

While one form of useful evidence may be quantitative measures, they do not, in and of themselves, become the criteria for verification. It is the structural design of the numbers, the context and way in which they are spoken or written that reflects the symbolic image of their mathematical properties. My African friends, for example, speak of "reading" a number, not of counting a number. Their mathematical processes are expressed in image symbols rather than abstract symbols. As yet, no method, to my knowledge, has been developed to express the meaning of these image symbols in standard English form.

Unlike squares, triangles, etc., affective-oriented measures appear as forces or rhythmic circles arrived at through situational experiencing. Thus, affective researchers must circularize cause-and-effect models, statistics, and current econometric techniques, connecting their symbolic imagery with their affects. An analogous process occurs for non-affective-oriented researchers. They sometimes make numerical adjustments, for example, in the results of their econometric forecasting models in order to bring the predicted numerical results into closer harmony with the forecaster's perception of economic reality. This ability to make such refinements is hopefully developed by the process of osmosis during graduate training and nurtured subsequently by specialized immersion in the discipline. Kuhn (1970) makes a similar observation in speaking about experience presented during education and professional initiation. He claims that "we have too long ignored the manner in which the knowledge of nature can be tacitly embodied in whole experiences without intervening abstraction of criteria or generalizations". One aspect of this tacit knowledge I term "economic sense." Its use, however, is generally referred to as the practice of the "art" of economic research.

In contrast, affective researchers embody and nurture this ability and it is an integral, systematic part of verification in the use of any data, quantitative or not. As indicated previously, there is control or discipline over the possible distortion by the research in his analysis. It is the collective experience or judgment of the affective community as a whole in the form of proverbs, folk wisdom, etc. This proverbial repertoire, therefore, provides the principles and generalizations that ensure the correspondence of the analysis with the area of affective reality.

For example, consider "The price of your hat ain't the measure of your brain." This is the principle that external symbols, *per se*, are not reliable indicators of individual abilities. In economic parlance, the renumeration of a factor, in and of itself, does not measure its marginal product. Alternatively, consider the role of proverbs as a decision rule for researchers in whether to recommend the allocation of housing funds to the community or external firm. One principle which embodies this Afro-American characteristic of affirmation by negation (something "bad" is good) is the following: "If you're White, you're right; if you're Black, step back." Stated differently, any proposal originated by the Afro-American community as a community which improves their own welfare in their own estimation will have a very high probability of not being funded for successful implementation. Therefore, the proposal is verifiably good for increasing black collective welfare and should be recommended.

Non-affective-oriented researchers, on the other hand, would prefer to generate some quantitative proxy of collective black utility. For example, if during riots only externally owned businesses were looted and burned, then the monetary value of these businesses might be one proxy measure of the value of the collective community preference for acquiring their own productive facilities. This value may offset the loss in housing units that results from the lower output of the community firm. In contrast to the need for some quantifiable measure, affective researchers as participant observers in the community know through Affect–Symbolic Imagery the value that the community gains through producing their own housing. In similar fashion, they know the value of the non-market, reciprocal repair work, construction, etc. done in the community that never appears in the gross national product, since it cannot be verified by conventional measures of quantification.

PEDAGOGICAL STYLES

There are at least two suggestions that flow from the foregoing. First, affective groups respond more readily to a teaching style that is termed "call and response." This refers to an arrangement where the professor is simultaneously a teacher of the class and a student in the class. It is a pedagogical technique consistent with the affective orientation of affiliative relations or inter- and intra-personal utilities. During this teacher-as-teacher presentation of the material, whether in the interrogatory or declarative voice (the call), students are free to speak to what you say and/or to what other students are saying (the response). These latter responses inform and educate the teacher-as-student. This of course is the teaching arrangement that characterizes, for example, many African-American church meetings or Native-American powwows or Hawaiian gatherings.

The second pedagogical style involves becoming, as much as is feasible, a member of the affective group whom you are teaching through "in-dwelling" their set of affective-oriented traits. One may undertake this rather difficult task in the Jungian sense of "I am and I am not and that which I am not is also part of me." Such undertaking should facilitate the teacher seeing better the inherent power of the current economic paradigms as well as their significant limitations. In turn, these limitations should provide knowledge of the nature of the difficult avenue that affective-oriented groups of students must travel if they wish to arrive at a common destination of gaining a powerful category of analyses together with a way of critiquing this category.

CONCLUSION

This chapter has set forth some ideas about teaching affective-oriented groups that devolve from a consideration of their language, their values, and their knowledge production. Limited validity but never absolute validity may be defended for these affective traits. Consider, for example, the actual case of a group of affective-oriented African Americans who decided to put on a community festival in Los Angeles one year. They planned together, they worked together. Since they had little money, each member of the community donated their respective skills and/or materials for various tasks. Some tasks demanded more time and effort than others. The festival was a resounding success. Next year, the local government provided funds to put on the festival. Unfortunately, community members began to set a money value on their formerly donated services. Competition based on self-interest emerged among members of the community. Each sought to maximize his/her *own* acquisition of money. People demanded justification for why some members were receiving more money than they. The festival had become an object divorced from themselves. Acquisition of numerical dollars determined their self-worth rather than the growth in the harmony of interpersonal and collective relationships. Affect and symbolic imagery had disappeared. The festival became a resounding failure and has not been held since, to my knowledge. Analysis of this behavior is susceptible to affective-oriented techniques. Such behavior, however, points to the area in which research is critically needed, namely, the specification of the dynamic process which characterizes the economic movement from affective behavior. In terms of the community festival, what is the nature of the mechanism that switched them away from affective-oriented behavior? Such research is vital to the maintenance and growth of affective-oriented, collective welfare.

BIBLIOGRAPHY

Areaw, E. O. and Dundes, A. (1964) "Proverbs and the Ethnography of Speaking Folklore," *American Anthropologist* 66, 2: 70.

Dixon, V. J. (1973) "A Determination of Investment Priorities in Urban Black Communities: Bedford Stuyvesant," unpublished thesis, Princeton University.

Johnson, H. G. (1992) "An Economic Theory of Protectionism: Tariff Bargaining, and the Formation of Customs Unions," *Journal of Political Economy* 73: 256–83.

Kuhn, T. (1970) "Reflections on my Critics," in Imre Lakatos and Alan Musgrave (eds) *Criticism in the Growth of Knowledge*, Cambridge: Cambridge University Press.

17 Race, gender, and economic data

Carolyn Shaw Bell

RACE AND ETHNICITY AS ECONOMIC VARIABLES

Economists have studied economic events by looking at demographic variables for a long time. But all too frequently analysts and other data users do not realize the deficiencies in what look like excellent quantitative measures—the black population, single mothers who are Hispanics, families of Vietnam veterans, so forth. In fact, changing social attitudes have changed language, including that used to collect data on people's racial and ethnic identities. It is quite impossible, for example, to compare the number of black people today with that existing before 1970 because the term "black" was not used. Many earlier tabulations show white and non-white, with Negro as a subset of non-white. In common speech, the term "colored people" was preferred, "Negro" being a more formal term.[1]

Until 1960, census enumerators visited households to collect data; following specific instructions, they determined race by direct observation. For example, in 1890 they were cautioned to write "white, black, mulatto, quadroon, octoroon, Chinese, Japanese, or Indian.... The word 'black' shall be used to describe those persons who have three-fourths or more black blood; 'mulatto,' those persons who have from three-to five-eighths black blood, and so on." Beginning in 1920 the term "Negro" appeared instead of "black," and "A person of mixed White and Negro blood was to be returned as Negro no matter how small the percentages of Negro blood; any mixture of white and other is reported as 'Other' " (USBC 1989).

By 1970 self-identification accounted for most of the census data, but many people, especially the older population, preferred "Negro" and "colored people" to the new term "black." When the census, hoping to obtain more accurate identification, asked people to identify themselves as white, black, or other, some unknown number opted for "other." Enumerators were instructed, on the other hand, to classify anyone using the terms "Chicano, LaRaza, Mexican–American or Moslem" as white. By 1990 self-identification allowed a person to select one of fifteen racial types listed, including "Black or Negro."

Analysts who compare different groups implicitly or explicitly assume them to be distinct and mutually exclusive, but this is not necessarily so when the term "other" occurs. (The alternative is to list every possible choice.)[2] Overlap is particularly likely with data on the Hispanic origin of people. The 1980 census listed categories and a residual "Other Spanish/ Hispanic" category; ten years later a respondent could write in a specific entry. None of these categories is racial, and analysts should be careful to make this clear.

Decisions about the design and execution of the decennial census reflect pressure from a variety of sources, including ethnic groups wishing to be recognized and congressional representatives wanting to reduce costs. Elsewhere, surveys picking up racial or ethnic data have to meet other considerations.

Currently, the decennial census relies on self-identification for both racial and ethnic heritage and accepts categories based on national origin or socio-cultural groups. But other surveys follow different formats. The Current Population Survey, conducted by the Bureau of the Census to pick up data on employment, household earnings, family composition, income, etc., uses four racial groups (and only Black, not Black or Negro) and twenty-one ethnic origin categories, including "Afro-American (Black, Negro)" and "Central or South American (Spanish countries)" along with the less ambiguous German, Italian, and so forth. The Survey of Income and Program Participation uses White, Black, and "other races," including American Indians, Japanese, Chinese, Filipinos, Pacific Islanders and "any other race except White and Black."

The Center for Disease Control, charged with monitoring disease trends and identifying groups at risk, uses a very simplified system of White non-Hispanic, Black non-Hispanic, Hispanic, Native American, Asian and Pacific Islander, and unspecified (Del Pinal 1992: 1, citing Buehler *et al.* 1990).

As this book goes to press, the Office of Management and Budget is receiving comments on a proposed new directive on statistical standards for race and ethnicity: the target date of January 1997 is probably optimistic. Congressional hearings, held in 1993, and a National Academy of Science report from the Committee on National Statistics have prompted many suggestions, e.g. adding "Middle Easterner" to the ethnic categories, changing "Black" to "African American," adding a "multiracial" category for self-identification, and changing the term "Hispanic" to refer to a racial rather than ethnic category.

As can be seen from the examples, race and ethnic identification pose complex issues. So far, there has been general agreement on three principles, applicable to whatever finally emerges as the new standard. First, none of the racial or ethnic categories denotes scientific or anthropological identification. Second, the entire process of determining racial or ethnic classifications must be guided by respect for the individual and for individual dignity: self-identification will be used as far as possible. And finally, whatever identifications are made will not in any way determine eligibility for any federal program.

In fact, of course, data on race and ethnicity have been used to monitor the impact of the Voting Rights Act, mapping new congressional districts in states, monitoring the behavior of banks under the Home Mortgage Disclosure Act and the Equal Credit Opportunity Act, and implementing federal affirmative action programs. These issues far transcend the problems of economists wishing to analyze economic events using race or ethnic categories as variables. But the economist should be warned: the data are probably not what they seem.

GENDER AS AN ECONOMIC VARIABLE

Classifying people by gender at least poses no problem of overlapping groups. Self-identification with two choices, male or female, is the common practice.[3] Other issues, however, reflect cultural and language changes. The set of ideas (or stereotypes) associated with the terms "girl," "woman," "female," has so changed that today no certainty exists about any characteristics aside from purely biological features.

The Current Population Survey, the source of data used in many economic research efforts, collects data monthly from some 60,000 households, a probability sample of the entire population. The primary data usually come from one person reporting for the entire household. The initial contact, an interview visit, records background information; later questions may be asked over the telephone. SIPP (data for individuals collected from over 22,000 households three times yearly for two and a half years) also combines an initial interview with later telephoned inquiries.

First, the person reporting may not know everything necessary to provide information for everyone in the household. That black male youth are undercounted by the Census of Population is partly attributed to this: it is not clear to what household, if any, a teenager belongs and so he goes unreported altogether. Which is more likely—that a woman is ignorant about the details of her husband's or son's job or that a man is ignorant about the details of his wife's or daughter's job? The amount of error in the basic interview data has not been estimated.

A second problem was partly solved when the CPS questionnaire was revised in January of 1994. For many years the first question asked was "What were you doing during most of last week—working, keeping house, going to school, or something else?" This question was repeated for each member of the household. Aside from the choices offered, the interviewer could record other activities *if volunteered by the respondent*. Those tabulated included with a job but not at work, looking for work, unable to work, retired, or other.

If the answer to the first question was "working" there followed a series of questions beginning "Did you do any work at all last week?" This query could pick up someone with a brief work stint who did not identify the *major* activity as "working." The interviewer then asked about hours, wages, occupational and job history details.

The entire approach left the definition of "work" itself open to a variety of interpretations. The word has a complex usage: studying, therapy, exercise, practice of a skill—all require work, quite aside from homework or housework.

Other problems exist. Anyone working a forty-hour week who sleeps eight hours a night cannot, truthfully, select working as the major activity. But few answers involve this precision: most people answer in terms of a "work week" of five or six days, not seven. *Because* of that latitude, the option "keeping house" was particularly troublesome.

Measuring accurately and honestly over seven days, many employed woman answered "keeping house" rather than "working." Although some employed men could also select this alternative, "keeping house" is expected for women and not for men. Evidence that this option affected the validity of the data came years ago when analysts could not find that the increasing number of women in the labor force led to an increasing number of retired women workers. For their major activity, most selected "keeping house" rather than working.

The new CPS questions begin "Last week did you do any work for pay?" and the Department of Labor boasted that the revision would count women's employment more accurately. For example, a new pool of discouraged workers has turned up among women who cite child care or family responsibilities as reasons for not working but who, in fact, want a job, are available for work, and have looked for work during the previous year. Evidently anyone working in the field of labor economics needs to be thoroughly familiar with both the present survey and its predecessors.

For an introductory course in economics the entire topic of employment data, survey methods, and how people answer questions usually interests students and can provide a highly useful learning experience. For example, role-playing in class, with a census interviewer and two loquacious respondents, or entertaining a speaker from the local census office, or arguing about the meaning of part-time and full-time work all serve to illustrate the importance of good data.

TOPICS WHERE GENDER MATTERS

Consumption spending

Although periodic surveys of income and spending date back to 1895, they have occurred at irregular intervals, reflecting congressional interest and understanding of what the statistics show. BLS achieved some degree of insulation from such pressures in establishing the ongoing Consumer Expenditure Survey (CEX,) now used to revise the Consumer Price Index (CPI). Spending patterns have been analyzed for two-earner families, for single-mother families, and so on. But despite their interest in the consumption function or the index of consumer sentiment at the macroeconomic level, economists have mostly ignored consumer spending, not least because it comes close to marketing, business activity, and other uncouth issues.

Colin Campbell, on the other hand, thinks that consumption is denigrated first because economists focus on production and second because the Puritan work ethic has colored the field. But he also points out that consumption is seen as women's work and hence trivial, that satisfying genuine needs is allowable but that gratifying wants or desires is not essential, as well as being worth less because it is performed by women.

He chides economists for overlooking the most remarkable thing about technological change, which is not that innovation occurs, but that consumers continually change what they hanker after. "No modern consumer, no matter how privileged or wealthy, can honestly say that there is nothing that he or she wants. It is this capacity to continuously 'discover' new wants that requires explaining" (Campbell 1994: 507).

CEX data provide a link between micro- and macroeconomic analysis, and the June 1990 *Monthly Labor Review* contains an excellent introductory article explaining the tie-in of CEX data to national income and product estimates from the Bureau of Economic Analysis in the census.

Poverty measures and data

Economic welfare looks very different for men and women, in view of data on income and wealth. Measuring poverty in the United States today is neither art nor science. Mollie Orshansky,[4] who developed the measure of poverty now in use over three decades ago, spent years urging that it be revised. Her work had been so modified and adjusted as to lose all resemblance to the rigorously objective measure she had created.

In 1955 the Department of Agriculture carried out a monumental study of food consumption, including both expenditure and nutritional data. Analysis showed that the average family or household used about one-third of total expenditures for food items. With information on what American families actually ate, the department's nutritional experts drew up family food budgets with menus and shopping lists to provide all essential nutrients. Orshansky's measure used the food plan for an economy diet, priced it out in actual stores, multiplied the total by three, and identified the result as a measure for total family expenditures at the edge of poverty. More objective than any previous measure, this method could calculate poverty-level incomes for families of different sizes, on farms and in urban areas. Adopted by the Council of Economic Advisers in 1965, this measure has been used since, adjusted only by the change in the CPI.

Questions about the poverty index have been raised by many, including Congress, which asked the National Academy of Sciences (NAS) to investigate. The standing Committee on National Statistics of the Commission on Behavioral and Social Sciences and Education of the National Research Council, the research arm of the Academy, created a special panel whose report, *Measuring Poverty*, was published in 1995. The panel's findings touch on most microeconomic issues of concern today, including the distribution of income, medical and health services, employment, and income maintenance programs. With or without congressional adoption the report will evoke considerable debate.

As of 1995, poverty measures consist of a set of dollar values, called "thresholds," which can be compared to a family's income to determine its poverty status. Holding that a redefinition of poverty cannot, and probably should not, produce figures very different from these, the panel calculated a poverty measure that would produce the same number of poor people. But the recommended method differs sharply from that in current use, especially in its treatment of several items which have special meaning for women. Throughout, data for 1992 collected in March 1993 were used.

First, "resources available" to the family or individual are defined as after-tax money income *plus* the value of "near-money" benefits: e.g. food stamps but not Medicaid, and *minus* expenses needed to earn income. Such expenses include child care, other work-related expenses, and out-of-pocket medical care costs, including health insurance premiums. Second, the poverty threshold is determined for a base family of two adults and two children as a percentage of median annual expenditures (as shown in the CEX) for such families on food, clothing, and shelter. The report calculated poverty thresholds for different types of families with an equivalence scale reflecting the fact that children typically consume less than adults and that economies of scale exist in household management (Citro and Michael 1995: 4–6).

The report deserves careful reading and analysis, but some implications are obvious for the economics of race and gender. Those who criticize welfare, and the women receiving welfare, frequently blame the poverty measure as unrealistic. Those who attack the current poverty measure frequently refer to racial or gender characteristics of the population that is poor. Aside from this, there is honest dispute about how to treat benefits, area differences in the cost of living, and home ownership.

First, the reference family chosen by the panel is that old familiar four-person, two adult/two children model. The panel argues that this third largest type accounts for 20 percent of all the people, more than the 17 percent of the population living in married couple households, and more than one-adult households which account for 10 percent of the population (Citro and Michael 1995: 101–2). So there is an implicit judgment in this reference family that poverty should be measured somehow in terms of the *whole* population.

Of the families below the poverty level as of 1993, over half report a female householder and no spouse present and accounted for 37 percent of the poor people; those in married couple families for 35 percent and single individuals the remainder. Single women with families have more children than do the married couple families: 8 million as opposed to 5 million. Ninety percent of the single women families received some form of means-tested assistance; 72 percent of the married couple families did (USBC 1994: xviii).

Unlike the total population, poverty describes a mostly female group of people. Changes over time reinforce this: the number and percent of families below the poverty level have dropped steadily since 1959, while the number of families headed by women has more than doubled.[5] It is not clear that creating a poverty measure from the experience of married couples with children, who are mostly non-poor families, is defensible.

Poverty thresholds for different sized families are calculated by weighting children at 0.70 of an adult and allowing for economies of scale by raising the total number of adult equivalents to a power between 0.65 and 0.75. The panel condemns the existing measure for implicitly recognizing economies of scale for the first child but significant diseconomies for the second, with scale economies appearing for the third through fifth child. The new measure states clearly that all equivalence scales are arbitrary and justifies its choice with reference to the existing literature (Citro and Michael 1995: 159–82).

A major change in the poverty measure defines the economic resources available to the family as disposable income (available for buying the essentials of food, clothing, and shelter) rather than gross money income. Disposable income is calculated by deducting taxes, expenses for child care, and medical insurance premiums from gross pay.

Very often women choosing between welfare and working face similar calculations, and working through such a choice would be a useful exercise for an economics class dealing with the supply of labor. In any case, the NAS report should be attended to, so that the new poverty measure is properly appreciated.

Sloppy language has created both stereotypes and dangerous thinking: one example refers to "the feminization of poverty." This phrase suggests that more women are now poor, or that poverty has affected women and girls more than it previously did. Such a conclusion is nonsensical, given that women outlive men. Before Social Security payments were indexed in 1972, almost one out of three older people were poor, most of them being women. While poverty among older adults has dropped to about 12 percent, female-headed households now account for most of the poverty population.

Older adults in the population

Equally inept language refers to "the elderly living on fixed incomes." By definition, almost everyone in this country over sixty-five years of age receives Social Security benefits or SSI, and by law these are not fixed, but move upward with a 3 percent or less change in the Consumer Price

Index. People over sixty-five contain, like any other population group, some who are well off, some who just get along, and some who are poor. But practically none of them live on a fixed income.

The rapid increase in the number of elderly people, predominantly female, has been well publicized but with little appreciation, because of inadequate data and insufficient analysis. For example, the rising number of grandparents who are caring for children, typically with neither parent present, is ignored in welfare policy debates.[6] Neither AFDC as presently constituted nor any of the major attempts to reform welfare recognizes grandparents as caregivers. (Should grandparents be forced to take a job or register for training? Should they be denied benefits if another grandchild is added to the family?) Women far outnumber men in this role of caregiver. (Mullen 1995; AARP 1995.)

The major source of information on older adults, the Social Security Administration, has much more data on men than on women. A ten-year study of 11,000 Americans, aged fifty-eight to sixty-three in 1969, is still being extensively used to analyze retirement decisions and behavior. The database covers men and single women: married women are included only as their husbands' dependants. Very little research on the retirement behavior of women exists, and findings for men do not necessarily apply to women.

Most age distributions top out with an open-ended class "sixty-five and over"; the appearance of the class interval "sixty-five to seventy-four" became necessary when this open-ended class grew unwieldy in size. People over seventy-five (or over eighty-five) are just beginning to receive attention: recent data show that the fastest-growing segment, those over eight-five, do not threaten Medicare since they remain healthy and die quickly. Women, of course, outnumber men in this group. In 1992 the 13 million men over age sixty-five included 4.7 million over seventy-five. The 18 million women over age sixty-five included 10 million over seventy-five (USBC 1994). The excess of females over males is greater at successively older ages.

A significant proportion of these *older* older women have incomes below poverty, but there are major data lacks, especially about the composition of the household. The phenomenon of a seventy-year-old woman caring for her ninety-five-year-old mother and her ninety-three-year-old aunt gets little attention beyond the anecdotal evidence of social workers and outreach agencies serving the elderly.

This is the kind of policy issue that can be made alive to students, who can use their newly acquired economic analysis of income transfers. Let them try to get sufficient data to properly evaluate income and need for these families!

Gender differences in basic needs

Most developed countries measure poverty by calculating the resources needed to maintain a family, based on actual expenditure data. Such figures make little sense in a developing nation, especially if most water sources are impure and most women cannot read or write. A new topic for economists has therefore arisen, the study of basic needs or measures of material well-being.

Three typical indicators of basic needs are life expectancy, literacy, and infant mortality. Elaborating such a list calls for more specification: for example, survival, health, autonomy (discussed in terms of schizophrenia and literacy), water, nutrition, housing, health services, security (emotional, psychological, physical), education, reproduction (Dogal and Gough 1991: 267). Some gender differences have been noted: reduced life expectancy among women because of poor care, very little participation of women in legislative or executive branches of government, a double burden when market work does not lessen home work, and wide variation in women's education in Third World countries.

Bruce Moon (1991: 248) summarizes the issue:

> Any inequality—whether cultural, sectoral, geographical, or sexual— would lower basic needs relative to a society in which resources and therefore life choices are more evenly distributed. Moreover, given the importance of women for all development processes—especially their particular centrality to problems of infant mortality, health care, nutrition— discrimination in the treatment of women can be expected to have major consequences for basic needs.

Despite this, basic needs analysis more often than not omits any mention of gender differences or of women.[7] The other analytical problem is that a poor country does not have reliable data.

INDIVIDUALS AND GENDER—MORE THAN A DATA PROBLEM

Most survey data look at families, households, or consumer units. Sampling begins at the household level; economics and sociology distinguish families from individuals, hence these three units appear in most basic sources: the decennial census, the Current Population Survey, the Survey of Incomes and Program Participation (SIPP), the Consumer Expenditure Survey, the National Longitudinal Surveys on employment, the Michigan Panel Survey of Income Dynamics, and surveys of health, financial status, crime, and so forth. Collecting data and analyzing economic events and conditions by families or by households is well entrenched.

After the Bureau of the Census abandoned the practice of defining the head of the family or household as the husband, it substituted a reference person, usually called a householder. This person owns, is buying, or rents the living quarters, or, if no such identification is possible, the householder is any adult member of the household. No matter how "the householder" is defined, using a reference person to collect information does not provide similar (or any) information about everyone in the household, and many tabulations are therefore suspect. "Family Income by Level of Education" is a good example: the householder's educational level may or may not be descriptive of anyone else in the household.

Because data are collected for the family or household, most analyses of labor force participation and/or the income earned by working ignore the individual's participation. Except for the occasional circus act, families do not hold jobs and earn wages; the individual does both (see Bell 1974, 1981). The existing data on families and households do not allow any analysis of the contributions of men and of women to income, and the spending and saving decisions of men and of women from income, and the decisions about employment of individuals. The Luxembourg Income Study group provides a notable exception. This database, which makes cross-country comparisons and analysis safe, presents information for households and families, but also provides data for individuals.[8]

Women are particularly apt to be shortchanged by a household or family frame of reference, because of the persistence of stereotypical thinking. Try the statement "Both wife and husband are employed in 59 percent of the families" (USBC 1993a: 77–8). Most people (including economists) calculate that if both spouses work in 60 percent of the families, then 40 percent are supported by a man. But the statement does not say that at all. In fact, the 53 million married couple families in 1992 included 8 million without *either* a wife *or* a husband at work. Most were retired, but younger student couples are also included. Another 3 million married couple families reported that the husband is not employed but the wife is.

The economic contribution of both men and women gets underestimated when the household or family income shared consists of more than money receipts. The more people in a household, the more non-recorded income can exist. Two kinds of error exist. One is the omission of all kinds of household production—the do-it-yourself assembling, repairing, modifying, cooking, freezing, and filing that accompany expenditures and enable consumption or use of the products. Home-based services proliferate not only among the poor to substitute for high-priced market goods, but among people with higher incomes. Home production uses household capital—appliances, including computers and automobiles, to produce goods and services for use within the household (USBC 1993a: 77–83).

Gross domestic product is understated by more than just household production, since all volunteer effort goes non-recorded—coaching Little League baseball, lobbying for NRA, serving on the church vestry, being a Big Sister or a small business consultant. Much of the private investment in building human capital is also omitted; think of the people learning a language, or how to wallpaper a room, or how to cook squid, from television, from local classes, or from home study.

The second error in analyzing economic events with household or family data consists of ignoring the distribution of income *within* the household or to other households. Any figure for per capita income probably bears little resemblance to the actual real income for each family member. This would need to be derived from consumption expenditure and capital accumulation data on an individual basis. Private transfer income in both money and real terms also exists, and again data do not. SIPP provides some clues about real income transfers: 44 percent of the men and 56 percent of the women help some household member with personal care, getting around outside, preparing meals, keeping track of bills or money, and doing housework. In 1986 some 6 million people provided such care to a household member but 15 million people helped someone outside of the household (USBC 1990).

CHILD CARE AND HUMAN CAPITAL INVESTMENT

Data on child care nearly always assume that child care is an issue for women. In labor market analysis, women's employment is analyzed in terms of the presence of children, or of young children. Industrial relations experts discovered the need to hire and keep skilled women workers and firms have built day-care centers, invented programs to care for sick children, welcomed family leave legislation, and so on.

The new poverty measure allows payments for child care by employed family members to be subtracted from family resources: the amount, equal to actual expenditures from the CEX, is capped at the wages of the lower-paid adult family member. Survey data on child care have always shown that much comes from family members or relatives. With varying financial arrangements, the data suggest that many grandmothers care for children so that their mothers can buy food and clothing and shelter. That is the rationale for subtracting child care expenses from resources.

But neither the NAS report or any other analyst has provided estimates of the contribution of the grandmother—or the father or mother or big sister—who supplied the child care to the value of home production and income. Child care also needs analysis in terms of human capital formation. It may not be the case that GDP increases all that much when a kid goes to pre-school rather than staying with grandma.

The mother, most likely to provide most child care, was recognized by Alfred Marshall: "The most valuable of all capital is that invested in human beings; and of that capital the most precious part is the result of the care and influence of the mother, so long as she retains her tender and unselfish instincts, and has not been hardened by the strain and stress of unfeminine work" (1890: VI, 4.3) Marshall would have disapproved, it goes without saying, of the existence of millions of single-parent families, supported chiefly by women. He would also have taken issue with those who insist that women work in order to receive welfare.

And he would clearly have supported the claim that basic needs, or a poverty level income for single mothers and their families, must be calculated with an additional dimension to that for a family with two adults. Clair Brown's first brilliant analysis (1977) of the time-poor demonstrated that a single mother, lacking another person to help, cannot allocated time flexibly or efficiently.

The Luxembourg income study recognizes that poverty defined by money income does not adequately describe the lack of resources available to a single mother. The new *Measuring Poverty* report devotes an entire appendix to this issue, noting that child care services provided the single mother as a condition of employment are no solution. Being time-poor is not just needing child care during the workday, it is giving up the command over time that being the sole support of a dependent child entails.

I would argue that the poverty threshold for a single mother with two children (a three-person family) be higher than that for a married couple with one child (also a three-person family). It is impossible to substitute money for time, but a larger income would certainly help. More important, single mothers with children could be perceived as extra poor, rather than as undeserving. I would also argue for a special allowance for single mothers of dependent children, to be funded with a special tax on all males above the age of puberty. Since no adult male can prove that he has *not* fathered a child currently in need, all adult males (except those medically certified as sterile) should contribute.

CONCLUSION AND IMPLICATIONS

Analyzing gender, racial, and ethnic issues in existing data must begin with questioning the most basic definitions of racial and ethnic categories, and of families and individuals. It is all too easy for the analyst of economic events to overlook misidentification and unknown characteristics when working with socio-demographic variables. Familiarity with these issues should at least prevent economists from collecting flawed data.

NOTES

1 See Henry Louis Gates's enchanting memoir, *Colored People*, (1994). I grew up in a New England town where I learned never to refer to colored people or Negroes as "black," since this would have been as insulting as the term "nigger." It was not until I reached college age that I read poetry and novels using the term "black" with approval—and the slogan "Black is Beautiful" came into being some three decades later.
2 For an excellent discussion of the race–ethnic problem see Del Pinal (1992).
3 The increase in gay and lesbian households, especially those containing children, has not brought any hard data on their number, let alone other aspects of their existence. Although it seems obvious that self-identification could, within the existing survey framework, provide useful data, it seems equally obvious that such a procedure is politically impossible.
4 Her name is practically unknown, and could be respected by students as familiar with it as with the Phillips curve, Okun's misery index, and Engel's law.
5 Over half the poor families are headed by a woman, and two-thirds of the individuals counted as poor are white (USBC 1993b: 6–7).

i

6 As of March, 1993, adults over sixty-five were responsible for one million families with children under eighteen.
7 See, for example, Coate and Rosati (1988). The quotation from Moon is the only mention of gender differences or women in the entire monograph.
8 An excellent introduction to these data is Smeeding *et al.* (1990).

BIBLIOGRAPHY

American Association of Retired Persons (1995) *Grandparents as Caregivers: Summary of a Working Meeting*, Washington, DC: American Association of Retired Persons.
Bell, C. S. (1974) "Economics, Sex, and Gender," *Social Science Quarterly* 55, 3: 615–31.
——(1981) "Demand, Supply, and Labor Market Analysis," *Journal of Economic Issues* XV, 2 (June): 423–34.
Brown, C., writing as Clair Vickery (1977) "The Time-poor: A New Look at Poverty," *Journal of Human Resources* 12, 1: 27–48.
Buehler, J. W., Berkelman, Ruth L., Stroup, Donna F., and Klaucke, Douglas N. (1990) "The Reporting of Race and Ethnicity in the National Notifiable Diseases Surveillance System," *Public Health Reports* 105, 1 (January–February): 102–3.
Campbell, C. (1994) "Consuming Goods and the Good of Consuming," *Critical Review* 8, 4: 503–20.
Citro, C. F., and Michael, R. T. (eds) (1995) *Measuring Poverty: A New Approach*, Washington, DC: National Academy Press.
Coate, R. A., and Rosati, J. A. (1988) *The Power of Human Needs in World Society*, Boulder, CO: Lynne Rienner.
Del Pinal, H. (1992) *Exploring Alternative Race–Ethnic Comparisons in the Current Population Surveys*, Series P23–182, Washington, DC: Bureau of the Census.
Dogal, L. and Gough, I (1991) *A Theory of Human Need*, New York: Guildford Press.
Gates, Henry Louis (1994) *Colored People*, New York: Knopf.
Marshall, Alfred (1890) *Principles of Economics*, eighth edition, New York: Macmillan.
Moon, B. E. (1991) *The Political Economy of Basic Needs*, Ithaca, NY: Cornell University Press.
Mullen, F. (1995) *A Tangled Web: Public Benefits, Grandparents, and Grandchildren*, Washington, DC: Public Policy Institute, American Association of Retired Persons.
Smeeding, T., O'Higgins, M. and Rainwater, L., eds (1990) *Poverty, Inequality, and Income Distribution*, Washington, DC: Urban Institute Press.
US Bureau of the Census (1989) *Two Hundred Years of US Census Taking: Population and Housing Questions, 1790–1990*, Washington, DC: Government Printing Office.
——(1990) *The Need for Personal Assistance with Everyday Activities: Recipients and Caregivers*, Current Population Reports, Series P70–19, Washington, DC: Government Printing Office
——(1993a) *Money Income of Households, Families, and Persons in the United States, 1992*, Current Population Reports, Series P60–184, Washington, DC: Government Printing Office.
——(1993b) *Poverty in United States, 1992*, Current Population Reports, Series P60–185, Washington, DC: Government Printing Office.
——(1994) *Household and Family Characteristics, March 1993*, Current Population Reports, Series P20, Washington, DC: Government Printing Office.

Index